*not
your
mama's*™ *Stitching*

not your mama's™ Stitching

The cool and creative way to stitch it to 'em

by Kate Shoup Welsh

BICENTENNIAL
1807
WILEY
2007
BICENTENNIAL

John Wiley & Sons, Inc.

Published by Wiley Publishing, Inc., Hoboken, New Jersey

No part of this publication may be reproduced, stored in a retrieval system or transmitted in any form or by any means, electronic, mechanical, photocopying, recording, scanning or otherwise, except as permitted under Sections 107 or 108 of the 1976 United States Copyright Act, without either the prior written permission of the Publisher, or authorization through payment of the appropriate per-copy fee to the Copyright Clearance Center, 222 Rosewood Drive, Danvers, MA 01923, (978) 750-8400, fax (978) 646-8600, or on the web at www.copyright.com. Requests to the Publisher for permission should be addressed to the Legal Department, Wiley Publishing, Inc., 10475 Crosspoint Blvd., Indianapolis, IN 46256, (317) 572-3447, fax (317) 572-4355, or online at http://www.wiley.com/go/permissions.

Wiley, the Wiley Publishing logo, Not Your Mama's, and related trademarks are trademarks or registered trademarks of John Wiley & Sons, Inc. and/or its affiliates. All other trademarks are the property of their respective owners. Wiley Publishing, Inc. is not associated with any product or vendor mentioned in this book.

The publisher and the author make no representations or warranties with respect to the accuracy or completeness of the contents of this work and specifically disclaim all warranties, including without limitation warranties of fitness for a particular purpose. No warranty may be created or extended by sales or promotional materials. The advice and strategies contained herein may not be suitable for every situation. This work is sold with the understanding that the publisher is not engaged in rendering legal, accounting, or other professional services. If professional assistance is required, the services of a competent professional person should be sought. Neither the publisher nor the author shall be liable for damages arising here from. The fact that an organization or Website is referred to in this work as a citation and/or a potential source of further information does not mean that the author or the publisher endorses the information the organization or Website may provide or recommendations it may make. Further, readers should be aware that Internet Websites listed in this work may have changed or disappeared between when this work was written and when it is read.

For general information on our other products and services or to obtain technical support please contact our Customer Care Department within the U.S. at (800) 762-2974, outside the U.S. at (317) 572-3993 or fax (317) 572-4002.

Wiley also publishes its books in a variety of electronic formats. Some content that appears in print may not be available in electronic books. For more information about Wiley products, please visit our web site at www.wiley.com.

Library of Congress Cataloging-in-Publication Data:

Welsh, Kate, 1972-
    Not your mama's stitching : the cool and creative way to stitch it to 'em / by Kate Shoup Welsh.
      p. cm.
    ISBN-13: 978-0-470-09516-4 (pbk.)
    ISBN-10: 0-470-09516-4
    1. Embroidery. 2. Cross-stitch. 3. Needlepoint. I. Title.

TT770.W42 2007
746.44—dc22
                                                2006101579

Printed in the United States of America

10 9 8 7 6 5 4 3 2 1

Book design by Elizabeth Brooks
Cover design by Troy Cummings
Interior photography by Matt Bowen
Illustrations by Joni Burns
Wiley Bicentennial Logo: Richard J. Pacifico
Book production by Wiley Publishing, Inc. Composition Services

For Gladys

Free bonus pattern available online!

Can't get enough stitching? Access one more *Not Your Mama's Stitching* pattern at www.wiley.com/go/notyourmamas.

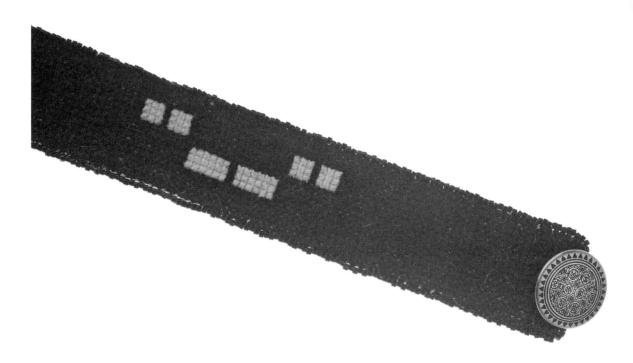

Additional stitching resources online!

At www.wiley.com/go/notyourmamas, you can also find additional stitching resources—books, magazines, instructional Web sites, and online storefronts—as well as a series of alphabet designs for use in your projects.

Contents

CHAPTER EIGHT

Present Tents: Nifty Needlecraft Gifts

Acknowledgments

The gestation period of any book involves the contributions of many, *many* people. For this book, much credit is due to Cindy Kitchel, who kindly gave me my first job in publishing and continues to inspire me with her poise, humor, and smarty-pantsness. Cindy also doubled on this project as a stunt stitcher, for which I am incredibly grateful. Roxane Cerda, my acquisitions editor, has crossed the line from client to friend; her contributions to this title span from moral support to project designs. And it goes without saying that project editor Donna Wright's encouragement, suggestions, and patience throughout have proved invaluable. Thanks are also due to Christina Stambaugh, who provided design direction; designer Elizabeth Brooks; layout technician Amanda Spagnuolo; graphics imaging technician Brent Savage; proofreader Betty Kish; indexer Lynnzee Elze and Carol Pogoni, the book's copy editor, who saved my ass on numerous occasions.

Then, of course, there are those people who had the unfortunate luck to live with or otherwise encounter me during the writing process, most notably my amazing and supportive husband, Ian, who always makes me feel smart and beautiful, even when I totally am *not*; and my brilliant, hilarious, and gorgeous six-year-old daughter, Heidi. Thanks also to the rest of the fam: Barbara Shoup (who, in addition to birthing me, also stunt-stitched for this book), Steve Shoup, Jenny Shoup, Jake Plant, Jim Plant, the Pfeiffers, the Weitz boys, the Goodales, the Caudells, Sue Welsh, Jay Welsh, Rae Terry, Caitlin Welsh, and Tommy Grim. No girl could ask for nicer relatives. Super special appreciation to Joan Warrick, whose skills as a seamstress are trumped only by her skills as a friend. Finally, undying gratitude to a few key members of my buddy list: Dan Barden, Sol Blickman, Kate Bova, Sally Chalex, the Cupps, the Other Cupps, the Dellingers, Betsy Haas, Heather Hauptman, Waddy Potthoff, the Snidermans, Bill Warrick, the girls of the DKG (especially Kitty Jarrett, yet *another* stunt stitcher), and the Friday Night Yogis. Thanks for tolerating me.

Introduction

◆◆◆

The Stitch Is Back

Stitch Hunt

Meet Rosey Grier, who, after being introduced to the joys of needlepoint in the early 1970s, quickly developed a passion for it. Luckily, Rosey had plenty of time to devote to the craft, having retired in 1967 after a successful career as . . . wait for it . . . *a pro defensive tackle* in the NFL. If anyone thought Rosey Grier was a girly man for publicly practicing needlepoint—hell, he even published a book about it, *Rosey Grier's Needlepoint for Men*—they probably kept it to themselves.

As it happens, Rosey wasn't the first person to develop a keen interest in needlework. In fact, needlecrafts have been around practically since Neanderthals roamed Earth. But although needlework—a.k.a. *stitching*—has enjoyed a long history, it all but died out during the first half of the 20th century. And unfortunately, in the years following its revival in the 1960s, the majority who joined the stitching bandwagon (Rosey Grier notwithstanding) either a) collected Hummel figurines, b) believed that showering was for the *bourgeoisie*, c) participated in Renaissance festivals, or d) all of the above. That is, they weren't chic, like you.

Recently, that's begun to change, thanks to a spike in interest among hip types in needlecrafts like embroidery, cross stitch, and needlepoint, which are the foci of this book. Indeed, needlecrafts have become *cool*. And of course, like many "cool" things—shoes come to mind—needlecrafts are also addictive. For one, the thread used in stitching is soft and colorful, and everyone knows that handling soft, colorful objects is habit-forming. Plus, stitching can provide an immediate rush. Forget knitting. Making a single sweater takes longer than growing out a bad haircut. With stitching, you can crank out some of the simpler pieces in the time it takes to refresh your highlights. Finally, after a long day earning 22 percent less than your male counterparts, what better way is there to unwind than stitching? And although certain stitching techniques do require some skill, it's possible to make many beautiful pieces armed only with the ability to poke a needle through fabric. To sum things up, if you like soft, colorful things and can be trusted with a needle, stitching is for you.

How This Book Is Organized

If you've opened this book, I'm assuming you're interested in learning more about stitching. Either that or you're trapped under a bookshelf and this is the only book you could reach while awaiting rescue. Regardless, this book is designed to get you up and running. Part One starts with a brief history of stitching, the upshot of which is that your slavish devotion to the craft is in fact the result of thousands of years of evolution and is therefore excusable. From there, you'll discover the various tools and materials that no stitcher should be without. Then it's on to a discussion of basic stitching skills such as starting a thread, tying off, and so on. Finally, you'll explore myriad embroidery, cross stitch, and needlepoint stitches. As you'll quickly learn, stitching can be as simple—or as complex—as you want it to be—kind of like a Starbucks order.

With those skills under your belt, you're ready for Part Two. Here you'll find 24 projects, ranging from "tattooed" tank tops to snarky stitched sayings. Each contains step-by-step instructions, an indication of the skills necessary to complete the project, a complete list of the materials you'll need, an estimate of how much those materials will cost, and a ballpark figure of the level of commitment required to complete the design. You'll complete projects described as "Flirtation" in less time than it takes to paint your toes; "Love o' Your Life" projects take longer to finish, but result in heirloom-quality pieces (unless you botch them up); a project categorized as a "Fling" falls somewhere in between.

Who This Book Is For

If you've never stitched a stitch, let alone completed a needlepoint pillow, this book is for you. That's not to say, however, that if you're an intermediate or even an advanced stitcher, you won't enjoy this book—especially Part Two, "Projects." With designs ranging from the ridiculously simple to the sublimely complex, there really is something for everyone. Well, okay, maybe not *everyone.* This is, after all, *Not Your Mama's Stitching.* That means if you have hosted a Pampered Chef party without feeling at least a little bit embarrassed, this may not be the book for you. But if you're cool, you're hip, and you want to learn how to make some kick-ass stitched pieces, read on.

Whatever, Little Miss Know-It-All

If you're already a seasoned stitcher, I'm guessing you can safely skip the first part of this book, which covers the ins and outs of various types of stitching. I should warn you, however, that you'll be missing out on some serious laughs. Or if not laughs, per se, at least a chuckle or two. Or maybe not. Whatever. If, however, you're new to this whole stitching thing, I urge you to read Part One before moving forward. But, I mean, it's up to you. Seriously. No judgment.

· Part One ·

Basic Training

Chapter One

◆◆◆

Back Stitch to the Future

op quiz: What Upper Paleolithic invention arguably enabled humans to conquer the earth?

A. The monkey-operated traffic signal
B. The mastodon-powered vacuum cleaner
C. The triceratops juicer
D. String

If you answered D, String, you're correct—although I think we can all agree that the triceratops juicer also played a pivotal role (at least, it did on *The Flintstones*). While old-school anthropologists have generally cited the invention of stone and metal tools in the evolutionary success of knuckle-draggers—indeed, the word "Paleolithic" is really just smart-people speak for "Old Stone Age"—recent scholarship indicates that theory may be as much hooey as the urban legend about eating Pop Rocks with soda. Instead, many anthropologists now believe it was *string*—as in spun plant or animal fiber—that enabled these Cro-Magnon grunters to ascend to the top of the food chain.

Given this new understanding of its importance, I could reasonably argue that *my* interest in string—specifically, in the string used in needlecrafts—is simply a product of latent survival instincts, the outcome of eons of evolution, as much a result of my DNA as my hair color (pre-highlights, of course). Whether this is in fact true remains to be proven, but it certainly *sounds* adequately scientific in the event my bankruptcy attorney questions my needlecraft-related purchases. In case you, too, find yourself cross-examined about your stitching stash, this chapter—while by no means a thorough account of the history of needlecrafts—contains enough historical information to snow any jury.

Weave Are the World

Look, I'm sure there are skeptics among you. I mean, if Captain Caveman was facing a marauding, ferocious beast, odds are he wouldn't extract a length of freaking *fiber* from his fur to fend it off; he'd probably opt for something sharp and hard. Plus, it's not like early people-ish types needed to use string to sew up animal skins and fur for clothing; some proto-Einstein of an earlier epoch had already figured out how to use critter sinew and needles made of bone for that purpose. So what gives?

Here's the deal: String was invaluable to early humans because it had so many uses. One, it could be employed to entertain cave kittens for *hours*. Plus, in the event one of our early ancestors had important stuff to remember, she could tie string around her index finger as a cue. But perhaps most importantly, in the words of renowned paleontologist Dr. Elizabeth Wayland Barber, string "opened the door to an enormous array of new ways to save labor and improve the odds of survival."

And how. The development of string yielded such handy items as snares, nets, and, ultimately, such tools as the bow and arrow—all of which enabled humans to hunt from afar rather

It's to Dye For

It was only a matter of time–in this case, a loooooooong time–before the neutral, Armani-inspired palette of Paleolithic fashion became *so* last era. Enter the ancient Chinese who, sometime before 3000 B.C., figured out how to whip up red, black, and yellow dyes. Subsequent discoveries in other pockets of the world yielded a yet broader palette. Ancient Indians used indigo to create blue dye, while the Phoenicians produced a vibrant purple dye by cracking open the mollusks that littered the Mediterranean coast and extracting the mucus within. Coastal people in Mexico also used shellfish to obtain colorant, but their approach involved a bit more foreplay: tickling and blowing on the creatures until they obligingly spit out their own dye. Other Central and South Americans employed the bodies of cochineal insects to concoct various shades, as did the Egyptians.

As you might guess, the process of extracting the materials necessary to formulate dye involved more labor than tutoring Kevin Federline for the SATs. In order to produce a measly 1.5 grams of purple colorant, the aforementioned Phoenicians bludgeoned some 12,000 mollusks to extract their dye snot. Even those of us with only a cursory understanding of simple economics can conclude that this dye was as prized as an Hermès Kelly bag, and priced accordingly. Read: If you weren't a Hilton sister, you could forget about wearing anything brighter than beige.

than engaging in hand-to-paw combat. This increased the likelihood of their continued existence a gazillion-fold. Also, string could be used to lash together planks in order to build a raft, which, along with the aforementioned nets and with newly invented fishing lines, could be used to haul in great quantities of fish.

Most importantly, with the invention of string came the ability to *weave*—that is, cross horizontally situated threads, called *weft threads*, and vertically situated threads, called *warp threads*, in an over-under fashion in order to create textiles. These textiles could then be used to construct lightweight containers for carrying food, making the whole "gathering" thing a bit easier (although constantly being asked "linen or mammoth hide?" by the bagger guy at the grocery checkout probably became annoying). These containers could also be used to *store* food, which meant that with a little foresight, early people could hoard enough eats when the pickings were good to withstand the inevitable downturn.

In addition to being used to construct lightweight containers, woven string could be used to fashion washable garments, reducing the need for smelly animal skins—a major victory for members of NETA (Neanderthals for the Ethical Treatment of Animals). String could also be woven into baby slings, thereby freeing the Wilmas of the world to berry-pick with *both* hands.

Just when did this so-called "string revolution" occur? It's hard to say. Unlike stone tools, which are incredibly durable, string and woven textiles are as ephemeral as the dewy skin of one's youth, susceptible to decay over time. So although experts date the oldest examples of fabric ever discovered to 16,000 B.C., secondary evidence such as impressions of early textiles on ancient fragments of clay indicates that string and woven textiles have been around *waaaay* longer. Some scholars contend that human-ish types began weaving at least as early as 40,000 B.C., and possibly much earlier.

Ancient Chinese Secret

Unless they personally claimed dominion over all they surveyed, ancient types could assume their clothing and household items would be free of any decorative stitching—an art form whose precise origins are as cloudy as Mel Gibson's judgment, but that appears to have originated in China circa 4500 B.C. No doubt spurred on by their early mastery over the silkworm, which yielded exquisite threads and fabrics, the Chinese have since enjoyed an impressive tradition of stitching. Heck, by the end of the Han Dynasty, which spanned from 206 B.C. to A.D. 220, just about everyone with a vagina was a pro. Over time, the decorative stitching techniques introduced by the Chinese oozed across

We Got the Bead

Although decorative stitching as a craft in its own right didn't materialize until 4500 B.C.-ish, humans embellished their clothing by stitching beads onto it much earlier. In fact, the fossilized remains of one Cro-Magnon hunter who lived circa 30,000 B.C. sported clothes, boots, and a hat decorated with Paleolithic bling: horizontal rows of ivory beads. You'll learn how to incorporate beads into your stitching in chapter 6 in the project "I'll Stop the World and Belt with You."

Asia to the Middle East—namely Egypt, Syria, Persia, Babylon, Israel, and Byzantium; trade and conquest spread it yet further, to such diverse regions as India, the Roman Empire, Africa, the Americas, and beyond.

Vestment Opportunity

Of course, like textiles in general, fabric containing decorative stitching, a.k.a. *needlework*, is transient and, unlike Dick Clark, subject to the ravages of time. Translation: Few early examples of it survive. In order to trace the development of needlework from China circa 4500 B.C., historians must rely on ancient paintings, sculptures, and literary sources. One early mention of decorative stitching appears in the Bible—namely Exodus, chapter 26, which, oddly enough, describes in excruciating detail the decorative requirements for a tabernacle.

Some of the earliest examples of *actual* thread work that have survived to the present day were produced in Europe in medieval times (as opposed to *at* Medieval Times, that restaurant chain where they re-enact jousts and stuff). Many artifacts from this era, most likely stitched with needles made of bronze, were commissioned by the Church and were therefore ecclesiastical (that's "church-y" to you and me) in nature: vestments, copes, albs, chasubles, surplices, stoles, *et al*. All were ornately stitched with vibrant colors, especially around the edges—hence, it was during this period that the term "embroidery," from the Anglo-Saxon word for "edge," was coined. Other embroidered pieces were made to order for royalty and similarly wealthy patrons for secular use: tents, banners, tabards, horse trappings, wall and bed hangings, and of

Hey! Whitey!

While the opus anglicanum style dominated the British Isles, opus teutonicum (Latin for "Teutonic work") took root in the area now called Germany. Embroiderers who stitched in this style produced monuments to blandness described as whitework—white thread on white fabric that yielded an effect Spinal Tap's Nigel Tufnel could only describe as "none more white." (Presumably to keep from falling asleep, Teutonic embroiderers broke the monotony of working these white-on-white pieces by developing new types of stitches, including the chain stitch, the buttonhole stitch, the encroaching Gobelin, and the long-arm cross, many of which are still used today.) Speaking of whitework, it's also a component of Norway's traditional Hardanger style, which is also characterized by cutwork—a form of needlework in which portions of the background fabric are cut away. Likewise, Danish Hedebo embroidery involves whitework, but also entails the drawn-thread technique in which certain warp and/or weft threads are removed from the fabric and the remaining threads are gathered together.

course garments of all types. (Sadly, few of these embroidered garments survive, as they were generally worn until they disintegrated into a stinking, festering pile of string.) In short, many of the embroidered goodies from this period served much the same function as illuminated manuscripts, jewelry, wall paintings, sculptures, etc.: to convey to others the extent to which you were wealthier and/or more powerful than they were.

Among the most advanced embroiderers of the time were the English; one early example of their skill is an incredibly detailed stole and maniple from the tomb of St. Cuthbert at Durham, which dates from A.D. 906-ish. (In time, this British style would be called *opus anglicanum,* Latin for "English work.") A more famous example of early needlework—also believed to have been produced by English stitchers—is the Bayeux Tapestry, which depicts the Norman conquest of England using 626 human figures, 190 horses, 35 dogs, 506 birds and critters, 33 buildings, 37 ships, 37 trees or groups of trees, and 57 Latin inscriptions. A whopping 231 feet long (that's 39.6 Gisele Bündchens to you and me), the tapestry, which was probably commissioned in the 1070s by the half-brother of William the Conqueror, consists of eight colors of wool threads embroidered on linen fabric—making the whole "tapestry" aspect of its name a bit of a misnomer, as the images that appear in tapestries are, by definition, woven, not stitched. Rather, the Bayeux Tapestry is among the earliest examples of *crewel,* which, although often assumed to be a needlework technique, simply refers to the type of wool used in an embroidered piece: crewel wool.

Courtesy Durham Cathedral

St. Cuthbert's maniple is among the earliest embroidered pieces to survive the ravages of time.

Courtesy Reading Museum

The Bayeux Tapestry is among the oldest, most ambitious examples of embroidery. This portion of the "tapestry" depicts the Battle of Hastings.

Women's Work, My Ass!

Although it's true that embroidery has long been a diversion for girly types, plenty of men also practiced the craft. Take St. Dunstan, the 10th century ladies' man who designed and stitched his own embroidery patterns. Monks, too, were known to embroider. In fact, it is said that embroidery was *so* popular in monasteries and convents that the high clergy chastised monks and nuns alike for eschewing their devotional responsibilities in favor of their needlework projects. The truth was, embroidered pieces were so *de rigueur,* the royal, noble, and clerical types who commissioned them didn't much care *who* made them—man, woman, child, or other—as long as they were sufficiently fancy-schmancy.

To meet this demand, skilled embroiderers opened shops, some of which were familial in nature and many of which were staffed by both women and men. Other skilled embroiderers served in the employ of a particular patron. In time professional embroidery guilds, many with a membership consisting entirely of men, formed both to protect artisans and to ensure quality. As to the latter, only those who had endured a seven-year apprenticeship as well as a period as a journeyman were permitted to ascend to Master Embroiderer status—and that only after enlisting a priest to recommend him, paying a fee, and producing a sample of work that met the strict standards of the Wardens of the Guild.

That's not to say all early embroidery was stitched by a pro. Plenty of amateurs dabbled in the craft—especially noblewomen, who were among the few hobbyists able to afford the necessary supplies. Indeed, many a medieval queen was handy with a needle, including Queen Aelgifu, whose husband, King Canute, ruled England from A.D. 1016 to 1035; and Queen Edith, whose husband, Edward the Confessor, reigned from A.D. 1042 to 1066. (Later queens, too, practiced the art of embroidery, most notably Queen Elizabeth I and her rival for the English throne, Mary Queen of Scots.)

Urban Outfitter

In A.D. 1095, when Pope Urban II got a bug up his butt about Muslim Turks occupying Jerusalem, he rallied Christians to swarm the city and boot them out—a maneuver designed to ensure the safety of Christian pilgrims. Answering his call to arms, European nobles and serfs alike enlisted in vast numbers for the campaign that would eventually be called the First Crusade.

Not the most disciplined of troops, these Crusaders haphazardly slaughtered Jews and heretics whilst sacking turf already held by allies en route to Jerusalem. By the time they finally reached their destination more than three years after Pope Urban's rallying cry, the very Turks they had come to evict had already scrammed—expelled by the ruling Fatimid Muslims. Although these same Fatimids promised to protect Christian pilgrims in Jerusalem, the Crusaders, spoiling for a fight, opted to conquer the city and claim it as their own—a feat that would have thrilled Pope Urban had he lived to hear the news. This new Christian-ruled kingdom of Jerusalem would endure until 1291, when Islamic soldiers achieved their stated objective of cleansing the region of the infidel outsiders. (Whoa, *déjà vu!*)

Look, I know what you're saying: This is fascinating, but exactly how does it relate to embroidery? Simple. The Crusaders' eastward march exposed them to lands and cultures—and styles of embroidery—they'd never experienced before. Naturally, when the victorious Crusaders returned to their homelands, new embroidery styles, such as the Byzantine style (much of which was copied from the Persian style), came with them. Indeed, the influence of Byzantine art of all types, characterized by rich colors and ornate designs, can be found throughout Europe—at least in part the result of the First (and subsequent) Crusade.

Read the Twine Print

With an artistic oeuvre that spans *Three Men and a Little Lady* to *Police Academy 1–4*, Steve Guttenberg's contributions to society cannot be denied. But it was an earlier Gutenberg—namely Johannes Gutenberg—who *really* made a difference. By inventing the printing press in the 1440s, Gutenberg launched an information revolution the likes of which would not be repeated until Al Gore invented the Internet. In fact, because the ability to produce many copies of a book meant that information and ideas could spread more quickly than bird flu, many consider Gutenberg's invention to be the turning point from the Middle Ages to the early modern period, an era characterized by rapid technological progress, a rise in scientific thought, secularized civic politics, the nation state, and the emergence of Protestantism.

Protestantism in particular benefited greatly from the advent of the printing press. Case in point: Just weeks after being nailed onto the door fronting Wittenberg's Castle Church in 1517, printed copies of Martin Luther's *95 Theses*, which dogged the Catholic Church's practice of *indulgences* whereby the wealthy could pay down their time in purgatory by filling the church's coffers, had circulated throughout Germany. Soon thereafter, copies of Luther's treatise had surfaced as far away as Italy, France, and England. This momentum eventually

Speaking of Henry VIII . . .

Among the most famous embroidery traditions is *blackwork:* black thread stitched onto white fabric. Sometimes called *Spanish work* after its area of origin, the blackwork aesthetic was deeply influenced by Islamic Moors, who ruled portions of the Iberian Peninsula from the 8th century until 1492, when they were vanquished by the forces of Ferdinand II of Aragon and Isabella I of Castile. Interestingly, although blackwork's origins lie in Spain, it is more closely associated with Tudor England. According to legend, if not actual fact, Ferdinand and Isabella's daughter, Catherine of Aragon, brought blackwork to England upon her (ultimately doomed) marriage to Henry VIII, and its popularity in the British Isles endured for nearly a century thereafter. For examples of blackwork from this period, peruse Hans Holbein's portraits of Henry VIII and his many wives; the prevalence of blackwork in these paintings likely explains why the double-running stitch commonly used in blackwork was subsequently christened the *Holbein stitch.*

spawned the Protestant Reformation, thereby creating four new religious institutions that opposed the papacy: the Lutheran church, the Calvinist church, the Anabaptist church, and the Anglican church.

Of course, many Protestants objected specifically to the pomp associated with Catholicism, *i.e.*, the aforementioned vestments, copes, albs, chasubles, surplices, and such, many of which were—you guessed it—embroidered. If you've ever torn a picture of your ex to pieces, you might be able to relate to those religious reformers who, after England split from the Catholic Church during the reign of Henry VIII, destroyed some of Britain's finest examples of ecclesiastical embroidery. (Note, however, that even the most zealous reformers did not thereafter stalk said examples of ecclesiastical embroidery for six months.)

In a kooky full circle–type scenario, even as the printing press indirectly marginalized ecclesiastical embroidery by aiding in the proliferation of Protestantism, it nurtured the growth of secular embroidery. Specifically, with the advent of the printing press, common-born embroiderer wannabes—a growing population, thanks to a changing economy in which the merchant and gentry classes prospered—could embroider garments and domestic objects using printed pattern sheets and, later, books containing embroidery patterns. One such book was *A Clef des Champs* by Jacques le Moyne, which included illustrations delineated with pin pricks that allowed for tracing (a technique called *pouncing*). Other books—such as Conrad Gessner's *Icones Animalium*, which contained a selection of hand-colored woodcuts depicting animals—served as inspiration, as did Pierre Pelon's *La Nature et Diversité des Poissons*, which portrayed marine critters. In addition to disseminating patterns, books also occasionally *displayed* them. That is, embroiderers were known to stitch designs—usually monograms, insignias, and coats of arms—directly onto bookbindings.

Free Samplers!

Although books with patterns had become available, most young girls still learned the fundamentals of embroidery from their mothers or other women in their household, perfecting stitches by working *samplers*—bits of cloth on which various techniques, borders, and motifs were practiced, later serving as reference pieces for the stitcher. Although early samplers—a word derived from the Latin *exemplum*, meaning "an example to be followed"—were literally scraps of fabric on which stitching techniques were refined, over time they developed into more sophisticated pieces that were an art form all their own, featuring a variety of designs, stitches, shades, and materials. In fact, the oldest dated sampler known to survive, stitched by one Jane Bostocke in 1598, is so prized it is housed in London's Victoria and Albert Museum.

In the 18th and 19th centuries, younger needle wielders completed samplers as part of their school curriculum in order to prepare for impending wifehood or domestic servitude, sticking to simple sampler themes such as alphabets, numerals, and such. The ladies of the day, however, stitched samplers that were more complex, featuring Biblical verses, pictures, even maps. As their designs became more elaborate, sampler stitchers used fewer and fewer *types* of stitches to complete them—eventually settling on counted cross stitch as the technique of choice. (You'll learn more about counted cross stitch in chapter 4, "Stitch Hitter: Your Guide to Cross-Stitch, Embroidery, and Needlepoint Stitches.")

Gros Point Blank

For those with sensitive *derrieres*, cushions were the primary source of comfort until the 17th century, when furniture upholstery was invented. Furniture makers quickly realized, however, that most fabric woven in the traditional manner was too delicate for such use. To rectify this, a new type of canvas was developed that was coarse and evenly woven, with holes large enough to accommodate yarn of varying thicknesses—more mesh than fabric. When stitched using techniques originally developed in the 16th century to copy Turkish rugs—primarily tent stitches—this new type of fabric proved as tough and durable as Jackie Chan; thus, needlepoint as we know it was born.

True to its roots, many early needlepoint pieces served as furniture upholstery, often with designs featuring flowers and faces (the latter presumably representing the origin of the phrase "Hey baby! Come sit on my face!" commonly shouted by modern-day construction workers). To render the details of these designs, stitchers used a technique called *petit point* (French for "little stitch"), essentially a tent stitch that diagonally crossed a single thread intersection on the canvas. Larger, less-detailed designs required less precision, hence the common use of the *gros point* (French for "big stitch") technique. This method, which yielded larger, coarser stitches, involved applying tent stitches that diagonally crossed *two* thread intersections. (You'll learn more about tent stitches and other needlepoint techniques in chapter 4.)

Needlepoint canvas also proved ideal for the *bargello* stitching style, also called the Florentine stitch, the Hungarian point stitch, or the flame stitch. Although the details of bargello's roots are as murky as Heather Mills McCartney's past, we do know that it achieved prominence during the 14th century in Hungary and surfaced in Italy sometime thereafter. In any case, unlike gros point and petit point needlepoint pieces, which tend to be pictorial in nature, bargello needlepoint is typically geometric, featuring repeated patterns of long, parallel stitches that step up and down the canvas. Depending on the "steepness" of the steps, the result ranges from a sharp zigzag pattern to a fluid, rolling design that resembles waves or flames (hence the name "flame stitch"). Bright colors are often used, with graduated shades creating a sense of depth.

You Say You Want a Revolution . . .

If you watch *Project Runway,* you probably already know that the fashion cycle involves six distinct phases: innovation, rise, acceleration, general acceptance, decline, and obsolescence. During, say, the Upper Paleolithic, fashion cycles lasted eons. Literally. I mean, who has time to think about hemlines when the prospect of survival is iffy at best? As human-ish types matured from hunting and gathering to farming and settling, however, they could turn their attention from such mundane matters as outwitting carnivores in order to survive to a far more critical issue: personal style.

Interest in fashion only grew as civilizations intertwined through trade, contracting the fashion cycle from millennia to centuries to mere decades. Take Elizabethan England, where the nobility wore embroidery the way Lance Armstrong wears corporate logos: *everywhere.* Hats, jackets, hoods, gloves, scarves, bonnets, hankies, even undies—if an item was wearable, it was probably jazzed up with embroidery. By the middle of the 17th century, however, European fashion had begun to shift to a more ascetic aesthetic. Although embroidery remained popular, the demand for such ostentatious decoration declined.

Even as the fashion cycle shrank, however, it remained hostage to the inherently slow schedule of hand-craftsmen. There was the spinner, who manually manufactured the necessary thread to weave, sew, and embroider textiles; the weaver, who wove said thread into cloth; the tailor or seamstress, who sewed the cloth into an actual garment; and finally, only after all that was complete, an embroiderer, who carefully stitched designs on the garment to embellish it. Hell, by the time the UPS guy delivered the piece to its intended owner, it was practically *passé!*

The Industrial Revolution, which occurred between 1750 and 1830 (the precise dates differ by region), put the fashion cycle in hyper drive. Where the creation of embroidered goodies formerly required the patience and skill of several craftsmen, machines could now do the job in nothing flat. Case in point: the spinning jenny and, later, the spinning mule. Tended by only one factory laborer, a single spinning mule could fabricate thread that was stronger, truer in color, and had fewer flaws than its hand-spun equivalent—200 times faster than a hand spinner.

Of course, producing thread 200 times faster than before was as pointless as giving Lindsay Lohan a library card if weavers, tailors, and embroiderers couldn't keep up. Hence the invention of the *power loom,* a mechanized apparatus that wove textiles at warp speed (no pun intended); the sewing machine, which boosted output by a factor of 10; and the embroidery machine, which, while not as skilled as a human embroiderer, was close enough to fool the unschooled eye. Fueling all these changes was the windfall of natural resources now available thanks to the conquest and colonization of territory in the Americas and beyond. What was the result of this boost in raw materials, output, and efficiency? More embroidered goodies at lower prices—meaning that many people whose wardrobes formerly consisted of the bare essentials could now afford multiple pieces that looked quite like those belonging to their betters.

Here's Lud in Your Eye

Not surprisingly, many artisans who had previously enjoyed a decent living rebelled against such advances, occasionally turning the machines that replaced them into kindling. These protests, however, proved as futile as Kenny Rogers' attempts to stay young; the new factory-based modes of production were simply too profitable. (These protestors would be dubbed *Luddites* after one Ned Lud, who, in 1779, incited English workmen to destroy labor-saving machinery. Today, "Luddite" refers to any opponent of technological progress–think Ted Kaczynski.)

The Agony of Effete

Of course, not everyone embraced the changes wrought by the Industrial Revolution. Just as rich people today will happily spend $197 on a hand-painted T-shirt in SoHo but wouldn't be caught dead wearing a $4.92 Wal-Mart knock-off, the cultural elite of the day viewed mass-produced items with some degree of disdain. It wasn't just that the uniformity of these objects screamed soullessness (which, of course, they did). Mainly, the simple fact that working types could *afford* goodies like mass-produced embroidered garments and housewares made said garments and housewares anathema to the upper crust. This attitude gave rise to several anti-bling movements, most notably the Aesthetes, who eschewed ostentation on all fronts, and the Arts and Crafts movement, which celebrated hand crafts—including needlecrafts.

Indeed, the Victorian period saw a dramatic increase in the number of needlecrafts hobbyists—fueled, ironically enough, by the Industrial Revolution. For starters, the materials required to engage in such activities were now mass produced, making them considerably cheaper than before. Also, the ever-widening middle class that emerged as a result of the Industrial Revolution had the disposable income to purchase said needlecrafts materials. Plus, members of the middle class now had the leisure time to pursue such hobbies. In fact, stitching during this era conveyed what a BMW 5-Series did in the 1980s: upward mobility.

The most popular form of needlework for these proto-yuppies was *Berlin work*, a technique similar to needlepoint that involved applying tent and/or cross stitches to a painted meshy canvas using worsted wool. Indeed, Berlin work was as popular as Pokémon; it practically abolished all other types of embroidery. But as anyone who has spent a fortune on a pair of shoes one season only to despise them the next knows, the heart is fickle. By the 1880s, Berlin work had been almost completely replaced by cross stitch. As for traditional embroidery, it was for dorks only—although bead embroidery (*i.e.*, stitching beads onto fabric) was deemed acceptable.

Death and Threadsurrection

The early 20th century saw a sharp decline in the practice of needlecrafts—a trend that began in 1914 when some Serbian nut job triggered World War I by offing Franz Ferdinand (the Archduke of the Austro-Hungarian Empire, not the band) and his wife as they paraded through Sarajevo. Ensuing years saw some nine million souls extinguished by the war; the onset of the Russian Revolution in 1917; and a global influenza epidemic in 1918. Frankly, no one was in the mood for jazzing up their clothes and household items with chipper embroidery. And even if they had been, the bulk of the necessary supplies and materials were swallowed up by the war effort—although it is said that needlecrafts *were* a popular hobby among British soldiers in convalescent homes.

The 1920s brought a respite from the grim realities of war—at least for the victors. Scrimping and saving was *so* last decade. Embroidery re-emerged, often to decorate women's stockings—now clearly visible thanks to scandalously high hemlines. Its resurgence was short-lived, however; the

Embroidery Overlord

In the spirit of the Bayeux Tapestry, one Lord Dulverton of Batsford, England, commissioned an embroidered recounting of Operation Overlord, a.k.a. the Allied invasion of Normandy in 1944, a.k.a. D-Day. The Overlord embroidery, on permanent display at the D-Day Museum in Portsmouth, England, spans 83 meters–10 more than the Bayeux Tapestry stitched more than a millennium prior. (In yo' FACE, Anglo-Saxons!) Beginning in 1973, 20 embroiderers worked for 5 years to complete the piece, which consists of 34 panels that depict not only the invasion and subsequent liberation of Paris, but the back story beginning with the dark days of 1940.

stock market crash of 1929, after which the economies of the United States and Europe collapsed, put the kibosh on all the fun. Demand for purty needlecraft pieces fell, replaced in people's hearts by demand for the ever-rare calorie. The advent of yet another world war, largely the result of Adolph Hitler's successful marketing of a new and improved brand of evil, drove the urge to adorn yet further underground. Moreover, many women who might formerly have enjoyed needlecrafts left home to work in factories.

Even after the Second World War, needlecrafting was, for all practical purposes, a dead art. But like some lucky dead things—that Jason guy from *Friday the 13th* comes to mind—needlework would be resurrected. Specifically, the "Up with Earth" types who emerged during the 1960s rediscovered many decorative art forms—needlework included. These days, tons of people—many of whom, ironically, suck at other domestic endeavors such as cooking and cleaning—have tapped into their genetically programmed interest in string by exploring the joys of embroidery, cross stitch, and needlepoint. On behalf of all of us, welcome to the cave!

Next!

In the next chapter, you'll find out the most critical part of any undertaking: what you get to buy.

Chapter Two

◆◆◆

Talking Shop: What to Buy

There's no doubt about it: The best part of any new endeavor is finding out what you get to buy. In this chapter you'll get the low down on all the goodies you'll need to stock your stitching kit. First, however, let's take a moment to define our terms—namely, the terms embroidery, cross stitch, and needlepoint.

What You Talkin' 'Bout Willis?

To many, *embroidery* refers to any kind of needlework that involves using a needle and thread to stitch on fabric. That definition encompasses all types of stitching, including cross stitch and needlepoint. For us, however, the term embroidery will refer specifically to *free embroidery*, A.K.A. *surface embroidery*. Free embroidery is a style of needlework that involves applying decorative stitches to fabric without using the fabric's weave as a guide. (You'll learn more about the various types of weaves in a moment.)

In contrast, *cross stitch* refers to a technique in which stitches—usually x-shaped—are worked evenly, using the weave of the fabric as a guide for the place-ment of the stitches. Although some cross-stitch designs come pre-stamped on fabric, most are worked from a paper chart; the stitcher counts the stitches marked on the chart to determine where they belong on the fabric. (You'll learn more about using charts in chapter 3, "Technically Speaking: Needlework Techniques.")

Finally, *needlepoint* resembles cross stitch in that it involves evenly working stitches using the weave of the fabric as a guide. It differs, however, in that the fabric used is a mesh canvas. Unlike cross stitch, which typically leaves areas of the back-ground unstitched, needlepoint—which was invented to re-create the look of woven

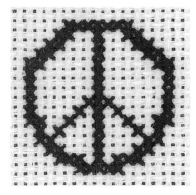

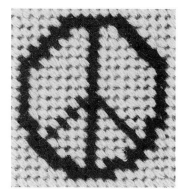

This is an example of
free embroidery, or plain old
embroidery for short.

This is an example of cross stitch.

This is an example of needlepoint.

tapestries—generally require that the canvas be entirely covered with stitching. Needlepoint designs are often printed or painted directly on the canvas, but some are stitched from a chart akin to those used in cross stitch.

Just Kitting

If you love woodland creatures, tigers, angels, kittens, patriotic symbols, aquarium fish, Precious Moments figures, trite sayings, or anything God related, you're in luck: There are eleventy-billion needlework kits on the market—some for needlepoint, some for cross stitch, and some for embroidery—that feature designs with one or all of the above. These kits contain just about everything you need to complete the design—fabric (some needlepoint kits ship with the design painted or silk-screened on the canvas, while some cross-stitch kits feature fabric with stamped designs); thread; any necessary charts or drawings; and perhaps even some stitching instructions. (Note that I say "just about everything" because kits typically *don't* contain the various tools required to complete a piece—i.e., scissors, hoops, etc. You're on your own for those. Fear not; you'll learn more about the tools of the trade a bit later in this chapter.)

If woodland creatures et al *aren't* your thing, you might have a harder time finding a needlework kit that interests you. Don't get discouraged! Despite the preponderance of unbelievably tacky (and not in that cool, kitschy way) kits, there are some real winners out there—kits that even *you* might be interested in buying. Take the fabulous Subversive Cross Stitch kits (www.subversivecrossstitch.com), which eschew the treacly quotes typically found on cross-stitch pieces—think "Home Sweet Home"—for sayings that are deliciously crass, as in "Homo Sweet Homo," and my personal favorite, "Pussy Got Me Dizzay." Or consider the exquisitely groovy Sublime Stitching embroidery kits (www.sublimestitching.com), with design themes that range from roller derby to dachshunds. (Speaking of Sublime Stitching, you're in luck.

The designer of Sublime Stitching kits, Julie Hart, graciously supplied a project for this book: chapter 7's "Coffee, Tea, or Me?")

In the event you *do* find a kit you like, consider these points before plunking down your hard-earned cash:

- Price If the kit costs more than your rent, you might reasonably think twice before buying it. If you really like it, however, you might justify purchasing it by telling yourself that stitching the piece will likely provide hours of entertainment, and that you'll be able to enjoy the finished product for years to come.

- Size Make sure the kit you're eyeing is a reasonable size. If you're an impatient type and have only a limited amount of free time to dedicate to your stitching, opt for a smaller piece. If, on the other hand, you have unlimited time and patience, buy a larger design. If you do go big, be aware that you might need special equipment such as a floor stand to actually stitch the design. (You'll learn more about floor stands later in this chapter.)

- Difficulty If this whole stitching thing is new to you, you'll probably want to go simple. Avoid kits that use a boatload of fancy stitches and a gazillion different colors.

- Instructions Are the instructions that come with the kit easy to understand? If charts are involved, do they use symbols, blocks of color, or some combination of both to indicate thread color? (You might find charts that include only blocks of color trickier to use, especially if the colors in the chart don't match up just so with the actual thread colors.) Finally, does the kit contain a full-color photo of the finished piece that you can use for guidance as you work?

If, after you've considered these points, you decide your kit qualifies for purchase, you're ready to skip ahead to the section "Meet the Needles!" later in this chapter. But if you have concluded that there are no kits on the planet that suit you, read on.

Test Pattern

Suppose your efforts to find a decent kit have been as unsuccessful as Tara Reid would be on *Jeopardy*. Don't despair. The selection of available needlework patterns—that is, the charts or drawings needed to complete a piece, minus fabric, thread, and the like—is more varied. In fact, you'll find whole *books* of needlework patterns, as well as Web sites that distribute them—sometimes free of charge. Indeed, you'll complete the projects in this book using the patterns we've supplied. (Note that in addition to paper-based patterns, iron-on patterns for embroidery are also available.)

If you find a pattern you like, odds are it will include information about what type of fabric and thread you should buy in order to complete the project. For example, if you've opted to complete a cross-stitch project, your pattern might indicate that you should use a 6 × 6-inch, white, 14-count Aida as your fabric and, say, DMC six-stranded cotton thread in the colors 310 (black), 166 (lime green), 307 (lemon), and so on. (Don't freak out if all this sounds like

Greek or Esperanto or some other crazy-ass language; you'll learn more about fabric and thread in a moment.) Simply bring the materials information with you when you visit your local needlework shop, tick each item off the list, and you're on your way.

Roll Your Own

So your hunt for a decent kit or pattern has ended in vain. Fortunately, you have yet one more option: creating your own. After you create your pattern, you'll need to track down all the necessary materials to complete the project: fabric, thread, and so on.

Design of the Times

You may well know what design you want your stitching project to incorporate. For example, maybe you want to stitch up a favorite saying, or an image of your favorite character on *Touched by an Angel*. Alternatively, maybe you know you want to start a stitching project but you're not sure what you want that project to be. In that case, for inspiration, check out old coloring books, comic books, art books, maps, nautical charts, catalogs, advertisements, photographs, greeting cards, and postcards—even wrapping paper.

When you're duly inspired, it's time commit your pattern design to paper. If embroidery's your gig, this is a simple matter of using colored pencils, markers, or even stamps to draw the design on a plain sheet of white paper. (If you need to enlarge or shrink a design, hit your local Kinko's and use the copier to do it.) After you do, you can use a water-soluble fabric pen or tailor's chalk to trace the design onto your fabric. A light box comes in *muy* handy here, although a sunny window will work in a pinch. (Often used to view film negatives, a *light box* is simply a box that has a light inside it and whose top is covered with translucent glass or plastic. If you're in the market for one, check out your local art-supply store.) Alternatively, transfer your design onto your fabric using run-of-the-mill tracing paper, a transfer pencil (that is, a special wax pencil designed specifically for this purpose, often found in the sewing section of your local craft store), and a hot iron. A third option is to transfer the design using carbon transfer paper and a ball-point pen. You'll learn more about transferring designs in chapter 3.

Hue Ado

Just about all designs involve color—which means you'll want to have some sense of what colors work together and what colors don't when constructing your design. You'll also want to ensure that you don't overwhelm your design with light colors or dark colors; instead, strive for a balance. For more information about color, see the section "Color Me Beautiful" later in this chapter.

Note: If your design involves lettering and you plan to use an iron to transfer it, the lettering in the design should be backward so that it appears correctly on the fabric. The same goes for designs that you want to face a certain direction in the finished piece—they should be drawn backward on the tracing paper.

If you're all about cross stitch, however, you'll need to commit your design to *graph* paper. Each square on the paper represents one stitch; simply fill them as needed with the desired color to chart your design. (When you determine exactly which thread colors you want to use for your design, take a moment to create a key for the chart, indicating the manufacturer and color number of each thread color used.) Then, rather than transferring your design directly onto your fabric, you'll simply refer to the charted design when stitching, counting off the squares on the chart to determine where on your fabric each stitch belongs. (To learn more about stitching from a chart, see the next chapter.)

If coloring in all those squares to create your cross-stitch chart strikes you as uncomfortably similar to guessing your way through a multiple-choice exam, try rendering a full-color drawing of your design on plain paper, placing a sheet of gridded acetate on top of the drawing, and making a color copy. The result will be your full-color drawing with a grid laid over it. (Okay, so some of the squares in the copy will probably contain more than one color. If so, just flip a coin to decide which color you'll use when stitching. Again, remember to create a key for your chart after you determine which thread colors you'll use.)

Either method will suffice if the design in your mind is fairly simple. If, on the other hand, your design is as complicated as the New York City metro transit system, consider using a computer program such as PC Stitch to convert digital images to needlework charts. Simply upload your favorite photo or other digital graphic into the software, answer a few questions, *et voilà* — a unique cross stitch, complete with a list of the type, brand, and color of thread needed to complete the design. Many of these programs also ship with clip-art and other tools to enable you to get your pattern just right. Some even help you keep track of your thread and other supplies, notifying you when you're running low.

If needlepoint is your craft of choice, you can use the same methods as cross stitchers do to generate a chart of your design. You can then use the resulting chart as a reference when stitching, again counting off the squares to determine where each stitch belongs. Frankly, however, counting stitches is a pain in the ass. For this reason, you might reasonably decide to paint your design directly onto your canvas. To do so, you'll need acrylic paints (they're waterproof, and they dry quickly) and a flat-top synthetic bristle paint brush (stick with sizes 1–4). You'll learn more about painting on canvas in chapter 3.

Materials Girl

Unless you're a mime, your stitching project will necessitate the use of some type of fabric, referred to among needle snobs as *ground fabric*. Just what type of ground fabric you need, however, differs depending on the needlework technique you plan to use. For example, if needlepoint is your bag, you'll need to stock up on canvas (hence the fact that "needlepoint" is often called "canvas work"). If you're more into cross stitch, then even-weave fabric is the way to go. Some types of even-weave fabric also work for embroidery, as does plain-weave fabric.

Leave It to Weaver

So what's the difference between canvas, even-weave fabric, and plain-weave fabric? It relates to how each type of material is woven, what types of fibers are used, and how those fibers, which are spun into threads, are spaced. Typically, a weaver manufactures fabric by first laying long threads on a loom from top to bottom. As mentioned in chapter 1, "Back Stitch to the Future," these vertical threads are called *warp threads*. Horizontal threads, called *weft threads*, are then woven across the warp threads from left to right and then back again, typically in an over-under fashion. The edge created by the weft thread's switchbacks is called the *selvage*. If cloth woven in this manner contains the same number of weft and warp threads per inch, that fabric is deemed *even weave;* if not, it's considered *plain weave*. As for canvas, it's merely a type of even-weave fabric whose holes are larger than the threads that separate them.

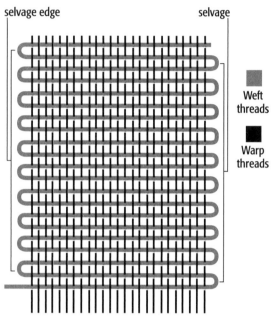

Warp threads run vertically (north/south), while weft threads run horizontally (east/west).

In addition to being divided into canvas, even weave, and plain weave, some fabric is also classified by *gauge* — that is, the number of threads or, depending on the type of fabric, the number of holes per inch. Gauge comes into play when you're choosing fabric for a charted cross-stitch or needlepoint piece. For example, the gauge of needlepoint canvas gen-erallly ranges from 7 to 22, with the higher number indicating the finer fabric. That is, the 7-count mesh, which contains 7 holes per inch, yields a very coarse stitch, while the 22-count mesh, boasting a whopping 22 holes per inch, results in an extremely wee stitch. For its part, cross-stitch fabric is generally available in gauges ranging from 18 to 36.

Because fine-gauge fabric contains more holes per inch, stitching a charted design on it results in a smaller finished item; if you're hoping to cover a bit more ground with your piece, opt for a lower-count fabric. Note that gauge is less of an issue with plain-weave fabric, which, as I mentioned, is used for embroidery. That's because, unlike needlepoint and cross stitch, which demand that stitches be carefully placed in the holes between the threads, embroidery stitches can be made willy-nilly. (If a plain-weave fabric is very tightly woven, however, you might want to stitch it using a finer thread.)

This was stitched on 18-count canvas.

(Legend for figure: Weft threads, Warp threads)

This was stitched on 14-count canvas.

This was stitched on 10-count canvas.

Stabilizing Influence

If you're starting an embroidery project and your heart is set on using a fabric that is stretchy, is loosely woven, or is otherwise unfriendly toward embroidery, you'll probably need to use a *stabilizing material* (sometimes referred to as *interfacing*) to ensure that your stitches lay properly. Stabilizers are generally temporary in nature–that is, they're meant to be removed from the fabric when embroidery is complete. This might explain why stabilizers are divided into the following four categories, each referring to how the stabilizer is removed from the fabric:

- ◆ **Tear away** Tear-away stabilizers work well on fabrics made of natural fibers or fabrics that are particularly soft. If however, your fabric is delicate, sheer, knit, loosely woven, or otherwise unstable, you'll want to opt for a different type of stabilizer.
- ◆ **Heat away** Delicate fabrics, sheer fabrics, and fabrics that aren't washable do well with a heat-away stabilizer.
- ◆ **Wash away** When wet, these stabilizers melt like the Wicked Witch of the West. (Note that some wash-away stabilizers can require several rinsings for complete removal.)
- ◆ **Cut away** Although you *can* remove this type of stabilizer from your fabric (by cutting it, natch), cut-away stabilizers can also be left on the fabric permanently to keep the fabric stable *after* the embroidery is complete. That makes this type of stabilizer ideal for projects that involve a knit fabric and are designed to be

continued

continued

worn, as it can prevent your design from stretching with multiple washings. Likewise, if the fabric you intend to use is thin, synthetic, and/or loosely woven, a cut-away stabilizer is the way to go. Finally, no matter what type of fabric you choose, cut-away stabilizers are great if the back side of the project will never be visible—like, say, if the piece is framed or sewn into a pillow. If you're looking to buy just one type of stabilizer, opt for the cut-away variety as it's a bit more adaptable than the others.

Stabilizers in all these categories are sold in a variety of weights, with heavier stabilizers being sturdier. If your design is particularly stitch rich—i.e., it is densely stitched—you'll want a heavier stabilizer. Designs that are a bit more stitch poor do fine with a lighter stabilizer. (If you find that the heavy interfacing is just too much, but the lighter interfacing options aren't quite enough, you can use multiple layers of a lighter interfacing to attain the desired weight.) Finally, stabilizers in all these categories are also available in different forms:

- **Fusible stabilizers** Fusible stabilizers, my personal favorite, are ironed onto the fabric. (Note that some fusible stabilizers are double-sided—that is, in addition to using them to stabilize the fabric on which you are stitching, you can also use them to fuse the stitched fabric to *another* piece of fabric.)
- **Non-fusible stabilizers** These are generally attached to fabric using a basting stitch. (You'll learn about basting stitches in chapter 4, "Stitch Hitter: Your Guide to Cross-Stitch, Embroidery, and Needlepoint Stitches.")
- **Adhesive-backed stabilizers** You apply an adhesive-backed stabilizer to fabric by sticking it on.
- **Liquid stabilizers** Washable stabilizers also come in liquid form; you simply brush the liquid directly onto the fabric and wait for it to dry.

Although stabilizers are generally applied to the back side of the fabric, some—especially water-soluble ones—can be applied to the front side. When used in this way, stabilizers are called toppings.

Plain Jane Weave

So you're planning to embroider a full-scale replica of the Bayeux Tapestry. You know you need plain-weave fabric—but the question remains, what *type* of plain-weave fabric? Because plain-weave fabrics can be made from just about any type of fiber, your range of plain-weave fabric choices is as broad as J. Lo's ass. That said, certain plain-weave fabrics work better than others for embroidery. In particular, fine cotton, woven cotton, Dupion silk, Tussah silk, and linen make good candidates. When considering your fabric options, just remember that odds are your embroidered stitches won't completely obscure the fabric underneath—which means you'll want to go for a material whose color enhances rather than clashes with your design. Put another way, that bolt of orange-and-lime paisley print you salvaged from your Aunt Edna's attic might be put to better use elsewhere. Like inside your fireplace.

Even-Weaven

Even-weave fabric, used primarily by cross stitchers (as opposed to, say, cross-*dressers*), is a type of plain-weave fabric whose warp and weft threads are precisely the same thickness. Put another way, the gauge of even-weave fabrics is the same regardless of whether you count from top to bottom or from left to right. Even-weave fabrics suitable for cross stitch include the following:

- ◆ Single even-weave fabric Available primarily in cotton or linen, single even-weave fabric is composed of single strands of intersecting threads. Gauges typically range from 18 to 36.

- ◆ Hardanger Hardanger fabric is woven in a similar fashion to single even-weave fabric, except that pairs of threads are used. Gauges are limited to 22 or 24 threads per inch—which in this instance equals 11 or 12 holes because the threads are in pairs.

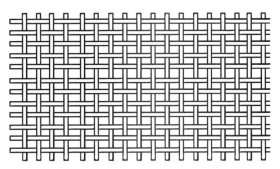

The threads in single even-weave fabric intersect in an over-under fashion.

- ◆ Aida Like single even-weave and Hardanger fabric, the threads in Aida cloth are woven in an over-under fashion. Rather than using single threads or pairs of threads, however, groups of three or more threads are used. Gauges generally range from 8 to 18 squares (that is, groups of thread) per inch.

- ◆ Binca Binca fabric is just like Aida fabric but features a coarser gauge—typically six squares per inch, but sometimes eight squares per inch.

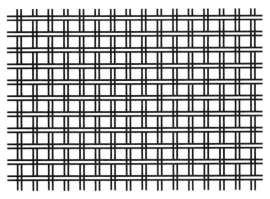

Hardanger fabric is woven using the same technique as single even-weave fabric, but using pairs of threads.

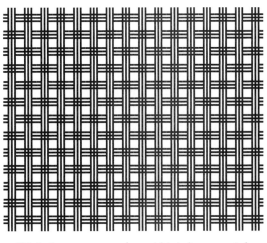

Aida is the most commonly used fabric for cross-stitch projects.

As with embroidery projects, cross-stitch work does not typically cover the underlying fabric; indeed, the fabric itself generally serves as the design's background. That means you'll want to choose your fabric—its type and its color—carefully to ensure that it doesn't clash with your stitching.

Canvas the Area

As I mentioned, canvas is simply a type of even-weave material whose holes are larger than the threads between them. Because one of the characteristics of needlepoint is that the stitched design obscures the canvas completely, the color of your canvas is less of a concern than it would be if you were embroidering or cross stitching—although if dark threads comprise the bulk of your design, you might want to use darker-colored canvas just to be sure no naked white canvas peeps through. Of greater interest are the canvas's gauge, stability, and quality (good-quality canvas contains smooth thread that won't snag stitches). Here are some options:

- ♦ **Mono canvas** This type of canvas is woven in the same manner as single even-weave fabric: with single threads that intersect in an over-under fashion. Gauges typically range from 10 holes (coarse) to 22 holes per inch (fine).

- ♦ **Interlock single canvas** Like mono canvas, interlock single canvas is generally offered in gauges ranging from 10 to 22, and is woven with single threads. Instead of crossing in an over-under fashion, however, the weft threads in interlock single canvas—or, more precisely, the *plies* of the weft threads (you'll learn more about plies in a moment)—are woven *around* each other for increased stability. As an added perk, the edges of interlock canvas tend not to unravel when cut—a problem that commonly occurs with mono canvas.

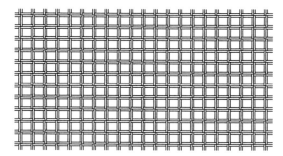

The plies of the weft threads in interlock single canvas wrap around each other.

Double canvas is similar to Hardanger fabric, except that the pairs of thread are split.

- ♦ **Double canvas (a.k.a. Penelope canvas or duo canvas)** Like Hardanger fabric, double canvas is woven in an over-under fashion with pairs of threads. Unlike Hardanger fabric, however, the pairs of threads in double canvas are split during the weaving process. In addition to offering improved stability, this type of canvas has smaller holes, making for more precisely placed stitches. Gauges for double canvas typically range from 7 to 10.

Get Wasted: Using Waste Canvas

Yet another type of canvas is *waste canvas*. Although it sounds gross, like the threads comprising the canvas are made of fecal matter or some other noxious substance, waste canvas is in fact just canvas that's designed to fall apart when damp. You use waste canvas to stitch counted designs (think cross stitch or needlepoint) onto plain-weave fabric rather than even-weave fabric or canvas. Simply use a basting stitch (see chapter 4 to learn how) to attach the waste fabric onto the plain-weave fabric and stitch up your design (make sure the waste canvas is large enough to provide a decent margin around the design space). When you're finished, spritz the canvas with water like it's been a bad kitty, and then use tweezers to pull the threads of the waste canvas out from under the stitched bits.

The Unusual Suspects

In addition to woven fabric, other types of more unusual materials are available for needlework projects:

♦ Plastic canvas Generally available in gauges of 7, 10, and 14, plastic canvas is extremely stable and can easily be cut into nifty shapes ("a hat, a brooch, a pterodactyl!"), making it ideal for children or other immature types, like your roommate's boyfriend.

♦ Vinyl Aida (a.k.a. vinyl weave) Although it sounds like the name of a fetish opera, vinyl Aida is in fact just Aida-style material made of vinyl, resulting in added durability. Gauges range from 14 to 18.

♦ Perforated paper If you're looking to cross stitch a note card, bookmark, or wee framed design, perforated paper, which typically has a gauge of 14, is a great way to go. Note, though, that it's as fragile as Nicole Ritchie. If your piece is likely to experience some abuse, opt for a different material.

The Fabric of Your Life

Now that you have some sense of what types of fabrics are available for stitching, it's time to decide what type and, if you're planning to needlepoint or cross stitch, what gauge is right for your project. Use this table to narrow down your options.

Choosing Your Fabric

Stitch Type	Fabric Options	Gauges
Cross stitch	Aida	8–18
	Binca	6–8
	Hardanger	22 or 24

continued

Stitch Type	Fabric Options	Gauges
	Single even-weave	18–36
	Perforated paper	14
	Vinyl Aida	14–18
Embroidery	Hardanger	N/A
	Plain-weave	N/A
	Single even-weave	N/A
Needlepoint	Double canvas	7–10
	Interlock single canvas	10–22
	Mono canvas	10–22
	Perforated paper	14
	Plastic canvas	7, 10, and 14

Technicolor Yarn

Thread is composed of lengths of wool, cotton, silk, linen, or synthetic fiber called *plies*. These plies are twisted, or *spun*, together to create *strands*, which are in turn combined. A thread's weight depends on the thickness of the plies, the number of plies in each strand, and the number of strands in the thread. Stitchers have more thread options than Carrie Bradshaw has shoes—from very fine cotton thread to wool that's heavier than Refrigerator Perry. Visit your local craft store to see (and feel) the myriad of threads available for you to use. The thread you choose depends on the following:

Skein Deep

Depending on its type, needlework thread is typically sold by the *skein* (i.e., a continuous length of loosely coiled yarn) or ball or, in some cases, by single lengths (especially handy if your project requires just one 12-inch strand of 4,029 different colors). Note that although you might be tempted to pilfer from your grandma's knitting stash, refrain; yarn designed for knitting and crocheting tends to be too stretchy for needlework, and might not block properly.

- ♦ **The stitching technique you plan to use**
  Different styles of stitching—i.e., embroidery, cross stitch, needlepoint, or what have you—call for different types of thread.
- ♦ **The type of fabric you've selected** If you've opted for a fabric that is woven extremely finely, you'll want to steer clear of bulkier thread.
- ♦ **The effect you want to achieve** Be sure to consider whether you want your piece to appear textured or smooth, shiny or matte, and choose your thread accordingly.

Strip It Good

Regardless of what type of thread you use, if it contains multiple strands, you might need to *strip* it—that is, separate the strands—and then recombine the stripped threads side by side rather than twisting them back together so that the thread will lie better. To strip your thread without winding up with a tangled mess *à la* Courtney Love's coiffure, first cut a 15- to 18-inch length of it. Then pinch the end of one strand and carefully pull it out of the thread. Repeat as needed until all the strands have been stripped. Before recombining the strands, ensure that your project demands the entire batch; sometimes only a few strands are needed. For example, if you plan to use Persian wool on, say, 12-count or 14-count canvas, two strands of the yarn will usually do the trick. Other times, you'll need to *add* strands to your thread; for example, nine strands of six-stranded cotton floss works well for 13-count canvas. Also, be aware that you can combine strands of different types of threads—for example, lining up a strand of six-stranded floss with some crewel wool—to achieve some interesting effects.

♦ **Your piece's ultimate destiny** If you're planning to stitch up a piece to upholster that chair you pilfered from Great Aunt Mabel's attic, you'll want to use more durable thread; ditto if you intend to sew your piece into, say, a throw pillow. If, however, your stitched masterpiece is meant to be framed and admired from afar, you can use more delicate thread. If your finished piece will be worn, avoid threads that shrink, bleed, or otherwise deteriorate when washed; ditto thread for pieces meant to serve as table or bed linens, tea towels, and so on. (Note that threads whose color stands up to laundering are called *color fast*. Be aware, however, that even some color-fast threads bleed the first time they hit water. For this reason, it's good practice to rinse these threads before stitching with them.)

As the Wool Turns

If you like to think of yourself as "old school," then wool may well be your thread of choice. Spun principally from the fur of sheep and goats, this material has existed since well before the Iron Age. When stitched on canvas or fabric, wool yields a soft, matte look. Although there are several types of wool thread, or *yarn*, the following are most commonly used for needlework:

♦ **Persian yarn** The most popular and versatile type of wool thread, Persian yarn is available in a wide range of brilliant colors. Assembled with three strands, Persian yarn is easy to strip and recombine. Persian yarn, generally used in needlepoint projects, is typically too heavy for embroidery or cross-stitch pieces. One reliable brand of Persian yarn is Paternayan.

- **Tapestry yarn** Although tapestry yarn contains four strands, it is not meant to be stripped. The result is a stitch that's as smooth as Tim Meadows in *The Ladies Man*. Used for needlepoint, tapestry yarn works best with 10- to 13-count canvas. Proven brands of tapestry yarn include Appleton Tapestry Wool and DMC Lain Colbert.
- **Crewel wool** While Persian and tapestry yarn are best suited for needlepoint, crewel wool, composed of a single thread containing two plies that cannot be stripped, can be used for needlepoint, embroidery, and cross stitch. (Indeed, as mentioned in chapter 1,"Back Stitch to the Future," the embroidery technique often called "crewel" is so named because it uses crewel wool.) Threads of crewel wool can be combined to create heavier stitches. One trusted brand is Appleton Crewel Wool.
- **Silk/wool blends** Also suitable for needlepoint, embroidery, and cross stitch, silk/wool blends are smoother than pure wool but heftier than pure silk. Look for brands such as J.L. Walsh, Felicity's Garden, Silk and Ivory by Brown Paper Packages, and Impressions by The Caron Collection.

Linenist Leanings

Like wool, linen, which is spun from flax, has enjoyed a long and varied history. In addition to being used for garments, books, printed money, and even shields, linen has been employed as thread by crafty types for thousands of years. Although its natural color ranges from ivoryish to tannish to brownish to grayish, linen thread, which is characterized by its lovely sheen, can be dyed any number of hues. With a texture that can vary from soft and smooth to stiff and rough, linen thread tends toward springiness.

Linen thread is sold in a variety of sizes, indicated by two numbers. The first number refers to the thread's weight—the lower the number, the heavier the thread—while the second number designates the number of plies in the thread. (Note that although linen thread does contain plies, it should not be stripped.) Lighter weights, such as 10/2, work well for cross stitch, with heavier weights being suitable for needlepoint. But be warned: Linen thread can be somewhat uneven in width. Moreover, poorer-quality linen yarn may contain *slubs*—that is, small, randomly occurring knots. (Not to be confused with *scrubs*, like in that song by TLC.) Popular brands of linen thread include Rainbow Linen from Rainbow Gallery and Flax 'n Colors from The Thread Gatherer.

Cotton Club

In addition to being among the cheaper threads available, cotton is washable, easy to work with, and available in myriad colors. It's also extremely adaptable, with most varieties suitable for needlepoint, embroidery, or cross stitch. One additional benefit of cotton thread is its smoothness, which is the result of a process called "gassing." (This gassing process differs somewhat from the gassing process your brother uses to clear out a room, which is in no way related to smoothness.) Here are the types of cotton thread you'll likely consider using for a needlework project:

- ◆ Six-stranded floss This six-strand thread is the most common type of cotton thread. Often called "embroidery floss," it's available in a vast spectrum of hues and boasts a nice luster. The most widely used brands of six-stranded floss are DMC, Anchor, and Presencia Finca Mouline.
- ◆ Pearl cotton Called *coton perlé* by fancy-pants types, pearl cotton is a softly twisted thread that's characterized by its sheen (not its *Charlie* Sheen, thank God). Unlike other types of cotton thread, pearl cotton is not meant to be stripped. It is, however, available in a variety of sizes ranging from 12 (super skinny) to 3 (pleasantly zaftig). As with six-stranded floss, popular brands of pearl cotton include DMC and Anchor, as well as Overture from Rainbow Gallery.

Got Silk?

If you've got a bit of extra cash burning a hole in your purse, silk thread is the way to go. Although it's true that silk is made by worms—which, let's face it, is pretty much totally disgusting—it's also smoother, stronger, and all-around purtier than wool, linen, or cotton. Distinguished by its incredible gloss (a product of the fiber's molecular structure), as well as by the extraordinary colors achieved during the dyeing process, silk is manufactured in weights similar to pearl cotton thread.

Although a type of silk called *reeled silk* or *pure filament silk*, which is simply unwound from silkworm cocoons as is—sometimes in lengths up to 1,000 yards (that's slightly less than a kilometer, for those of you who understand the metric system)—can be used for needlework, *spun silk* is the more common choice. Rather than being a continuous length of fiber, as reeled silk is, spun silk is, well, spun. That is, it is composed of shorter plies and strands of silk that are spun together, resulting in thread that is less smooth than reeled silk but easier to stitch. Proven brands of spun silk include Silk Mori from Kreinik Mfg. Co., Soie d'Alger from Au Ver a Soie, Splendor from Rainbow Gallery, Silk 'n Colors from The Thread Gatherer, and Soie Cristale by The Caron Collection.

Chartsy Fartsy

So you have a drawer full of DMC floss—but the pattern you're working with calls for Anchor thread. In the immortal words of Keanu Reeves in *Speed*, "What do you do? What. Do. You. *Do?*" Option A is to suck it up and buy all new thread. But a better alternative is to use a conversion chart to determine which DMC thread colors most closely mirror their Anchor counterparts (and vice versa). Similar charts can be found for converting, say, DMC thread to Paternayan wool. Because these charts would consume more pages than James Joyce's *Ulysses*, I'll urge you to find them on the Internet; in the search engine of your choice, simply type "thread conversion chart" and click one of the 100,000+ hits returned.

Silk Road

If you're looking for natural beauty and luster (and hey, what girl *isn't?*), silk thread is the way to go. Its smooth surface reflects light–an effect that is only enhanced by the fiber's translucent qualities. Plus, it's as strong as Linda Hamilton in *Terminator 2*. That said, if you're stitching with silk, you'll want to keep a few things in mind:

♦ Silk is prone to damage from the abrasion that naturally occurs during the stitching process. To mitigate this, use a needle that's a bit bigger than normal, the idea being that the needle will create a larger hole in the fabric, allowing the silk to pass through a bit more cleanly.

♦ If you're working with canvas, avoid resting the silk on it; otherwise, the rough warp and weft threads may snag it.

♦ Opt for stitches that play up the thread's shine. Stitches that involve combinations of long and short elements work well, as do stitches that turn different directions.

Faking It

In contrast to the aforementioned threads, all of which are made of natural fibers, there are also tons of synthetic threads available. Some are fuzzy, like Charleston thread by Needle Necessities. Others—like Marlitt thread by Anchor, as well as DMC rayon floss—are shiny, like silk. Still others are metallic, like DMC's line of metallic floss. (Speaking of metallic things, threads made of actual gold, silver, and copper—materials that needleworkers of old used in their more *chi chi* pieces—do exist, although they'll cost you.)

Choose or Lose

I mentioned that the type of thread you choose depends on myriad factors—the stitching technique you plan to use, the type of fabric you've selected, the effect you want to achieve, the finished piece's ultimate destiny, blah-de blah-de blah. Indeed, some threads won't even work for certain techniques or fabric types. Take Persian wool: It's way too thick for embroidering on plain-weave fabric or cross stitching on, say, 18-count Aida material. In contrast, size 12 pearl cotton would be too skinny to cover the mesh of, say, a 10-count needlepoint canvas.

Adding to the confusion, many threads can be split into smaller strands or combined with others. This means that in addition to figuring out what type of thread to use, you also have to figure out how much of it you need for proper coverage! Worse, the number of strands required can vary by stitch. For example, if you plan to use an upright stitch on your piece, such as a bargello stitch, you might need more strands than if you opt for a diagonal one, such as a tent stitch. (You'll learn all about different types of stitches in chapter 4.) It's more confusing than filing your taxes! For this reason, I've included the following tables, which offer suggestions on what types and gauges of fabric to use with what kinds of thread, as well as how many strands are needed for diagonal stitches versus upright ones. Note that the operative word here is "suggestions"; if you discover that you prefer a lighter or heavier stitch—and lots of people do—by all means subtract or add strands as desired. (If only the IRS were equally obliging . . . .)

Persian Wool Coverage

Fabric	Gauge	Number of Strands/Stitch
Canvas	18	1/diagonal 2/upright
Canvas	14 or 12	2/diagonal 3/upright
Canvas	10	3/diagonal 4 or 5/upright

Crewel Wool Coverage

Fabric	Gauge	Number of Strands/Stitch
Canvas or linen	18	1/diagonal 2/upright
Canvas or linen	14	2/diagonal 3/upright
Canvas or linen	12	3/diagonal 4/upright
Canvas or linen	10	4 or 5/diagonal 5 or 6/upright

Six-Stranded Cotton Coverage

Fabric	Gauge	Number of Strands/Stitch
Linen	36 or 32	1/diagonal 1/upright
Linen	28	1 or 2/diagonal 1 or 2/upright
Linen	18	2 or 3/diagonal 2 or 3/upright
Single even-weave	25 or 24	2/diagonal 2/upright
Hardanger	22	2/diagonal 2/upright
Canvas	18	3 or 4/diagonal 5 or 6/upright
Canvas	14	5 or 6/diagonal 6 or 7/upright
Canvas	12	6 or 7/diagonal 7 or 8/upright
Aida	18	2/diagonal 2/upright
Aida	16	2/diagonal 2/upright
Aida	14	3/diagonal 3/upright
Aida	11	3/diagonal 3/upright
Perforated paper	14	3/diagonal 3/upright

Silk Thread Coverage

Fabric	Gauge	Number of Strands/Stitch	
Canvas	18	3 or 4/diagonal	4 or 5/upright
Canvas	14	4 or 5/diagonal	6 or 7/upright
Canvas	12	7 or 8/diagonal	8 or 9/upright
Canvas	10	8 or 9/diagonal	9 or 10/upright
Aida	16	2/diagonal	2/upright
Aida	14	3/diagonal	3/upright
Aida	11	3/diagonal	3/upright

It follows, then, that the amount of thread you need to purchase for a given project will vary depending on how many strands of it are required per stitch. That is to say, if you're using three, rather than six, strands of six-stranded embroidery floss, you'll only need half as much.

Speaking of determining how much thread to buy for a project, if you're stitching a design of your own creation and you didn't use a computer program that automatically calculates how much of each color thread is required to complete the design, you'll quickly discover that unless you have a Ph.D. in math (which, it goes without saying, I do *not*), you're basically screwed. The problem is the number of variables involved: fabric count, thread type, number of strands, type of stitch, blah blah blah. My advice? Corner your favorite salesperson at your local needlecrafts store and make her figure it out. Barring that, take a wild guess on what you think you'll need and then buy twice as much—maybe more if you're dealing with thread that varies by dye lot. (You'll learn about dye lots in a moment.)

Color Me Beautiful

In addition to determining what type of fabric and thread will work best for your project, you must also decide what colors to use. Odds are you'll have given this some thought already—namely, when you designed your, er, design. What you might not be prepared for, however, is the range of hues available of any given color. That is, you won't just find red DMC thread; you'll find red DMC thread ranging in value from very light to very dark including Red, Rose, Bright Red, Dark Red, Deep Red, Orange Red, Coral Red, two shades of Red

We've Got a Bleeder . . .

In addition to regularly dyed thread–that is, thread that is one color and one color only–*overdyed* thread is also available. Overdyed thread is dyed by hand to achieve a variegated effect. A skein of overdyed thread typically features light and dark hues within a single color family, but might instead include several colors that bleed from one to the next, creating a variegated effect. (Incidentally, you can also make your own variegated thread by threading strands from different-colored skeins of thread onto a single needle.)

Copper, three shades of Garnet, and six shades of Cranberry. Good designs feature a variety of hue values; that is to say, designs that use primarily dark values or light values will look as unbalanced as Tom Cruise.

In addition to ensuring that the color values are balanced, you'll want to make sure the colors themselves don't clash. In fact, you might want to consider researching color theory at least a little so you don't wonder why burnt sienna and periwinkle threads look vomitous on orange fabric. One way to explore color theory without forking over art-school tuition is to park yourself in front of a display of paint chips at your local hardware store—especially the ones created by interior designers to demonstrate which diverse colors work well together. Then hit your local needlework shop armed with the paint chips that really caught your eye in the hopes of finding threads and fabrics that match. Beyond that, look to fashion, food, and home magazines for color-combination ideas.

Meet the Needles!

Unlike hard drugs, which may or may not require the use of a needle, pretty much all stitching projects do. Don't assume, however, that the needle that came with the sewing kit you filched from your hotel room in Las Vegas will do the trick. Different types of stitching require different types—and sizes—of needles. At the very least, you'll want these types of needles on hand:

- ◆ Tapestry needles Ideal for needlepoint and cross stitch, tapestry needles are characterized by large eyes and blunt ends. Sizes range from 28 (smallest) to 13 (largest).
- ◆ Chenille needles Chenille needles are similar to tapestry needles in that both types feature large eyes. Chenille needles are also sized similarly to tapestry needles. But while tapestry needles are characterized by a blunt end, chenille needles are sharper than Kate Moss' elbows, making them great for embroidery.
- ◆ Embroidery needles Sometimes called crewel needles, embroidery needles are super sharp and have long eyes. These needles, which range in size from 1 (thick) to 12 (thin), have a finer shank than their chenille needle counterparts.

Tapestry needle.

Chenille needle.

Embroidery needle.

Choosing Your Needle Type

Stitch Type	Needle Options
Needlepoint	Tapestry needle
Embroidery	Chenille needle Embroidery needle
Cross stitch	Tapestry needle

In addition to these needles, you might also want to keep a few other types around:

- ◆ Beading needles If you plan to embellish your stitched piece with beads, you'll want to keep some beading needles, available in a variety of lengths, around. The distinguishing characteristic of a beading needle is that its eye is the same width as the rest of the needle, which is itself as fine as George Clooney. This enables the needle to pass easily through particularly wee beads. Beading needles, which feature a sharp end, range in size from 10 to 16 with 10 being the thickest and 16 being the finest.
- ◆ Sharps These all-purpose needles are handy for hand-sewing your stitched pieces into various nifty objects (i.e., pillows, bags, beer cozies, etc.).

Be aware that like fine cutlery and love, needles are prone to tarnish. That's because many are plated with nickel. Eventually they'll become rougher than Nitro from *American Gladiator*, snagging your thread and fabric, and will need to be replaced. If this pisses you off, you can suck it up and buy gold-plated needles. They're much smoother than their nickel-plated counterparts, and they last waaaay longer.

Punch Drunk

More a cousin than a sibling to the aforementioned needles, punch needles are in fact hollow shafts with a point and eye on one end and a handle on the other. Thread is drawn through the end of the handle of the punch needle, down the needle's shaft, and then through its eye. Punch needles are used specifically for the punch-needle stitching technique, in which thread or yarn is punched through the ground fabric from back to front, creating a shag carpet-like effect. Smaller-sized punch needles work well with cotton floss, while larger sizes accommodate yarn and even ribbon.

Welcome to the Size Is Right!

As I mentioned, the type of needle you use depends on your stitching technique. What *size* you use depends on other factors. In the case of needlepoint and cross-stitch projects, your needle size will depend largely on—you guessed it—the gauge of your fabric and, by extension, the weight of your thread. Use these tables as your guide:

Choosing a Tapestry Needle for Your Needlepoint Project

Canvas Gauge	Needle Size
10-count	18
12-count	20
14-count	22
16-count	22
18-count	22
20-count	24
22-count	24

Choosing a Tapestry Needle for Your Cross-Stitch Project

Fabric Gauge	Needle Size
7- or 8-count Aida	18
10-count Aida	20
11-count Aida	22

continued

continued

Fabric Gauge	Needle Size
14-count Aida	22
16-count Aida	22
22-count Aida	24
18- to 25-count single even-weave	24
25- to 32-count single even-weave	26
36- to 40-count single even-weave	28
22-count and up Hardanger	28

Determining which needle size is right for your embroidery project involves a bit of experimentation on your part. (Whoa! Put your pants back on! Not *that* type of experimentation!) Your objective is to use the largest needle possible that doesn't muck up your fabric.

Better Threader

If you opted for shop class over home-ec in middle school like I did, odds are you'll consider chucking stitching as a hobby the first time you try to thread a needle. Refrain! Instead, rush to your local needlework shop and buy a needle threader, which usually looks like a cheap game token with a wire loop on one end. Simply pass the wire loop through the eye of your needle, feed your thread through the wire loop, work the needle free of the threader, and you're good to go.

On Rules and the Ignoring of Them

Of course, these tables are only guidelines, and as anyone who has spent significant time in juvenile detention knows, guidelines are meant to be summarily ignored. Specifically, *these* guidelines should be ignored if you are stitching with a particularly fragile type of thread. Instead, opt for a larger needle so that when you poke the needle through the canvas or fabric, the needle will enlarge the hole, allowing the delicate strands to then pass through the enlarged hole unmolested. Likewise, toss these guidelines out the window if you're needlepointing or cross stitching on waste canvas and the underlying fabric is, say, bed linen or something similar. In that case, you'll simply want to use a sharp. (If the underlying fabric is jersey or woven, a tapestry needle should do the trick.)

Go Tell It on the Mounting

Mounting refers to attaching your fabric to a hoop, scroll frame, or stretcher frame to keep it as taut as Melanie Griffith's face. In addition to making stitching a bit easier, it also reduces the amount of distortion that naturally occurs during the stitching process. Here's the scoop on each of your mounting options:

- ◆ Hoops These devices are ideal for cross stitching or embroidering on non–even weave fabrics like silk, cotton, and blends, and on even-weave fabrics such as linen, Aida, and Hardanger—but less so for needlepointing on canvas, which performs better on scroll frames or stretcher frames. Hoops consist of two wood, metal, or plastic rings, one of which fits snugly inside the other. The best hoops for stitching are ones with a screw mechanism on the outer ring, which enables you to keep the fabric taut. Hoops are sold in a range of diameters, but generally top out at 12 inches; working with hoops that are much larger than 8 inches in diameter, however, can be tricky unless you plan to clamp it to a table or stand. (That said, there's no law against un-mounting a large piece of fabric from a smaller hoop when you finish stitching one area of a design and re-mounting it to begin stitching the next—although doing so could mark up your fabric and squash your stitches a bit.) If you do decide to use a hoop with your project, consider keeping some tissue paper or cotton strips handy; you can use them to protect your fabric while it's in the hoop. (For details, see the section "Mount Up: Mounting Your Fabric" in chapter 3.)

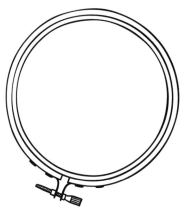

Hoops are ideal for embroidery or cross-stitch projects.

- ◆ Scroll frames Sometimes called *roller frames,* scroll frames often consist of two round scroll bars with fabric tape or webbing, which you use to attach your fabric—although some feature slots through which the fabric is fed. These round scroll bars are

Scroll frames are a bit more substantial than their hoop brethren.

attached with a pair of screws or bolts to a pair of flat side bars. To use the scroll frame, you attach the top and bottom edges of your fabric—be it even-weave fabric for cross stitch, non–even weave fabric for embroidery, or canvas for needlepoint—to the scroll bars, roll the scroll bars until the fabric is drum tight, and then tighten the screws or bolts as needed to maintain the tension. Optionally, you can then use *frame clips* to attach the fabric to the sides of the scroll frame. As you finish stitching one area of the fabric, simply loosen the screws or bolts and remove the frame clips, scroll the stitched area of the fabric up or down, and tighten the bolts or screws and re-attach the clips to continue working elsewhere; doing so won't harm your stitches unless they are raised or otherwise three dimensional.

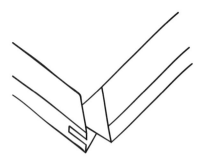

♦ **Stretcher frames** You can assemble your own stretcher frames, which look a bit like picture frames, from stretcher bars, sold in pairs at art-supply stores as well as craft stores. Each stretcher bar should be an inch or so longer than the edges of

You build your own stretcher frames from stretcher bars using the interlocking joints in the corner.

the fabric. For example, if your fabric is 18 × 18 inches, you'll want two pairs of 19- to 20-inch stretcher bars. Simply attach the pair of horizontal bars to the pair of vertical bars using the interlocking joints on the corners, and then attach your fabric to the bars using a staple gun or needlepoint tacks. (Note that you should avoid mounting fragile fabric on stretcher frames, as stapling or tacking the fabric to the frame will almost certainly damage it. Stretcher frames work best with hardier plain-weave and even-weave fabrics and with canvas.)

If you really want to go crazy, invest in a table or floor stand for your hoop, scroll frame, stretcher frame, or Q Snap. That way, rather than using one hand to hold the hoop or frame or whatever and stitching with the other, you can use *both* hands to stitch. Good stands allow you to adjust the height and the angle for more comfy stitching.

Survival Tools

Science-y types used to say that our ability to use tools was one significant behavior that sep-arated us from the apes—until Jane Goodall spied a chimp using a stick as a tool to fish for termites underground (which, by the way, he then ate). Regardless of whether you're a *homo sapien* or a *pan troglodyte* (or just a regular troglodyte, like your ex-boyfriend), these are the tools you'll want around for stitching:

Q Snaps Up

Q Snaps are yet another option for mounting your fabric. Like stretcher frames, they're composed of modular pieces—in this case, four plastic tubes, called *elbows*, which are available in a variety of lengths—that you join together to form a square or rectangle. Once the elbows have been joined, you use clamps to attach your fabric to them, rolling the clamps away from the center of the fabric to tighten it. The benefit of using Q Snaps over stretcher frames is that you don't have to staple the fabric, which means you can work on different areas as needed.

- **Scissors** You'll need a pair of embroidery scissors, which are particularly sharp and feature fine, smooth points, for cutting thread. You'll also want a pair of fabric shears for slicing and dicing your fabric. Because some people have meatier fingers than others, try out a few different brands of each to see what fits best before forking over your cash. Note that as with most things, the cheaper the scissors are, the more they'll suck.

- **X-Acto knife** An X-Acto knife can come in handy when cutting or trimming plastic canvas.

- **Tweezers** If you plan to work with waste canvas, keep some tweezers handy so you can more easily remove the canvas from the fabric after you finish stitching. They're also great for picking out errant threads in your piece. Opt for the kind with super-fine points.

Embroidery scissors are as dainty as Audrey Hepburn.

Fabric shears are much more substantial than embroidery scissors and work well for cutting fabric.

- **Pins** Make it a point to keep a few pins of various types around. They make great placeholders when you need to mark a specific spot on your fabric, and can also be used to hold threads aside as you work in order to keep them out of your way. You'll also need pins when it comes time to block your piece.

- **Pin cushion/emery** If your piece is particularly complicated, requiring you to change colors more often than Madonna changes her image, you might want to thread several needles with the various necessary colors, then stick the threaded needles in a pin cushion or emery. (An *emery* is similar to a pin cushion but is filled with a very gritty material; stowing your needles in one of these will keep them sharp and shiny. If you've ever bought one of those tomato pincushions and wondered about the little strawberry that came with it, the strawberry is an emery.)

- **Magnet** A magnet can serve the same purpose as a pin cushion or emery: to park multiple threaded needles. Magnets are also handy in the event you drop a needle; simply wave the magnet near the needle to pick it up.

- **Thimble/finger shield** The accident prone should consider investing in a thimble and/or a finger shield to avoid pricks while doing needlecrafts. (Unfortunately, avoiding pricks elsewhere, like in bars or at work, is not as easy.)

- **Laying tool** When working with multiple plies of thread on a single needle, you might want to use a laying tool to ensure that the threads remain parallel rather than twisting as you stitch. (This

Using a laying tool helps ensure your threads remain parallel.

process is called "laying" the thread. Although it is a common practice among needle-crafters, I suspect it is less fun than laying some other things, like Daniel Craig, that new James Bond guy.) If you don't feel like shelling out for a laying tool, a large tap-estry needle works in a pinch.

♦ **Tape** Tape is an essential item; you'll tape up the cut edges of your piece to prevent fraying. Drafting masking tape and painter's masking tape are a bit less sticky than regular masking tape and therefore your better options, but masking tape will work in a pinch.

♦ **Ruler and/or tape measure** These are essential when it comes time to cut your fabric.

♦ **Stitch converter** Using this nifty device, a sort of stitcher's slide rule, can help you determine how large a design will be; simply indicate the number of stitches across or down the design and the gauge of your fabric.

♦ **Gentle detergent** While not technically a "tool," gentle detergent (think Woolite or something similar) is essential for any stitcher. You'll use it after you complete your stitching projects to remove any dirt or grime, without damaging the fabric or thread.

♦ **Iron** In addition to using a hot iron to transfer an embroidery design or apply a stabi-lizer onto fabric, you'll also use it to press the creases from your finished piece (after washing the piece with the aforementioned gentle detergent, of course).

♦ **Staple gun** A staple gun comes in incredibly handy for blocking your piece, as well as for mounting a piece on a stretcher frame. (You'll learn about blocking and mounting in chapter 3.)

♦ **Sewing machine** Okay, this is not *required* for needlework, but it's definitely a "nice to have"—especially if you want to use your needlework designs to fashion bags, pillows, or what have you.

Destination Organization

As soon as you accumulate even a modest collection of fabric, thread, needles, and such—espe-cially if you've gone a little crazy and bought way more than you need—you'll see why it's a good idea to keep them organized. Failure to implement some type of system results in chaos; unless you're an anarchist—not that there's anything wrong with that—you'll go mad. This section outlines where and how to store your stitching-related goodies.

Benign Neglect: Properly Storing Unused Fabric

It happens to all of us: we go a little crazy buying fabric and wind up with more than we could reasonably use in a decade. When you experience this, you'll want to make it a point to take special care of your surplus to ensure it doesn't become damaged, soiled, mildew-y, or develop some other type of taint. First, roll up any unused fabric right-side-in, wrap the rolled fabric with a layer of acid-free tissue, and secure the bundle by loosely tying a piece of yarn around it. If the fabric in question is canvas or even-weave cloth, pin a scrap of paper on the fabric that indicates its gauge. Finally, resist the temptation to seal this fabric burrito in a plastic bag; like children, fabric needs to breathe. Instead, store it as is in a dry, well-ventilated area, away from sunlight (to prevent fading).

Monster Stash

Trust me on this: Failing to develop an organization and storage system for your thread will result in certain disaster. Okay, "disaster" is a little strong. I mean, we're not talking Hurricane Katrina here. But as God is my witness, I can promise you that you will be severely inconvenienced. For one thing, if you don't organize your threads, you won't be able to keep track of what colors you have—which means you'll almost certainly end up shelling out for colors you've already bought. Secondly, failing to organize and properly store your thread almost guarantees it'll become as dirty and tangled as Owen Wilson's hair. Here are some suggestions:

- A *hardware storage cabinet*—the kind that have a boatload of tiny drawers, typically used for screws and nails and stuff—works extremely well for storing thread. To keep track of which colors you have on hand, stick a label on each drawer indicating the precise color(s) stored—including the color number assigned by the manufacturer. (If you really want to go crazy, upgrade to a wooden storage box; you can even find some designed specifically for storing embroidery floss.)

- Not to be confused with "Bobbitt," as in "Lorena," *bobbins* are great for storing thread—especially cotton floss and the like. (Avoid the cylindrical bobbins used for sewing thread; instead, opt for the flat kind, which are designed especially for needlework thread.) Many embroidery bobbins feature "write-on" margins, where you can write down the thread's color number. These bobbins can then be stored in a plastic compartmentalized caddy or on a *snap ring,* which looks like a big key ring that snaps open and shut. As an added bonus, this system is somewhat portable. (In case you didn't notice, the key to both of these systems is marking the color number alongside the thread. By doing so, you can avoid buying thread for a project that you already own.)

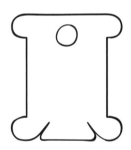

Floss bobbin.

In addition to purchasing at least one long-term thread-storage solution, I suggest you pick up a fist full of *project cards*. Sometimes called *master cards* or *thread cards*, project cards are oblong cards that feature several holes along the right margin through which you can affix lengths of cut thread. Next to each thread hole is a space for noting the thread's color number. Some project cards also feature a series of holes along the left margin that enable you to store the project card in a loose-leaf binder; others feature a magnet on one end for easy needle storage and retrieval. Any time you start a new project, you'll want a few of these handy to organize the thread for that specific project. (Note that if you're crafting on a budget, you can make these yourself by excising a box top from a cereal box and punching some holes through it.)

Needle Me This

So you don't wind up with needles in your couch cushions, on your floor, or, say, between the first and second metatarsal bones in your foot, keep a needle case—these can be store-bought or made by hand—in your stitching kit for storing extras. In addition to preventing debilitating podiatric wounds, some needle cases can also help you keep track of your needles by type and size, while others feature magnets for easy needle retrieval in the event you drop one. Alternatively, if you're a reduce/reuse/recycle type, used Altoid tins, Tic-Tac boxes, and prescription bottles make great containers for needles and various other stitching doo-dads such as pins, needle threaders, and the like.

Don't Be a Tool

You know how cosmetic companies inevitably include a makeup bag whenever they run a "gift with purchase" promotion? Those bags are great for housing your stitching tools—shears, embroidery scissors, tweezers, pin cushion, magnet, thimble, blah blah blah. If you just can't wait for the next Clinique Bonus Time, hoof it to your local CVS to buy an el cheap-o cosmetic bag.

Pattern Recognition

If you wind up with enough paper needlework patterns to cover a sleeping homeless person, consider investing in a loose-leaf binder to store them. If you're really feeling anal-retentive, categorize them by design theme or by type (i.e., cross stitch, embroidery, or needlepoint) and separate the categories with dividers.

Next!

Now that the important matter of shopping for needlework supplies is complete, you're ready to learn what to do with them. The next chapter covers techniques that every stitcher with a modicum of self-respect should master.

Chapter **Three**

◆◆◆

Technically Speaking: Needlework Techniques

You've spent this month's rent on needlework supplies; it's time to put those goodies to use! In this chapter you'll master general needlework techniques that apply whether you're working a needlepoint project, a cross-stitch piece, or an embroidery heirloom. (As for the ins and outs of working certain types of needlework stitches, those are covered in chapter 4, "Stitch Hitter: Your Guide to Cross-Stitch, Embroidery, and Needlepoint Stitches.")

The Anal-Retentive Stitcher: Setting Up Your Work Environment

Remember Phil Hartman—God rest his soul—as the Gene, Anal-Retentive Chef on *Saturday Night Live?* He spent the whole sketch *preparing* to cook—cleaning the cooking surface, tidying the countertop, ensuring that his peppers were chopped just so—but never actually managed to place a single pot in the oven. Although Chef Gene might have taken things a little far, he may have had a point; at the risk of sounding like an anal-retentive stitcher, I suggest you take some time to prepare your work environment for best results. Just don't get so carried away that you never manage to start—let alone *finish*—your piece.

Most importantly, make sure you have adequate lighting. This not only helps you see your piece but also prevents the development of crow's feet around your eyes due to squinting—an obvious *Glamour* magazine *Don't.* Although you *can* go big and buy a needlework-specific light from your local needlecrafts store, a regular run-of-the-mill desk lamp that allows you to adjust its position may well do the trick. Lamps with those clippie doodads are great if you plan to work with a stand; likewise, travel reading lights work well with scroll frames. The type of bulb you choose—halogen, daylight, fluorescent daylight, LCD, or whatever—is a matter of personal preference. Also, if your eyesight sucks, consider a magnifying light, or else keep a magnifying glass handy.

Beyond that, consider the following:

♦ Ensure that your seat (your chair, not your *derrière*) has adequate cushion for your seat (your *derrière*, not your chair).

♦ Good posture is key. That's not to say you should stitch with a book on your head, but do make an effort to sit up straight.

♦ Do not—I repeat, do *not*—let your cat near your stitching. Ditto small children. They will not understand the critical difference between "unbelievably expensive silk thread" and "exciting new toy."

Cut and Run: Preparing Your Materials

Easy, tiger. I know you're itching to stitch. Before you begin, however, you need to organize your thread, as well as cut, tape, and mount your fabric. You may also need to transfer your design onto your fabric.

Don't Let the Thread Bugs Bite: Organizing Your Thread

In chapter 2, "Talking Shop: What to Buy," I urged you to purchase project cards, a.k.a. *master cards* or *thread cards*—oblong cards that feature several holes along the margin for affixing lengths of cut thread. If you're planning to work on a project that involves more than a few colors of thread, now's the time to pull those puppies out so you can organize your skeins. (Note that some needlework kits presort the thread and attach it to project cards for you, which is a serious bonus and means you can ignore these steps.)

1. Using a permanent marker, label the holes along the margin with the manufacturer number of each thread color in your project. Write the numbers in numerical order; that way, when you're looking for a particular color later, you'll be able to find it easily.

2. If you'll be working from a chart, draw the chart's symbol for each color next to its number.

3. Sort your threads into the same order as the labels on the project cards.

4. Feed the first color thread through the hole next to the corresponding label and tie it in a loose knot to secure it. Repeat for the remaining color threads in the project.

Eyes on the Size: Preparing Your Fabric for Cutting

Regardless of the type of needlework you plan to do—embroidery, needlepoint, or cross stitch—you'll need to cut your fabric to size before you begin. First, however, you might need to wash and iron it. Here's how you figure out whether your fabric is okay as is or needs some prepping:

- If you're stitching directly on a pre-manufactured item, such as a bib or towel or onesie or whatever, washing and ironing it *before* you stitch is a good idea to prevent shrinkage later. Ditto if you're embroidering on a plain-weave fabric that is prone to shrinking. Don't worry about being all careful; just toss them in your washer and dryer as you would any regular garment.

- If you're stitching on needlepoint canvas or on Aida or a similar fabric designed specifically for cross stitch, do *not* wash it first. Doing so will remove the starch from the fabric, which makes it harder to stitch. Ironing, however—especially with steam—isn't a bad idea if your fabric suffers from any stubborn creases, although it's not strictly required.

After you've washed and/or ironed your fabric—or not—you're ready to trim it to size . . . almost. First, you need to determine how large your stitched design will be. If, say, you're embroidering a design you've mapped out on paper, simply use your ruler to measure the design. Determining the final size of a cross-stitch or needlepoint design stitched from a chart, however, is a bit trickier—primarily because the size of the stitched design will depend on the gauge of your fabric or canvas. Fortunately, you can use the stitch converter I told you to buy in chapter 2 to figure it out. Simply indicate the number of stitches across the design and the gauge of your fabric to determine the width of the design, and the number of stitches down the design and the fabric gauge to determine the height.

If you ignored my advice and failed to purchase said stitch converter *(loser)*, follow these steps:

1. Using the needlework chart, count one row of stitches (i.e., from left to right). Let's pretend for the sake of example that the total number of stitches in a single row is 100.

2. Next, count one column of stitches on the needlework chart (i.e., from top to bottom). Here, pretend there are 150 stitches.

3. Check your fabric's gauge. Ideally, this information will be immediately available to you because a) the fabric is still in its original packaging or b) as directed in chapter 2, you wisely pinned a piece of paper onto the fabric indicating its gauge when you put it in storage. If said information is not immediately available, you can determine the gauge yourself; simply line up your ruler on the fabric and count the number of holes or squares in 1 inch. For this example, let's pretend we're dealing with 18-count Aida fabric.

4. Divide the number of horizontal stitches (here, 100) by the gauge of the fabric (in this example, 18). Let's see . . . carry the one . . . got it: 5.5555555555. For some added wiggle room, round up to the next half inch—here, 6. *Et voilà!* You have determined that the design will be 6 inches wide-ish.

5. Divide the number of vertical stitches (in this case, 150) by the gauge of the fabric (again, 18). The result: 8.33333333. Once more, round up to the nearest half-inch—8.5.

So you're dealing with a design size of 6 × 8.5 inches. Does that mean your fabric's measurements should match? *Nyet.* To ascertain your *fabric size,* add a margin of 4-ish to 8-ish inches all the way around—unless your design is particularly large or small, in which case you might use a slightly larger or smaller margin, respectively. These margins will come into play when you block your piece, frame it, make it into a pillow, or whatever.

Finally. You're ready to cut—that is, *after* you mark the correct measurements on your material using a fabric pen or a pencil. Then, using your shears, get snippy.

She's a Grainiac

When cutting the fabric, make it a point to *cut on the grain*—that is, along the warp and weft threads comprising the canvas. Otherwise, when you're finished stitching your piece, it'll be as skewed as the programming on Fox News. Even blocking the piece might not help; fabric that was stitched while skewed tends to want to remain that way. (You'll learn about blocking later in this chapter.) Even if you do manage to straighten things out, it may result in distortions around your stitches.

Ready and Stable: Applying a Stabilizer

I mentioned in chapter 2 that if you're starting an embroidery project and your fabric is stretchy, loosely woven, or otherwise embroidery averse, you'll want to apply a stabilizing material (or *interfacing*) to the fabric in order to ensure that your stitches lay properly. How, exactly, you apply said stabilizer depends on whether your stabilizer is fusible, nonfusible, adhesive-backed, or liquid. Because the specific instructions for applying all these stabilizers vary by manufacturer, I won't get into the specifics here. However, here are some general points to get you started:

- **Fusible Interfacing** To apply a fusible interfacing, use a hot iron—think *Cotton* setting. Lightly misting the fabric with water will help the interfacing stick; if you go this route, place a thin towel such as a tea towel between the iron and the stabilizer to prevent the stabilizer from melting. Ditto if you are using fabric that's mixed poly-cotton; placing a tea towel between the iron and the fabric will prevent scorching.
- **Nonfusible stabilizers** Nonfusible stabilizers are generally attached to fabric using a basting stitch. For added sticking power, try using a temporary spray fabric adhesive to position the stabilizer before stitching it into place.
- **Adhesive-backed stabilizer** Applying adhesive-backed stabilizer is simple; just peel the protective paper from the stabilizer and stick it onto the back side of your fabric.
- **Liquid stabilizer** To apply a liquid stabilizer, simply brush it directly onto the fabric. (You'll need to wait for it to dry before you begin stitching.)

Transfer Student: Transferring Your Embroidery Design

You learned in chapter 2 that you can transfer an embroidery design that's been committed to paper onto your fabric by using tracing paper, a transfer pencil, and an iron. Alternatively, you might be able to trace the design (or draw it freehand) right onto the fabric using a water-soluble fabric pen, tailor's chalk, or carbon transfer paper and a ballpoint pen. Either way, you'll want the outline of the transferred design to be as accurate as Ru Paul's eyeliner so the stitching doesn't get all whopper-jawed. (As mentioned, if you need to resize the image before transferring it to your fabric, use a copier to do the job.)

Iron Efficiency

To transfer your design using your iron, do the following:

1. Place a piece of tracing paper on top of your design.
2. Using a transfer pencil, trace the design onto the tracing paper.
3. Place the tracing paper face down on the front side of your fabric, situating the drawn design where you want it to be stitched. Try lightly misting the fabric first. Also to prevent scorching, lay a thin towel over the tracing paper.

4. Apply a hot iron to the back side of the paper and towel to transfer the design. For best results, don't move the iron around while it's on the paper; instead, situate the iron for a few seconds on one spot, pick it up, place it on another spot for a few seconds, pick it up, and so on. (If your fabric is particularly delicate, you might want to opt for a slightly cooler setting to avoid damaging it.)

5. Carefully peel a corner of the tracing paper from the fabric to peek at the fabric. If the design appears clearly on the fabric, continue slowly peeling the paper off. If not, carefully lay the paper back down on the fabric in the same spot as before and repeat step 4.

The Amazing Trace

To trace a design onto your fabric using tailor's chalk or a water-soluble pen, do the following:

1. Place your paper design on a light box or use masking tape to tape it onto a sunny window. (If your fabric is sheer-ish, you might be able to skip this step.)

2. Lay or tape (again, using masking tape) your fabric over the back-lit paper design.

3. Using tailor's chalk or a water-soluble fabric pen, trace the design.

Alternatively, trace the design using carbon transfer paper like so:

1. Lay your fabric face up on your work surface.

2. Lay the carbon transfer paper, with the carbon side down, on top of the fabric.

3. Lay the pattern, design side up, over the carbon transfer paper.

4. Weigh down the layers of fabric and paper with a paperweight or with your hand.

5. Pressing firmly with a ballpoint pen, draw over the lines of your design to apply it to your fabric.

Paint Killer: Painting Your Needlepoint Canvas

Although a needlepoint pattern can be stitched from a chart, it's easier to work from a painted canvas—hence the fact that most needlepoint kits supply painted canvases instead of (or in addition to) charted designs. If you want to paint your design onto needlepoint canvas, do the following:

1. In order to protect the original design, make a photocopy of it. You'll work from that.

2. On the photocopy, trace over the outline of your design with darker lines so you'll be able to see them a bit better through the canvas.

3. Center your canvas over the copied design and tape it in place.

4. Using the underlying design as a guide, paint your canvas. As mentioned in chapter 2, acrylic paints are waterproof and dry quickly, making them ideal for painting needle-point canvas. Apply the paints with a flat-top synthetic bristle paint brush (stick with sizes 1–4). Avoid the Tammy Faye Bakker effect that results from spreading the paint too thickly, as too much paint clogs the holes in the canvas. (By the way, even if you apply a light touch, the paint will probably block the holes at least a little. This can change the gauge of the canvas a bit, which means you might need to reduce the number of strands in your thread.)

5. After the paint dries, separate the canvas from the paper design.

Caught on Tape: Taping Up Your Fabric

Regardless of what type of project you plan to complete—embroidery, needlepoint, or cross stitch—you'll want to use 2-inch wide tape to tape up the edges of your fabric. Drafting masking tape and painter's masking tape are a bit less sticky than regular masking tape and therefore your better options, but masking tape will work in a pinch. In addition to preventing it from unraveling like Michael Jackson, this also keeps your thread from catching on the edges of your fabric as you stitch.

Apply half the tape to the front of the fabric.

1. Cut a length of tape that's roughly as long as the right edge of your fabric.

2. On the front side of the fabric, apply half of the tape lengthwise to the right edge.

3. Turn the fabric over and fold the remaining tape onto the back side, pressing it until it sticks.

4. Repeat steps 1–3 for the left edge of the fabric.

5. If you plan to mount the fabric onto a hoop, repeat steps 1–3 on the top and bottom edges. (If you'll be using a scroll frame, you can skip this step.)

Mount Up: Mounting Your Fabric

You have three options when it comes to mounting fabric: a hoop, a scroll frame, or a stretcher frame.

Hoop de Do: Mounting Fabric onto a Hoop

To mount fabric onto a hoop, do the following:

1. Lay the hoop on a hard, flat surface.

2. Loosen the screw on the hoop enough to separate the outer hoop from the inner hoop and set the outer hoop aside. (On the off chance your hoop doesn't feature a screw—some don't—you can ignore the bits about the screw in these steps.)

3. Lay the fabric over the inner hoop.

4. If you're feeling all anal-retentive, consider laying a few layers of tissue paper over the fabric. Alternatively, wrap the inner and outer portions of the hoop in strips of cotton. This will prevent your fabric from being marked up by the hoop in any way.

5. Place the outer hoop on top of the fabric (and on top of the tissue paper, if applicable) and push down until the outer hoop fits around the inner hoop.

6. Tighten the screw on the outer hoop until the outer hoop is snug around the inner hoop.

7. Pull the ends of the fabric to tighten any slack, and then tighten the screw a bit more. Although some stitchers like to have a teeny bit of give in the center of the fabric, I like mine to be as taut as Jessica Alba's *derrière*, with the screw completely tight. You may want to experiment a bit to decide which approach works best for you.

8. If you covered your fabric with tissue paper, tear the paper away from the area you plan to stitch.

9. When you are finished stitching, remove the hoop by loosening the screw and extricating the outer hoop from the inner one.

Tangled up in Screw

When stitching fabric that's been mounted with a hoop, hold the hoop such that the screw is positioned at one o'clock. This will prevent threads from getting tangled up on the screw. Also, work with one hand on the bottom of the hoop to support it, and the other hand on top, working the needle.

Hoop Schemes

Not all fabrics are happy being hooped. For example, hoops tend to crush velvet. If you're stitching on such a material, try hooping a piece of adhesive-backed stabilizer instead of the fabric itself. Then peel the adhesive backing from the stabilizer, spritz a bit of temporary fabric adhesive on it for a bit of added stick, and press the back side of your touchy fabric onto it. In this way, you enjoy the benefits of using a hoop without damaging your fabric in the bargain.

Scroll in One

The scroll bars on some scroll frames require you to stitch your fabric onto them, while others feature slots through which you feed the ends of the fabric. For this reason, we'll cover actually attaching fabric to a scroll frame in slightly more general terms (check the instructions that came with your scroll frame for specifics):

1. Measure the top edge of the fabric and use a pencil to mark the center.
2. Repeat step 1 on the bottom edge of the fabric.
3. Find and mark the center of the top scroll bar on the scroll frame.
4. Repeat step 2 on the bottom scroll bar.
5. After lining up the center of the top scroll bar with the center of the fabric's top edge, attach the fabric to the bar. Depending on how your scroll frame is designed, you'll do this by sticking the fabric to the scroll bar's fabric tape, basting the fabric onto the scroll bar's webbing, or feeding the fabric through the slots in the scroll bar.
6. After lining up the center of the bottom bar with the center of the fabric's bottom edge, attach the fabric to the bar.
7. Insert the top bar into the appropriate slots on the roller frame's side bars.
8. Insert the bottom bar into the appropriate slots on the roller frame's side bars.
9. Rotate the top bar to roll the fabric into the correct position for stitching your design.
10. Tighten the two bolts on the top bar to hold it in place.
11. Turn the bottom bar to tighten the slack. Then turn it once more so the fabric is tighter than Mariah Carey's skirt.
12. Tighten the bolts on the bottom bar to hold it in place.
13. If your fabric is super big, you may also want to attach the left and right edges of the fabric to the scroll frame's side bars to further stabilize it. The easiest way to do so is to use special *frame clips* to clip the edges of the fabric onto the side bars.
14. After completing an area of the design, you can roll the worked area into the frame without damaging the stitches (unless they are raised, in which case you're S.O.L.). Just remove the frame clips used to stabilize the left and right edges of the fabric (if applicable), loosen the bolts attaching the top and bottom bars to the side bars, and roll the fabric upward or downward. When the fabric is placed correctly, tighten the bolts and reattach the frame clips (again, if applicable).
15. When you're ready to remove your fabric from the scroll frame, remove the frame clips (if applicable) and peel your fabric from the adhesive securing the fabric to the scroll bars, cut the stitches from the scroll bars' webbing, or work the fabric from the slot (depending on how the fabric was attached).

Stretch and Kvetch

You can assemble your own stretcher frame (it looks a bit like a picture frame) and mount your fabric onto it. Here's how it's done:

1. Assemble the stretcher bars comprising the stretcher frame using the interlocking joints on the corners.

2. After measuring each stretcher bar, mark its center point.

3. Measure all four edges of the fabric, marking each edge's center point.

4. Line up the marks on the fabric with the marks on the stretcher bars.

5. Tack or staple the fabric onto the stretcher bars at the four center points.

6. Continue tacking or stapling outward from the center point on one edge of fabric until that edge is completely attached to the stretcher bar beneath it.

7. Move to an adjacent stretcher bar and repeat step 6, pulling the fabric taut.

8. Repeat step 6 on the remaining two stretcher bars, again ensuring that the fabric is pulled taut.

9. If, as you work on your piece, the fabric on the frame becomes loose in the center, remove all the tacks or staples, reshape and tighten the fabric, and repeat steps 6–8 to reattach the fabric.

10. After you finish stitching, remove the tacks or staples to extricate the fabric from the stretcher bars.

Chart to Chart Chat: Understanding Needlework Charts

Cross stitchers and needlepointers among you will likely stitch from a *needlework chart*—that is, a diagram that describes how to complete your design—at some point in your needlecrafts career. In fact, you will use a chart quite soon if you plan to complete any of the cross-stitch or needlepoint projects in this book. With more complicated designs, these charts—which are often composed of a gazillion tiny symbols, always on a grid—might *look* as complicated as your feelings about your mother, they are actually quite simple to interpret:

♦ Each square on the chart represents a square on Aida (or similar even-weave) fabric or an intersection of warp and weft threads on needlepoint canvas.

♦ Each of the symbols that appears in these squares—for example, #, <, ^, *, and the like—represents a specific thread color. To interpret these symbols—that is, to determine which symbol represents which thread color—simply refer to the key provided with the chart.

♦ Cross-stitch charts can easily be used for needlepoint and vice versa.

- Cross-stitch charts frequently include empty squares, which indicate that no stitch is required on the corresponding square of fabric. (If you're using a cross-stitch chart to complete a needlepoint design, you'll want to stitch those areas intended to be left blank, most likely using white thread.)

- Some charts use special types of lines or symbols to indicate what type of stitch is to be performed on various portions of the design. For example, although most cross-stitch charts call for simple cross stitches, some designs also call for three-quarter stitches, one-quarter stitches, back stitches, French knots, and so on. These symbols or lines will be listed in the key accompanying the chart.

If you're dealing with a particularly large and complex design that will take you the better part of your youth to complete, you can expect your chart to suffer many indignities in the form of dirt, coffee stains, stray marks, and so on. Plus, you might make it a practice to mark off squares on your chart as you complete the corresponding stitches on your fabric (a highlighter works well for this) so you can see at a glance how much of your design you've managed to finish. Either way, the odds that you'll be able to reuse the chart later are greatly reduced. To contend with these inevitabilities, make a photocopy of your chart before beginning your project and work from *it* rather than from your original. While you're at it, enlarge the chart to prevent eyeball exhaustion. Then, store your original in a safe place for later use.

Let's Get This Party Started

Praise [insert deity of choice], you're ready to get started stitching—*if* you've transferred your design onto your fabric. In that case, you can pretty much thread your needle with the color of your choice and go at it. (See chapter 4 to explore the types of stitches that are available to you.) If, however, you'll be stitching from a chart, you'll need to decide where on your fabric you want to start stitching: in the center or in a corner.

- In the center Starting in the center of your fabric and beginning by stitching the elements in the center of your chart ensures you'll wind up with your design precisely centered on your fabric. To find the center, fold the fabric in half lengthwise and then fold it in half widthwise; the center is where the folds cross. This approach is especially effective if your design features a prominent foreground element near the center; stitch this foreground element first and work outward.

- In the corner Much like jigsaw-puzzle enthusiasts often like to piece together the border of a puzzle before filling in the center, some stitchers like to work from the outside in, stitching the areas around the edges of the chart first. This can be helpful because it defines the work area early on. Just make sure when you start stitching in a corner of the fabric that you've left an adequate margin.

Although you'll find needlecrafters who swear by one approach or the other, I prefer a more libertarian stance, which is to say you should start where you want.

Feed Your Thread: Threading Your Needle

You've decided where you want to start stitching. You have your thread, embroidery scissors, needle, and, ideally, your needle threader at hand. You're ready to Thread! That! Needle!

1. First, using a sharp pair of embroidery scissors, cut a 15- to 18-inch length of thread. (Going much longer than this tends to result in knotted, tangled, or weakened thread. Trust me. I've tried.)

2. If your thread is pearl cotton or some type of super-fuzzy yarn, determine the direction of the thread's *nap*—i.e., which way the fuzzies (that's a technical term) go. To do so, pinch one end of the thread and pass it across your palm in both directions. If the thread feels smoother when passed in one direction than in the other, that's the direction of the nap. (When you're finished, skip to step 5.)

3. If your thread is of a type that can be separated—for example, six-stranded embroidery floss—*strip it* by pinching the end of one strand and carefully pulling it out of the length of thread. Repeat as needed, until all the strands have been stripped.

4. Recombine the strands of your stripped thread. (Refer to the tables in chapter 2 to determine how many strands are required for your project.)

5. Moisten the tip of one end of your thread and then squeeze any excess moisture from it. (I usually just put it in my mouth. If that grosses you out, try keeping a glass of water or a wet sponge handy.) If you're dealing with thread that's been stripped, either end will do; if your thread has a nap, you'll want to moisten the end as shown here.

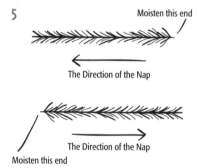

5

Moisten this end

The Direction of the Nap

The Direction of the Nap

Moisten this end

The top thread's right end should be moistened; the bottom thread's left end should be moistened.

6. Using your embroidery scissors, trim the moist end of the thread at an angle. This makes it a bit easier to thread your needle.

7. If you chintzed out on buying a threader, try poking the angled tip of the thread through the eye of your needle. If that doesn't work, hold the thread between your thumb and forefinger so that a stub of it sticks up. Then brush the eye of the needle over the stub and hope against hope that the stub will penetrate the eye. If *that* doesn't work, try threading through the *other* side of the eye. (As it turns out, there is a wrong and a right side to a needle.) As a last resort, you can try folding a wee piece of paper in half, placing the thread in the fold, and try passing the paper through the eye of the needle. Or you can just suck it up and buy a needle threader.

8. If you wisely purchased a needle threader, simply pass the threader's wire loop through the eye of your needle, feed the thread through the loop, and work the needle free of the threader.

By the way, you should make it a habit to change needles on a regular basis. Some needles tend to oxidize, turning black in the process; stitching with an oxidized needle can result in grayish schmutz on your piece. Likewise, make it a point to remove your needle from your stitching—or, at the very least, attach it to the fabric somewhere outside the design area—when you're finished for the day. That way, if the needle rusts while it's off duty, it won't soil your fabric.

Ready or Knot: Starting Your Stitch

With the needle duly threaded, your next task is to start your stitch. Perhaps the easiest way is to do the following:

1. Draw the needle through the fabric from back to front, leaving a tail that's an inch or so long on the back side.

2. Pass the needle through the fabric from front to back.

3. Begin your next stitch by again drawing the needle through the fabric from back to front, crossing over the inch-long tail from step 1 along the way.

4. Repeat steps 2 and 3 until the tail is completely covered with stitches.

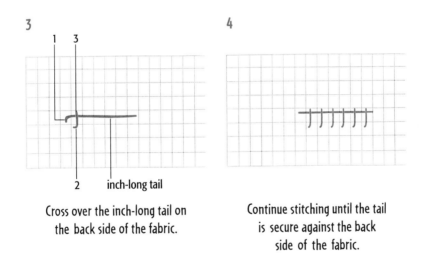

Cross over the inch-long tail on the back side of the fabric.

Continue stitching until the tail is secure against the back side of the fabric.

Another way to start your thread is to first tie a knot on the tail end of the thread to serve as a stopper. (Don't overthink this whole knot thing; any run-of-the-mill knot or two will do. Just make sure the knot is larger than the holes in your fabric.) Then, simply draw the thread through your fabric from back to front, allowing the knot to act as the stopper on the back side, and stitch away. Be aware, however, that serious needlework types will shun you. Plus, having a knot on the back of your fabric can result in a lump in the finished piece, especially if it's framed. Instead, use a *waste knot* or an *away waste knot* (see below) to start your stitching, regardless of whether your project involves embroidery, needlepoint, or cross stitch.

Waste Knot Want Knot: Working a Waste Knot

If you're preparing to work a stitch-rich area of your design, a waste knot is the way to go when starting a thread. Here's how it's done:

1. Tie a knot—any old knot will do—at the end of your thread, making sure the knot is larger than the holes in your fabric.

2. About an inch away from the spot where you plan to start stitching, and in the path of the stitches you intend to complete, pass your needle and thread through your fabric from the front to back. The knot will rest on the front side of the fabric.

3. At the point where you want to start your stitches, draw the needle through the fabric from back to front.

4. Pass the needle back through the fabric from front to back.

5. Begin your next stitch by again drawing the needle through the fabric from back to front, crossing over the thread that runs from the knot to the first stitch.

6. Continue stitching toward the knot. On the back side of your fabric, your stitches should cross the thread that runs from the knot to the first stitch.

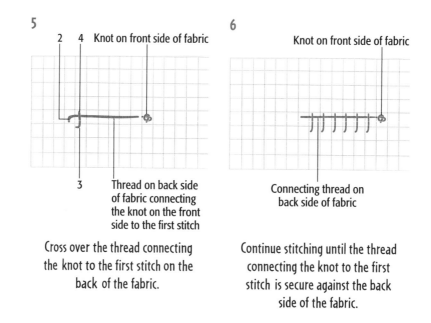

Cross over the thread connecting the knot to the first stitch on the back of the fabric.

Continue stitching until the thread connecting the knot to the first stitch is secure against the back side of the fabric.

7. When your stitches reach the knot, use your embroidery scissors to cut the knot off. (Be sure you snip only the knot! Cutting your fabric or your stitching along with it is the worst thing *ever* and will drive even the most stable girl to drink. Try turning the tip of your scissors away from your stitches to prevent this.) With the knot gone, continue stitching as normal.

Waste Away: Working an Away Waste Knot

If you're preparing to stitch a more sparsely populated area in your design, use an *away waste knot*. It's exactly like a regular waste knot, except, well, it's away—that is, rather than being placed an inch from your starting point, an away waste knot is placed 6 or 7 inches away. Here's the skinny:

1. Tie a knot—any old knot will do—at the end of your thread, making sure the knot is larger than the holes in your fabric.

2. Six or seven inches away from the spot where you plan to start stitching, and in the general path of at least some of the stitches you intend to complete, pass your needle and thread through your fabric from front to back. The knot will rest on the front side of the fabric.

3. At the point where you want to start your stitches, draw the needle through the fabric from back to front.

4. Pass the needle back through the fabric from front to back.

5. Begin your next stitch by again drawing the needle through the fabric from back to front, crossing over the thread that runs from the knot to the first stitch.

6. Continue stitching, crossing the thread that runs on the back side of your fabric from the knot to the first stitch whenever possible.

7. After you've secured the thread connected to the knot to the back of your fabric, use your embroidery scissors to cut the knot from the front of your piece. You'll be left with a tail of thread that's several inches long hanging from the back of the fabric.

8. Flip your piece over so the back side faces up, thread a needle onto the tail of thread hanging from the back, and weave the needle and thread in and out of the stitched area to secure the tail.

9. Again using your embroidery scissors, snip the excess thread in the tail.

Absolutely Stabulous: Using the Stab Method

Regardless of whether you plan to needlepoint, embroider, or cross stitch your piece, and no matter what type of stitch you plan to execute, you'll want to use the *stab method* to complete your stitches:

1. With your dominant hand, insert your needle into your fabric from back to front at a 90-degree angle.

2. If your fabric is attached to a stand, use your other hand to pull the needle and thread the rest of the way through the fabric. (If your fabric is not attached to a stand, this hand will already be occupied holding your mounted fabric; in that case, simply bring your dominant hand around to the front of the fabric to do the job.)

3. Using the same hand as in step 2, insert the needle into your fabric from front to back at a 90-degree angle.

4. With the same hand as in step 1, pull the needle and thread the rest of the way through the fabric.

Note: For specifics on working various types of cross-stitch, embroidery, and needlepoint stitches, see chapter 4.

Tie Master: Tying Off to End Your Thread

So a) you've finished stitching a particular area of your design and are ready to switch to a different-colored thread, b) you're ready to stop stitching altogether either to take a breather or to finish your piece, or c) you've stitched a length of thread until only a couple inches of it are left on your needle. Your next step is to *tie off* your thread—that is, secure it so your stitches don't unravel.

If you plan to continue stitching with a new thread in the roughly same spot where you've left off with the old one, simply do the following to tie off and start your next thread:

1. Draw the needle with the old thread still attached through the fabric from front to back.

2. Remove the needle from the thread and lay the remaining tail flat against the back of the fabric.

3. Thread your needle on a new piece of thread.

4. At the point where you want to continue stitching, draw the needle with the new thread through the fabric from back to front, leaving a tail that's an inch or so long on the back side.

5. Situate the tail from the new thread alongside the tail from the previous one.

6. Pull the needle through the fabric from front to back.

7. Begin your next stitch by again drawing the needle through the fabric from back to front, crossing over the tails of both the new thread and the old thread along the way.

8. Repeat steps 6 and 7 until both tails are covered. (If the tail from your previous thread is significantly longer than the tail on your new thread, you can snip the longer thread to size if you like.)

Alternatively, you can tie off using the *waste ending method*. (Again, this assumes you intend to continue stitching in the same basic area.) Here's how it works:

1. Draw the needle with the old thread still attached through the fabric from front to back.

2. About an inch away, and in the path that your next thread will travel, pull the needle back through the fabric from back to front.

3. Remove the needle from the thread and knot the thread to keep it from slipping back through the holes in the fabric.

4. Thread your needle on a new piece of thread and start it using the method of your choice.

5. As you stitch, cross over the previous thread that runs along the back side of the fabric to secure it. When your stitches reach the knot on the front side of the fabric, use your embroidery scissors to snip the knot.

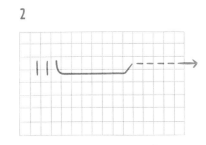

Pull the needle from the back of the fabric, shown here, to the front, about an inch away from your last stitch.

Another tie-off method—especially effective if you've just completed a particularly stitch-rich area—is to weave the remaining thread on your needle through some existing stitches on the back side of your fabric, much like you did to secure the tail end of your thread when using an away waste knot. Rather than simply drawing back through a row of stitches, try staggering things a bit. When you're confident the thread is secure, snip the excess. This approach works whether you plan to continue stitching or you're done for the day.

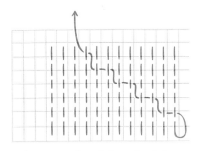

Draw your thread through existing stitches on the back side of your fabric to tie off.

Whichever method you choose to tie off, take a moment to snip any excess thread; otherwise, they may make your piece all lumpy when its framed.

Signing Off

A Bob Ross painting just isn't a Bob Ross painting if it hasn't been signed by The Master. For this reason, you should feel free to sign your own pieces–but using thread instead of paint. I like to use a coordinating shade to stitch my initials in the lower-right corner to make my mark.

Apocal-oops Now: Fixing Mistakes

It's inevitable: Someday, somehow, you will *totally* screw up while stitching. For example, if you're stitching from a chart, you might botch up your counting and wind up adding or dropping a stitch by accident—thereby offsetting each subsequent stitch by one. Hopefully you'll realize your mistake immediately, in which case you can simply undo the errant stitch. Here's how:

1. Remove the needle from your thread.

2. On the front side of the fabric, insert said needle underneath the errant stitch and lift to loosen the stitch.

3. Once the stitch is loose, continue pulling the needle upward until the tail end of the thread pops through the fabric from back to front.

4. Re-thread the needle and continue stitching, correcting your mistake as you go.

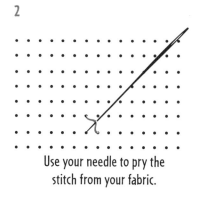

Use your needle to pry the stitch from your fabric.

If you don't immediately realize your mistake but notice it within a row or so, you'll want to undo each stitch you've added to the design since the mistake occurred. Just follow the preceding steps over and over (and *over*) until you reach the error. Be aware, however, that passing thread through fabric in this manner can weaken the thread, making it prone to breakage. For this reason, rather than rethreading the needle on the same thread, tie off and start a new one; then continue as normal, correcting the mistake as you work.

If you don't notice the mistake you made in the 9th row of your piece until the 24th one, do some hard thinking about whether the mistake is worth fixing. If you—and *only* you—will ever notice the error, let it go. If, however, you know in your heart of hearts that the mistake will greatly affect the design, and if you don't have it in you to set it on fire and call it a day, you'll have to suck it up and undo your stitches in order to fix the mistake. Rather than using your needle, however, save some time by removing the stitches with your embroidery scissors. Simply slip the sharp point of the scissors under each stitch, raising the stitch slightly, and then cutting it.

Of course, cutting your stitches opens you up to cutting your fabric along with it. If this happens to you, resist the temptation to hurl yourself in front of a moving train. Cuts involving a single canvas thread or a single fabric thread can be summarily ignored; just keep stitching *as though nothing happened*. If, by some slip of your scissors, you managed to sever multiple threads, try sticking a piece of cellophane tape over the threads on the front and back sides of the fabric. Then, using a particularly sharp needle, stitch right through the tape.

If a cut results in a larger opening, your best bet is to patch it. Note, however, that you might be S.O.L. if your piece involves embroidery or cross stitch. That's because the fabric in those types of projects is typically visible underneath the stitching, which means a patch probably would be too. If, however, your piece is needlepoint, you can patch it by cutting a square of blank canvas that's a bit larger than the area you want to mend. (Be sure this square of canvas is the same gauge as the canvas used in your project.) Then, precisely aligning the holes of this blank canvas with the holes in the back side of your piece, use a basting stitch to affix the patch. (You'll learn about basting stitches in chapter 4, in the section "Hand Job: Hand-Sewing Stitches.") Finally, stitch over the patch just as you would the original canvas. You can remove the basting stitches after the patched area has been completely stitched over; simply snip them using your embroidery scissors.

The Final Cut: Finishing Your Piece

Hey! You've just finished your needlework piece! What are you going to do next? Okay, going to Disneyland—that's obvious. But what about after that? Before you can truly call your piece complete, you'll need to do the following:

- If you applied a stabilizer to your piece, you'll need to remove it—unless you used a kind designed to remain in place.
- Look, no offense, but even the most fastidious girl has oil on her hands and skin—and chances are that oil found its way onto your fabric. For this reason, you'll want to clean your piece.
- If the corners of your piece aren't square, or if the edges of your fabric are all ripply—and not in a good way, like Matthew McConaughey's abs—you'll want to block your piece to eliminate any distortion.
- Obviously, you can't just tack your beautiful needlework on a wall and call it a day. Unless you stitched directly on, say, a onesie or a bib or a dog T-shirt or a placemat or a tea towel, you'll need to figure out how you want to present it. Do you want to sew it into a bag? Do you want to frame it? Should it become the front of a pillow?

Take It Off: Removing the Stabilizer

If you applied stabilizer (interfacing) to your piece, now's the time to remove it. How, exactly, this is done depends on whether the interfacing you used is designed to be torn away, heated away, washed away, or cut away.

- **Tear away** To remove tear-away stabilizer from your embroidered piece, hold the piece firmly in one hand while gently tugging the stabilizer with the other. As the stabilizer tears away, rotate the embroidered fabric as needed. If any loose bits of the stabilizer remain inside the design itself, don't sweat it; they're fine as is (unless the stabilizer you used was stiff, in which case you might want to use tweezers to pluck the stiff scraps out).

- ◆ **Heat away** There are two different types of heat-away stabilizers: woven and filmy. To remove a woven stabilizer, use a dry iron to apply heat—10 seconds at the Cotton setting should do the trick. The stabilizer will flake away; just brush the flakes from your piece (a toothbrush is an effective tool here). Filmy heat-away stabilizers simply disappear when ironed.

- ◆ **Wash away** Remove a wash-away stabilizer by, er, washing it. (Note that some wash-away stabilizers might require several rinsings for complete removal.)

- ◆ **Cut away** Although you *can* cut this type of stabilizer from your fabric, cut-away stabilizers can also remain on the fabric permanently to keep the fabric stable *after* the embroidery is complete. Likewise, if the fabric you intend to use is thin, synthetic, and/or loosely woven, or is designed to be worn and washed, a cut-away stabilizer is the way to go. No matter what type of fabric you choose, cut-away stabilizers are great if the back side of the project will never be visible—like, say, if the piece will be framed or sewn into a pillow. If you do decide to remove a cut-away stabilizer after use, move your scissors in a gliding motion rather than a cutting motion. Do leave a quarter inch or so of the stabilizer around the embroidery, and don't bother cutting any stabilizer within the confines of the design.

Wash Me: Cleaning Your Needlework

Obviously, if you never get your needlework dirty in the first place, you don't have to worry too much about cleaning it when it's finished. But unless you're stitching in a hermetically sealed room using robotic arms, that's probably not realistic. That said, there are a few things you can do to avoid soiling your work too much:

- ◆ Always wash your hands before stitching. Otherwise, you'll wind up with greasy fabric. (No offense.) Also, avoid using hand lotion before stitching, as lotion typically contains oil.

- ◆ If you're a snacker (guilty!), resist the temptation to nosh while stitching unless your design specifically calls for potato-chip crumbs. Keeping beverages nearby is also a recipe for disaster.

- ◆ Rather than leaving your fabric in its hoop for the duration of the project, remove it when you finish each stitching session. This helps prevent the inner walls of the hoop from marking your project, and helps prevent creases.

- ◆ When not stitching your piece, roll it up and store it in a baggie. To allow it to breathe, poke a few holes in the bag.

Even if you go to great lengths to ensure that your piece remains as clean as possible, you'll still want to wash it when it's finished—ideally by hand. Here's how:

1. In a large bowl, thoroughly mix a smidge of mild, colorless, fragrance-free soap (think Woolite, or use a soap made especially for needlework, available at your local needle-crafts store) with enough room-temperature water to cover your piece. Avoid using a metal bowl; otherwise, the metal in the bowl may react with the chemicals in the soap—which can affect the colors in your piece.

2. After the detergent has dissolved in the water, submerge your piece, swishing it around gently.

3. If your piece is as filthy as Colin Farrell's mouth, soak it (the piece, not Colin Farrell's mouth) for a half hour or so. Otherwise, a few minutes will do.

4. If, after soaking for 30-ish minutes, your piece is still marred by a stubborn stain, use a soft brush to gently scrub the spot. The key word here is *gently;* scouring the spot like it's incriminating evidence can damage the thread and/or the fabric.

5. Place the stitched piece under running cold water to rinse it, stopping when the water runs clear.

6. Don't even *think* about wringing out your piece. Instead, roll it up like a diploma and gently squeeze out the excess water.

7. Blot out yet more moisture by rolling the piece in a clean white towel.

8. Unroll the towel and lay your piece on it, ensuring the piece is as flat as Nebraska, and allow it to air dry.

9. While the piece is still a teeny bit damp, iron it. To protect the work, first spread a clean, fluffy, white towel on your ironing board. Then lay your piece face down on the towel. Finally, with a dry iron on a medium setting, iron the piece. Rather than sliding the iron back and forth across the piece, briefly press it down, lift it back up, move it to the next spot, and repeat.

10. After pressing the piece, lay it flat again and allow it to dry completely.

But what if your piece requires a bit more attention? Here are a few tips for handling stains:

♦ Blood If you're dealing with blood stains, first evaluate whether caring for your stitching is indeed your first priority—as opposed to, say, visiting the ER or calling the police. Assuming no one requires immediate medical assistance, dab a bit of hydrogen peroxide on the stain. Alternatively, soak the piece in a solution composed of 85 percent salt and 15 percent water, rinsing it with cold water afterward.

♦ Red wine Look, no judgment here. I mean, who *hasn't* gotten sloshed while stitching? If your evening of debauched crafting ends with a giant red-wine stain smack in the middle of your piece, quickly soak up what you can using a paper napkin. Then—here's the fun part—dump a pile of table salt onto the stain and gently rub it in, the idea being that the salt will absorb the stain. Finally, wash the piece ASAP following the steps above.

- ◆ **Rust** If you store your needle by drawing it through your fabric, you may wind up with the occasional rust stain (which is why you should not store your needle this way). To remove it, mix 1 teaspoon of oxalic acid (probably available at your local pharmacy) with 1 cup of hot water. Then dip a towel into the solution and use it to dab the solution on the stain. Finally, follow the steps above to wash your piece, rinsing it well.

- ◆ **Stray pencil marks** To erase these, brew a solution consisting of three parts rubbing alcohol and one part water, plus a half teaspoon of dishwasher detergent. Dip a towel in the solution, and then use the towel to dab the stain on your piece.

If all else fails, take your piece to a dry cleaner—preferably one that has experience dealing with such items. (Cleaners that handle furnishings are your best bet.) Ask around if necessary; *someone* will know how to fix it.

Jenny from the Block: Blocking Your Piece

For most pieces, washing and pressing will be all that's required. If, however, your piece is as distorted as Dick Cheney's world view, you'll need to *block* it to straighten it out. Note that if you stitched your piece on canvas, blocking is almost certainly required (unless you used straight stitches only, in which case you may get a bye).

To block your piece, you'll need a *blocking board*—that is, a flat surface that's strong enough to withstand the forces involved with pulling fabric. If the piece you need to block is small-ish, you might be able to use your ironing board as a blocking board. Otherwise, you'll need to buy a blocking board or, even better, make one yourself. Here's how:

1. Cover a piece of soft, fibrous board—Homasote's a good choice—with plastic wrap. (This is just to seal out any chemicals that ooze out of the board.) The board should be larger than the piece you're about to block.

2. Lay a piece of batting—that is, the stuffing material frequently used for quilting projects, available at your local crafts store—that's larger than the board on top of it, fold the edges under, and, on the underside of the board, staple them in place. (You'll need a staple gun for this.)

3. Place a layer of cotton fabric on the batting. Opt for checkered fabric; that way, you'll have a built-in grid when you're ready to block your piece. Stretch the fabric taut, ensuring that the fabric's grid print lines up with the edges of the board. Then, as with the batting, fold the edges of the fabric under and staple them in place on the underside of the board.

With your blocking board built, you're ready to block your piece. Here's how:

1. If the piece you're blocking needs to wind up an exact shape and/or size, draw a template, including lines to indicate the center points on each edge. Then, pin the template to your board and cover it with some type of transparent plastic to protect it.

2. If your piece was stitched on canvas, use a sponge and warm water to dampen the back side of the work. If your piece was stitched on plain-weave or even-weave fabric, soak it in cold water.

3. Lay your piece face down on your blocking board, aligning it with the template or with the fabric grid.

4. Use a rust-proof pin (that bit's important) to affix the top edge of the piece at its center point to the board.

5. Repeat step 4 to pin the bottom and two side edges of the piece to the board, each at its center point. Pull tight when pinning the piece—but not so tight you damage it.

6. Pin each corner of the work to the board; they should be square with the center pins you added in steps 4 and 5.

7. Working from the center of each edge outward, add more pins at 1-inch intervals. When you're finished, the piece should be as tight and flat as Sheryl Crow's abdomen. If your work is stitched on canvas, the warp and weft threads should be absolutely straight and intersecting at 90-degree angles.

8. Leave the piece pinned to the blocking board until it is completely dry.

9. When the piece is dry (this can take a few days), unpin it. If the piece has been properly straightened out, you're set. If not, try not to feel like a failure and block it again.

Ready, Frame, Admire: Mounting and Framing Your Piece

Look, I'm not gonna lie to you: Framing your piece—*really* framing it, all nice-like—probably requires a professional. If you've just worked a piece that you plan to pass down to your great-granddaughter, I urge you to hire out the job. Look for a framer who practices *conservation framing*, which, in addition to protecting your piece from UV light, bugs, humidity, and pollution, ensures that no acidic materials touch your stitching. (Even so, you should avoid hanging such heirloom pieces in heat, damp, or direct sunlight. That means your bathroom with the skylight and sun lamp is a bad location for a piece that took you 7 years to finish.)

If, however, your piece is of a more temporary nature (think: the office cubicle art in the "Cue the Violins" project, found in chapter 7. "Canvas the Area: Needlework for the Home"),

What Are My Options Here?

Obviously, when it comes to finished needlework pieces, framing isn't your only option. For example, you might instead opt for turning your piece into a throw pillow or a bag. For how-to details, see the projects "You Bore Me" (chapter 7) and "Laptop Dance" (chapter 6), respectively.

there's no reason you can't take a stab at framing it yourself. Your first step is to mount the piece either on a stretcher frame (remember those?) or on a board. (If you stitched your piece on a delicate fabric, mount it on a board rather than on a stretcher frame. If, however, you used a sturdier material, such as canvas, then a stretcher frame is a fine option.) After you've mounted the piece using the method of your choice, simply pop it into a frame.

Bring out the Stretcher: Mounting Your Piece on a Stretcher Frame

Mounting your finished piece on a stretcher frame is not unlike mounting an *unfinished* piece on one:

1. Assemble the stretcher bars comprising the stretcher frame using the interlocking joints on the corners. (Your frame should be slightly larger than the stitched area of your piece all the way around.)
2. Lay your piece face down on a flat surface and center the frame on the design area.
3. Fold the top unstitched edge of the fabric over the top bar of the stretcher frame and, using a staple gun, staple it on at the center point.
4. Repeat step 3 for the bottom and two sides of the fabric. When you're finished, the work should be stretched flat but not so much so that it's distorted.
5. Working from the center of each edge outward, add more staples at 1-inch intervals, stopping before you reach the corners.
6. Get ready, Miss Hospital Corners! It's time to make a triangular fold with the fabric in the top-right corner of the piece. Then, staple the fold into place.
7. Repeat step 6 for the remaining three corners. (Note that if you're a minimalist, or just lazy, you could reasonably stop here and not even frame your piece.)

Board Exams: Mounting Your Piece on Cardboard

Mounting the finished piece on cardboard—the way to go if your piece is super fragile—is a different animal, involving a process called *lacing*. To start, cut a piece of thick, acid-free cardboard to a size that's slightly larger than your stitched piece all the way around. Then do the following:

1. Optionally, place your cardboard face down on a thin layer of batting; this will create the pillow-y effect you sometimes see with framed needlework. Then fold the batting over and staple it to the back side of the board to keep it in place. (If you're planning to use glass with your frame, you'll want to skip this step as the pillow effect will be lost.)
2. Lay your piece face down on a flat surface, with the long edges of the piece on the top and bottom. (Obviously, if your piece is square, you can ignore that last bit.)
3. Center the board over the design area.
4. Fold the top and bottom edges of your fabric over to the back side of the board.

5. Along the top and bottom edges, insert pins into the *sides* of the board, as shown here, to fasten the fabric to the board.

6. Thread a sharp needle with strong thread. Then, in the bottom-left area, work a single back stitch, leaving a long tail. (You'll learn how to work a back stitch in chapter 4.)

7. Lace the two sides of the piece together as shown here, pulling firmly—but not so firmly as to distort the piece.

8. Finish with another back stitch, but don't tie off.

9. Repeat steps 4–8 to lace the short edges of the fabric together, folding the corners as you go.

10. Take a peek at the front side of the work to make sure it's positioned correctly; if not, tighten or loosen the lacing as needed. When everything looks copacetic, tie off and trim your excess thread.

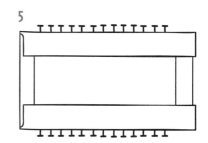

Pin your piece to the board. (Note that you'll want to push the pins all the way in, unlike what's shown here, which is meant to show you where the pins belong.)

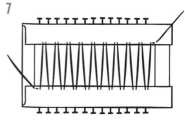

Lace the top and bottom edges of the fabric together.

You've Been Framed: Framing Your Piece

You've mounted your piece; now it's time to frame it using the store-bought, pre-made frame of your choice. First, though, you'll need to make a decision: glass or no glass? Although framing your piece under glass will protect the piece, even the most advanced nonreflective glass will detract from any nifty textured effects you've stitched into your piece. (Recall that if you opted to use batting when you mounted your piece, you'll want to opt out of using glass in order to retain the pillow-y effect.) You'll also want to decide whether to border the piece with a mat. If you do, make sure that a) the mat is acid free and b) the color of your mat doesn't clash with your piece and/or your frame (and/or your *décor*). Opt for a hue that appears somewhere in your design.

Your decisions duly made, do the following:

Lace Case

If the whole lacing thing seems like way too much of a pain in the ass, try affixing the unstitched parts of your piece to the back of the board using acid-free, double-sided tape. Use any leftover tape to prevent your boobs from popping out of your Oscar dress.

1. Pop open your store-bought frame and lay it face down on a flat surface.

2. Remove the backing and filler stuff. (If you've opted against glass, yank that out too.)

3. If you've chosen to use a mat, lay it face down in the frame.

Glassy Broad

If you decide to use glass, you'll want to choose a frame that's deeper than normal and that contains an extra stop inside—one for the glass and one for your piece. That way, your piece won't actually *touch* the glass. (Touching the glass is bad because condensation could make your piece all moldy—which looks nasty even on pieces that were green and fuzzy to begin with.) Alternatively, surround the piece with an acid-free mat to separate the fabric from the glass.

4. Lay your piece face down in the frame (make sure it's facing the right direction—i.e., it won't be upside down when you hang it).

5. Replace the backing and filler stuff (note that if your piece is thick, you might not be able to cram all the original filler back in; don't sweat it) and close the frame back up.

Next!

Finally! It's time to learn how to actually *stitch.* chapter 4, "Stitch Hitter: Your Guide to Cross-Stitch, Embroidery, and Needlepoint Stitches," walks you through all the best stitching techniques.

Chapter Four

♦◆♦

Stitch Hitter: Your Guide to Cross-Stitch, Embroidery, and Needlepoint Stitches

Y ou've organized your threads and prepared your fabric for stitching. You know how to thread your needle, how to start a thread, and how to tie one off (not to mention how to tie one *on*). That can mean only one thing: You're ready to learn some stitches, bitches! This section serves as a reference for several types of cross-stitch, embroidery, and needlepoint stitches—pictures and all.

I'll be straight with you: The stitches covered here, which range in complexity from as simple as Jessica Simpson to as difficult as Naomi Campbell, barely scrape the surface of the types of stitches you can attempt. Seriously, whole books are devoted solely to illustrate needlework stitches. (May I recommend Betty Barnden's *The Embroidery Stitch Bible?*) But if you master the ones shown here, you'll have an excellent foundation.

You Double-Crossing Stitch: Cross-Stitch Stitches

The most commonly used stitch in cross stitch is—wait for it—the cross stitch. Here's how it's done:

The cross stitch.

1. Start your thread in the bottom-left corner of the square you want to stitch, drawing your needle and thread through the fabric from back to front. (Okay, you can start in any corner, but I opted for the bottom-left one for the sake of example.)

2. Pull your needle from front to back through the hole diagonally up and to the right from the one through which your needle emerged in step 1.

3. From back to front, draw your needle and thread through the hole to the left of the one through which your needle passed in step 2.

4. Pass your needle through the only remaining hole around the square from front to back, crossing the stitch you completed in steps 1 and 2 en route.

Cross the stitch you completed in step 2.

You can execute the cross stitch in one of two ways. One is to work a row of half cross stitches (that is, repeat steps 1 and 2 above, but not steps 3 and 4) from left to right and then double back across the row to complete each stitch. Alternatively, you can complete each × shape one at a time. The former method is best if you're working on a solid block of color that will involve many rows. (Incidentally, to stitch a new row in a block, just work backward. That is, if the row you just completed went left to right, work the next row right to left.) If your stitches will be peppered throughout your design, however, the latter method applies.

Sergeant Peppered

Speaking of stitches that are peppered throughout a design: If, in order to complete such stitches, your thread must cross vast spaces in the fabric that will contain *no* stitches (think a half inch of empty fabric or more), then the thread will be visible when the design is complete. Even if it isn't, running your thread hither and yon across the back of your piece will almost certainly cause the fabric to pucker. To avoid such a gaffe, simply tie off your thread and start it anew for each stitch or take a roundabout way, weaving the thread through the backs of existing stitches.

In any case, regardless of which approach you choose, try to make it so your top stitch always slants in the same direction. That is, if, on your first stitch, the top stitch runs from the top-left corner to the bottom-right corner, *all* the top stitches in your project should slant the same way. It just looks better that way than when the stitches are all willy nilly.

Note: Incidentally, if you're stitching with overdyed floss, working half cross stitches across an entire row and then doubling back to complete the crosses results in a very subtle shading effect. Alternatively, completing each cross as you go emphasizes the floss's jazzy hues.

By the way, if you're looking to cover a bit more ground with your stitches—this may well be the case if you're working on an extremely fine-gauge piece of fabric, or if you suffer from ADHD—you can double them up. That is, rather than crossing a single square, each half stitch in your cross stitch can travel two squares.

Although most cross-stitch designs consist primarily of cross stitches, other types of stitches are sometimes used. These include the following:

♦ Fractional stitches
♦ Long-arm cross stitch
♦ Open herringbone stitch
♦ French knot
♦ Running stitches
♦ Back stitch

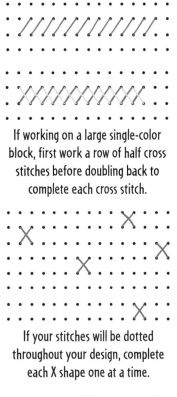

If working on a large single-color block, first work a row of half cross stitches before doubling back to complete each cross stitch.

If your stitches will be dotted throughout your design, complete each X shape one at a time.

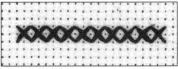

The double cross stitch.

Class Fraction: Fractional Stitches

If a cross-stitch design calls four rounded shapes, *quarter* and *three-quarter cross stitches* may be used. (Note that these are typically indicated by a small, special symbol placed in the corner of a square in your chart.) In addition, some designs also call for the use of half cross stitches (you learned how to stitch half cross stitches a second ago, when you executed a row of them before doubling back to cross them).

Quarter Patrol: The Quarter Cross Stitch

To complete a quarter cross stitch, do the following. (Note that the corner from which you start the stitch dictates the slant and placement of the quarter cross stitch.)

1. Start your thread in a corner of the square you want to stitch.
2. Pass your needle back down through the *middle* of the square in your fabric from front to back.

Three-Quarter Opera: The Three-Quarters Cross Stitch

A three-quarter cross stitch, which is really just a half cross stitch and a quarter cross stitch combined, works like this. (Note that the corner from which you start the half and quarter stitches comprising this stitch dictate its slant and placement.)

1. Start your thread in a corner of the square you want to stitch.
2. Pull your thread to the hole diagonally across from the one through which your needle emerged in step 1, and pass your needle and thread back through the fabric from front to back. (As you probably noticed, you just completed a half cross stitch.)
3. From back to front, draw your needle and thread through one of the two remaining holes surrounding the square.
4. Pass your needle back down through the *middle* of the square in your fabric from front to back.

Long Arm of the Law: The Long-Arm Cross Stitch

The long-arm cross stitch, which consists of one half cross stitch and one longer diagonal stitch works beautifully as a border. Here's the skinny on how it's done:

1. Start your thread in the upper-left corner of the square you want to stitch.
2. Pass your needle and thread back through the hole in the lower-right corner of the square. (As you probably noticed, you just completed a half cross stitch.)

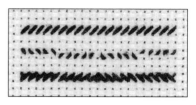

From top to bottom: the half cross stitch, the quarter cross stitch, and the three-quarters cross stitch.

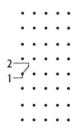

Start the quarter cross stitch from one of the holes surrounding the square, and finish it by passing your needle through the center of the square.

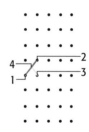

The three-quarter cross stitch is really just a half cross stitch and a quarter cross stitch combined.

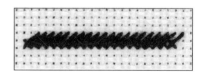

The long-arm cross stitch.

3. From back to front, draw your needle and thread through the lower-left corner of the square.

4. Here's where things change: Instead of passing your needle and thread through the upper-right corner of this square, pass it through the upper-right corner of the *next* square to the right (or, for an even more dramatic effect, the one after that).

5. To start the next stitch, pull the thread from back to front through the remaining corner of the first square (i.e., the upper-right corner); repeat steps 2–4 to continue.

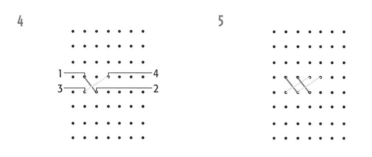

The top thread of the long-arm stitch crosses to the *next* square (to the right).

Continue with the next stitch.

Throw Me a Bone: The Open Herringbone Stitch

The open herringbone stitch also serves as an excellent border stitch, creating a lacy, zigzag effect. Here's how the open herringbone stitch works:

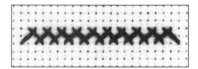

The open herringbone stitch.

1. Start your thread in the lower-left corner of the square you want to stitch.

2. Instead of passing the needle through the upper-right corner of the same square, pass it through the upper-right corner of the square situated diagonally up and to the right.

3. Draw your needle and thread through the hole immediately to the left from back to front.

4. Instead of passing the needle through the lower-right corner of the same square, pass it through the lower-right corner in the square situated diagonally down and to the right.

5. To start the next stitch, draw your needle through the lower-left corner of the same square from back to front; repeat steps 2–4 to continue.

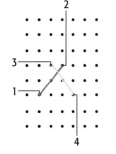

4

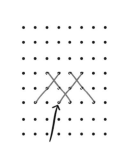

5

Work the open herringbone stitch.

Start your next stitch here.

Freedom Knot: The French Knot

French knots are a great way to add a bit of texture and dimension to any cross-stitch design (as well as embroidery designs), and often serve to simulate natural elements such as flower parts, eyeballs, or in the case of the project

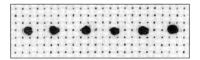

The French knot.

"Hoodie Two Chews" in chapter 5, rice. Four out of five experts agree: Mastering the French knot is trickier than simultaneously patting your head and rubbing your belly. Once you get the hang of it, though, you'll be set for life:

1. Draw your needle and thread through your fabric from back to front.
2. Point the tip of your needle toward the spot from whence the thread emerges from the fabric. Then, keeping the thread taut, wrap it around your needle two times, spiraling away from the fabric.
3. Insert the needle back through the fabric from front to back. (If your thread is relatively thick, and the holes in your fabric are small, you might be able to use the same hole as in step 1; if not, pull the needle through as close to the hole as you can.)
4. When the needle and thread are all the way through, pull the thread gently to tighten the knot.

If, after attempting a French knot, you're as lost as Paula Abdul on a camping trip, there are a few ways to cheat. My favorite is to replace the knot with a wee bead that's the same color as your thread. (You'll learn more about stitching with beads in the section, "The End All Bead All: Stitching with Beads," later in this chapter.) Another is to replace the French knot with a small cross stitch.

2

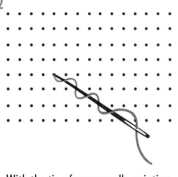

With the tip of your needle pointing toward the spot where the thread emerges from the fabric, wrap the thread around your needle two times.

3

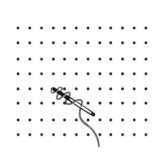

Draw the needle back through the fabric to create the knot.

4

The finished French knot.

Hit and Run: Running Stitches

Running stitches are used to outline areas in your cross-stitch design (as well as in embroidery designs) to better define them, as well as to create certain types of lettering. There are two main types of running stitches: the *running stitch* and the *double-running stitch* (sometimes called the Holbein stitch, as noted in chapter 1).

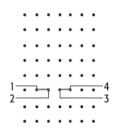

From top to bottom: the running stitch and the double-running stitch.

Run DMC: The Running Stitch

Here's how the running stitch works. (Note that you should complete all cross stitches, fractional stitches, and what have you in your cross-stitch design before working any running stitches to outline your design.)

1. Draw your needle and thread through your fabric from back to front.
2. In the next hole to the right, pass your needle through the fabric from front to back. (Note that I'm creating a running stitch that runs from left to right for the sake of example. Running stitches can also run right to left, top to bottom, bottom to top, even diagonally.)
3. In the *next* hole to the right, pass your needle through the fabric from back to front.
4. Again, in the next hole to the right, pass your needle through the fabric from front to back. Continue in this vein until the line is complete.

Work the running stitch.

Variation Sensation

Although the running stitch is pretty boring on its own, it does serve as the foundation for some pretty kick-ass variations, which could be implemented in cross stitch *or* embroidery. These include the whipped running stitch, the laced running stitch, and the interlaced running stitch. The *whipped running stitch* works like this:

1. Complete a line of regular running stitches. (I made mine from left to right.)

2. Starting at the point where you began the running stitch, draw a contrasting thread through the fabric from back to front.

3. Pass the needle under the first running stitch, from top to bottom, but don't pierce the fabric.

4. Pass the needle under the second running stitch, again from top to bottom. Continue in this manner until all the running stitches have been whipped.

5. When you finish the line of running stitches, simply pass the needle back through to the back of the fabric.

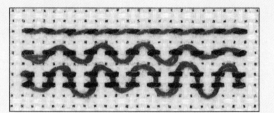

From top to bottom: the whipped running stitch, the laced running stitch, and the interlaced running stitch.

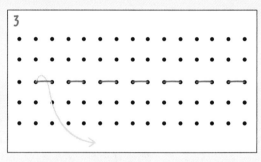

Starting the whipped running stitch.

The *laced running stitch* is similar to the whipped running stitch, except that instead of always passing through the running stitch from top to bottom, the laced running stitch alternates passing top to bottom with passing bottom to top. Like the laced running stitch, the *interlaced running stitch* passes through running stitches in alternating directions. However, instead of passing through a single line of running stitches, the interlaced running stitch travels between two parallel lines of running stitches.

Double or Nothing: The Double-Running Stitch

Whereas the running stitch results in a dotted line, the *double*-running stitch yields a line that's solid. Here's how it's done:

1. Repeat the preceding steps to complete a line of regular running stitches. (I made mine from left to right.)

2. Pull your thread back through the hole where you *started* your last running stitch, from back to front.

3. In the next hole to the left, pass your needle through the fabric from front to back.

4. In the *next* hole to the left, pass your needle through the fabric from back to front.

5. Again, in the next hole to the left, pass your needle through the fabric from front to back, and so on and so forth until the line is complete.

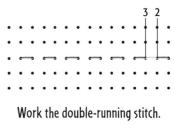

Work the double-running stitch.

Baby Got Back: The Back Stitch

Another stitch used to outline areas of a design is the back stitch, which looks suspiciously like the double-running stitch. Here's how it works:

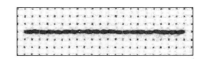

The back stitch.

1. Draw your needle and thread through your fabric from back to front.

2. In the next hole to the left, pass your needle through the fabric from front to back. (Note that I'm creating a back stitch that runs from left to right for the sake of example. Back stitches can also run right to left, top to bottom, bottom to top, even diagonally.)

2

Starting the back stitch.

3. Moving two holes to the right, draw your needle through from back to front.

4. In the next hole to the left, pass your needle through the fabric from front to back.

4

5. Again, moving two holes to the right, pass your needle through the fabric from back to front, yada yada yada, until the line is complete.

Continue the back stitch.

Stitchin' Confidential: Embroidery Stitches

The stable of available embroidery stitches is as large as Hugh Hefner's stable of Bunnies. In fact, remember all those stitches you learned for cross stitch? Every single one of them can be used in embroidery—the only difference being that you don't use holes in the fabric as your guide. In addition, the following families of embroidery stitches are but a smallering of stitch types:

♦ Line stitches
♦ Satin stitches

- Chain stitch
- Blanket stitches
- Feather stitches
- Couching stitches
- Woven stitches (needleweaving)

Note: The stitches in this section are worked left to right. If you're just starting out, I suggest you do the same. If you've tried your hand at embroidery before, however, don't hesitate to modify the steps as necessary to work right to left, bottom to top, or what have you.

Line Drive: Line Stitches

Line stitches are extremely important in embroidery, as they are typically used to define the pattern's border. This category of stitches encompasses the running, double-running, and back stitches you explored in the section "You Double-Crossing Stitch: Cross-Stitch Stitches," so I won't bother to repeat the ins and outs of those here. Two other types of line stitches, however—the *stem stitch* (sometimes called the *crewel stitch*) and the *split stitch*—deserve coverage.

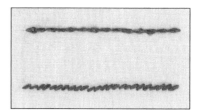

From top to bottom: the stem stitch and the split stitch.

Nice Stems: The Stem Stitch

To work the stem stitch, do the following:

1. For the sake of example, pretend you've applied a horizontal line to your fabric as a guide; then start your thread on the left end of the line.
2. Following the line, but at a slight diagonal, pass your needle back through the fabric from front to back. (Note that smaller stitches yield smoother lines, especially on curves.)
3. On the underside of the first stitch, about halfway across, draw your needle through the fabric from back to front.
4. Again, still following the line but at a slight diagonal, pass your needle back through the fabric from front to back. The length of this stitch should be identical to the one before it, and the two stitches should be snuggled up as close as Ashton Kutcher and Demi Moore.
5. Continue in this vein until the line is complete.

Work a stem stitch.

Split Ends: The Split Stitch

To work a split stitch, you'll need to work with thread consisting of an even number of strands, which should be untwisted. Do the following:

1. Again, for the sake of example, pretend you've applied a line to your fabric. Then start your thread on the left end of the line.

2. Following the line, pass your needle back through the fabric from front to back. (Note that smaller stitches yield smoother lines, especially on curves.)

3. About halfway across the first stitch, draw your needle through the fabric from back to front, splitting the thread comprising the first stitch along the way.

4. Still following the line, pass your needle back through the fabric from front to back. The length of this stitch should be identical to the one before it.

5. Continue in this vein until the line is complete.

Work a split stitch.

Satin Lover: Satin Stitches

Embroiderers make frequent use of satin stitches, which act as a smooth, solid filling for small-ish areas (think leaves, petals, and in the case of a couple projects in this book, worms). There are a few different types of satin stitches, including the *straight satin stitch, the slanted satin stitch,* and the *long-and-short satin stitch.*

From left to right: the straight satin stitch, the slanted satin stitch, and the long-and-short satin stitch.

Straight Up Now Tell Me: The Straight Satin Stitch

To work a straight satin stitch, often referred to as simply a "satin stitch" do the following:

1. For the sake of example, pretend you're stitching a square, the outline of which has already been transferred to your fabric. To begin, draw your needle and thread through your fabric from back to front in the bottom-left corner of the square.

2. Pass your needle back through the fabric from front to back in the *top*-left corner of the square. (Note that you could also work this stitch horizontally; I just went vertical here for the hell of it.)

3. Again starting at the bottom of the square, draw your needle through the fabric from back to front, just to the right of—but as close to as possible—the previous stitch.

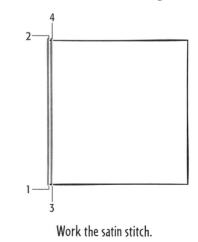

Work the satin stitch.

4. Run the thread parallel to the first stitch, with no fabric showing in between. Then, pass your needle back through the top of the square. Continue in this vein until the square is completely covered with satin stitches.

Slant Buy Me Love: The Slanted Satin Stitch

Slanted satin stitches are identical to straight satin stitches in that both are designed to completely cover the fabric underneath. The difference is that the slanted satin stitches are, er, slanted. Also, rather than starting a slanted satin stitch on the left side of the area to be stitched, as is the case with straight satin stitches, your center the first slanted satin stitch on the shape you're stitching to ensure a more consistent slant. Here's what to do:

1. Decide how steep you want the slant in your stitch to be (again, let's use the square for this example). For a more upright slant, start your thread closer to the middle of the base of the square; for a more dramatic slant, start closer to one of the corners.

2. Draw the thread through the line along the top of the square at the opposite point. That is, if you started the stitch 3mm to the left of center, finish it 3mm to the *right* of center.

3. Again starting at the bottom of the square, draw your needle through the fabric from back to front, just to the right of—but as close to as possible—the previous stitch.

4. Run the thread parallel to the first stitch, with no fabric showing in between. Then, pass your needle back through the fabric at the top of the square, immediately to the right of the previous stitch.

5. Continue in this vein until the area of the square to the right of your initial stitch is completely covered.

6. Again starting at the bottom of the square, draw your needle through the fabric from back to front, just to the left of—but as close to as possible—the center stitch you added in steps 1–2.

7. Run the thread *parallel* to the center stitch, with no fabric showing in between. Then, pass your needle back through the fabric at the top of the square, to the left of the center stitch. Continue in this vein until the area of the square to the left of your initial stitch is completely covered.

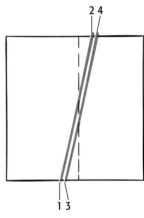

Work the slanted satin stitch.

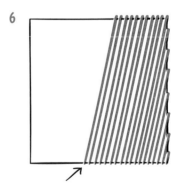

Start here after you fill in the right portion of the square.

The Long and Short of It: The Long-and-Short Satin Stitch

The long-and-short satin stitch is a bit different from its straight and slanted satin brethren in that the stitches are staggered, adding a bit of texture. Here's how it's done:

1. Again, using the square example, start your thread in the bottom-left corner of the square.

2. A few millimeters up, pass your needle back through the fabric from front to back. (Note that you could also work this stitch horizontally.)

3. Back at the bottom of the square, draw your needle through the fabric from back to front, just to the right of—but as close to as possible—the previous stitch.

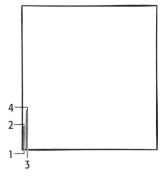

Stagger the first two stitches.

4. Run the thread parallel to the first stitch, with no fabric showing in between. After covering twice the distance as the first stitch, pass the needle back through the fabric from front to back. (As you probably guessed, this is where the "long" in "long-and-short satin stitch" comes from.)

5. Continue staggering the stitches until the base of the square is covered.

6. To launch a new row, begin at the left side of the square and, working from top to bottom, add one long stitch above the stitch you worked in steps 1 and 2. Begin by drawing the needle through the fabric from back to front, starting at the top of the new stitch.

Note: There's no law that says you have to start a new row on the same side of the square as the first row. I did it that way to make things a bit easier to explain.

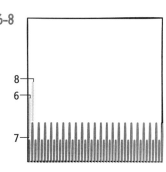

Begin the second row.

7. Draw your needle back through the fabric from front to back, piercing the tippy top portion of the stitch you added in steps 1 and 2 en route.

8. Add another long stitch to the row, this time piercing the top of the stitch added in steps 3 and 4 to complete the stitch. (Note that from now until you begin the top row in the square, you'll use long stitches only.)

9. Continue adding stitches in this manner until you complete the row.

10. Continue adding rows until only one more row is necessary to cover the square.

11. The last row of the square should be staggered in the same manner as the first row. To begin, draw the needle through the fabric from back to front. I started in the square's top-left corner.

12. Draw your needle through the fabric from front to back, piercing the tip of the stitch below it. (Note that whether the stitch you're working is a long stitch or a short stitch depends on the placement of the stitch below it.)

13. Add a second stitch, again starting from the line that defines the top edge of the square. If the stitch you added in step 12 was a short stitch, this stitch will be long—or vice versa.

14. Continue adding stitches in this manner along the top of the square to complete the row.

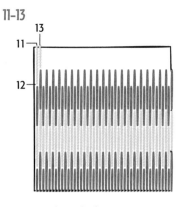

Start the last row.

Blame It on the Chain: Chain Stitches

If you've ever crocheted, you're probably familiar with working chain stitches in that context. Embroidered chain stitches are similar. In fact, some stitchers use a hook—called a *tambour hook*—that resembles a crochet hook to work chain stitches, although we'll be doing them with a plain old needle. Like the running stitch, chain stitches can be whipped for effect.

From top to bottom: the chain stitch and the whipped chain stitch.

Plain Chain: The Chain Stitch

Here's the skinny on the chain stitch:

1. For the sake of example, pretend you've drawn a horizontal line on your fabric. Then, start your thread on the left end of the line.

2. Pass your needle back through the fabric (going front to back) in the same spot as step 1. Instead of pulling the stitch tight, however, leave enough slack to create a small-ish loop. (It might help to pinch the loop between your thumb and forefinger to prevent it from following the rest of your thread through the hole.)

3. Just to the right of the initial stitch, draw your needle and thread through the fabric from back to front. Then pull the needle and thread through the loop you created in step 2.

Create a loop.

4. Create a new loop in the thread and pass the needle back through the fabric in the same spot as in step 3. Tug gently—you want the loop you made in step 2 to be pulled snug against the fabric, but you don't want the loop you made in *this* step to follow the rest of the thread through the hole.

5. Continue stitching in this manner until the chain is complete. For the last stitch, draw your needle and thread through the fabric from back to front, pull the needle and thread through the loop from the preceding stitch, and draw the loop snug against the fabric with a wee straight, horizontal stitch.

Work the next stitch in the chain.

Whips and Chains: The Whipped Chain Stitch

To embellish the chain stitch, try whipping it. This process is similar to whipping a running stitch:

1. Repeat the steps in the preceding section to complete a line of chain stitches, but make the chain stitches a bit longer and looser than you might otherwise. (It'll tighten up a bit as you whip it.)

2. Starting at the point where you began the chain stitch, draw a contrasting thread through the fabric from back to front.

3. Pass the needle and thread under the first chain stitch, from top to bottom, but don't pierce the fabric.

4. Pass the needle under the second chain stitch, again from top to bottom. Continue in this manner until all the chain stitches have been whipped.

Starting the whipped chain stitch.

Not to Be Confused with Michael Jackson's Child: The Blanket Stitch

A *blanket stitch* is similar to a chain stitch in that it also involves passing the needle through a loop on the front side of the fabric. The difference is that the blanket stitch does not pass back through the fabric via the original hole. The result is a series of L–shaped stitches.

Here's how the blanket stitch works:

1. When working blanket stitches, you'll follow an actual line on the fabric, as well as an imaginary line that runs parallel to it. To begin, start your thread on the left side of the *actual* horizontal line.

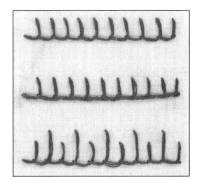

From top to bottom: the blanket stitch, the whipped blanket stitch, and the long-and-short blanket stitch.

2. Draw the thread diagonally up to the imaginary line and to the right, and then pass your needle through the fabric from front to back. Rather than pulling the thread all the way through, however, leave a loop in place.

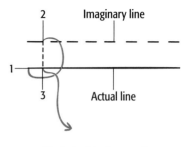

3. Directly beneath the hole through which the needle passed in step 2, on the actual line, draw your needle and thread through your fabric from back to front. Then pass the needle and thread through the loop you created in step 2. Pull tight to secure the loop, completing the vertical portion of the L shape. (I'll call this the *spine* so I don't have to keep writing "vertical portion of the L shape.")

Work the blanket stitch.

4. Repeat steps 2 and 3 to start the next stitch, continuing in this manner until the row is complete.

Like running stitches and chain stitches, blanket stitches can also be whipped; simply draw the thread through the bottom portion of the L shape from top to bottom. Blanket stitches can also be modified by varying the height of the spine, which creates a *long-and-short blanket stitch*.

Feather Report: Feather Stitches

The feather-stitch family—technically a branch on the blanket-stitch family tree—encompasses several stitches, including the *single feather stitch*, the (regular) *feather stitch*, and the *long-arm feather stitch* (also called the *Cretan* or *quill* stitch).

SWF, Feather Fetish: The Single Feather Stitch

True or false: The single feather stitch is really just a blanket stitch with slanted, rather than upright, spines. Answer: True! In fact, the steps to complete it are identical, with one exception: In step 3, rather than drawing your needle and thread through the fabric directly *beneath* the hole you created in step 2, you draw it through somewhere to the *right* of that point. Then pass the needle and thread through the loop created in step 2 and continue as normal.

Birds of a Feather: The Feather Stitch

The feather stitch differs from the single feather stitch in that rather than always pointing to one side, the spines of the stitch alternate sides. Here's how it works:

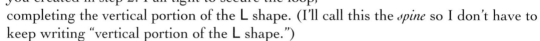

From top to bottom: the single feather stitch, the feather stitch, and the long-arm feather stitch.

1. When working feather stitches, you'll follow an actual horizontal line on the fabric, as well as two equidistant imaginary lines that run parallel to the actual one—one above and one below. To begin, start your thread on the left side of the actual line.

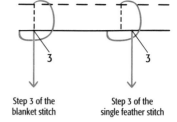

Step 3 of the blanket stitch

Step 3 of the single feather stitch

Rather than drawing your needle and thread through the fabric directly *beneath* the hole you created in step 2, as you did with the blanket stitch, draw it through somewhere to the *right* of that point.

2. Moving diagonally up and to the right, on the top imaginary line, pass your needle through the fabric from front to back. As with the single feather stitch (and the blanket stitch), leave a loop in place rather than pulling the thread all the way through.

3. Instead of drawing your needle and thread through the actual line directly beneath the hole you created in step 2, as you would for a blanket stitch, draw it through (from back to front) somewhere to the *right* of that point, as you did for the single feather stitch. Then pass the needle and thread through the loop you created in step 2. Pull tight to secure the loop, completing the slanting spine.

4. If you were continuing with single feather stitches, you'd repeat steps 2–3 to complete a stitch whose spine pointed the same way as the previous stitch's spine. But because the spines of feather stitches point in *alternate* directions, instead draw your thread diagonally *down*, to the bottom imaginary line, and to the right. Again, rather than pulling the thread all the way through from front to back, leave a loop in place.

4 and 5

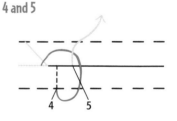

Work the alternating spines of the feather stitch and create the slant.

5. Rather than drawing your needle and thread through the actual line directly above the hole you created in step 4, draw it through (from back to front) somewhere to the right of that point. Then pass the needle and thread through the loop you created in step 4. Pull tight to secure the loop, completing the slanting spine.

6. Continue working the stitch in this manner until the line is complete.

Arm Yourself: The Long-Arm Feather Stitch

Like the feather stitch, the spines of the long-arm feather stitch alternate sides. In fact, the spines of long-armed feather stitches are identical to regular feather stitches except that they are, er, longer. You'd think, then, that the steps to complete the long-armed feather stitch would be almost identical—but you'd be wrong. The difference? Instead of drawing the thread up and to the right in step 2 and down and to the right in step 4, you draw the thread up or down and to the *left*, respectively. Then continue as normal, drawing your thread through the fabric in steps 3 and 5 where you would for a regular feather stitch.

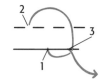

Draw the thread up (or down) and to the *left*; then continue as you would a regular feather stitch.

Couch Potato: Couching Stitches

Think about it: What better place is there to lie down than on a lovely, comfortable couch? Hence the term *couching stitches*. These stitches, generally used to create lines (although sometimes these lines are crammed together to make a fill), involve two sets of threads: laying threads and tying threads. The *laying threads*, which are typically thick and sometimes doubled (i.e., two threads are used rather than one), lie down, while the *tying threads*, which tend to be fine, secure the lazy-ass laying threads to the fabric. For a more subtle effect, use the same hue for both the laying and tying threads; using contrasting colors for these threads yields a punchier look. Regardless of your color selection, you'll need two needles — one for the laying thread and one for the tying thread — in order to complete a line of couching stitches.

Couched lines.

Big Comfy Couch: The Couching Stitch

Here's how couching stitches work:

1. For the sake of example, pretend you've drawn a horizontal line on your fabric. Then start your thread on the left end of your line. (Use an away waste knot here, with the knot situated on the right end of your line.)
2. Align the laying thread on the line on your fabric.
3. To the right of the spot through which you drew your laying thread in step 1 and just above the laying thread, draw the needle threaded with your *tying* thread through your fabric from back to front.
4. Cross the tying thread over the top of the laying thread and back down through the fabric on the other side to affix the laying thread to the fabric. (Note that here, the stitch you've used is essentially a very short straight satin stitch, but other types of stitches, including the cross stitch and half cross stitch, will also work.)

4

Laying thread

Couching thread

Cross over the laying thread to affix it to the fabric.

5. Continue in this manner, evenly spacing the stitches made with your tying thread. As you go, keep the

laying thread taut in order to ensure a line that's as firm as a neo-con's.

6. To turn a corner with your laying thread, add a stitch with your tying thread—but angle it. Then pull the laying thread in the new direction and add more tying stitches as normal. For rounder corners, tighten up the tying stitches as the laying thread rounds the bend.

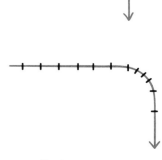

7. As you near the end of your line, draw the needle threaded with your laying thread through the fabric from front to back. On the back side of the fabric, align the laying thread with the remaining portion of the line drawn on the *front* of your fabric. (Okay, I know, you might not be able to *see* said line from the back of your fabric, but take your best shot.)

8. Continue stitching with the tying thread, this time crossing over the laying thread on both the front *and* back sides of the fabric to secure it.

9. Tie off the tying thread by weaving it in and out of the stitched laying thread on the back side of the fabric.

Turning a corner.

Mad Couch Disease: More Couching Stitches

Variations on the couching stitch include bunch couching, open pendant couching, and zigzag couching. For *bunch couching,* you simply bunch up the laying thread between each tying stitch. (You can be all tidy about it, or create a willier-nillier effect as shown here.) Open *pendant couching*—of which there are two varieties: open pendant couching and closed pendant couching—involves looping the laying thread between each tying stitch. As for the *zigzag couching stitch,* it simply involves offsetting each tying stitch to create a jagged line with the laying stitch. Couching stitches can also be worked in circles, creating a spiral or lollipop effect. (Mmmm. Lollipops . . . .)

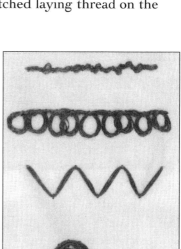

From top to bottom: bunch couching, open pendant couching, zigzag couching, and couching circles.

Give It the Old Weave-Ho: Basic Needleweaving

If you're looking to fancy up your piece, woven stitches are a great option. Used primarily as fillers—that is, to cover a lot of ground—they *look* complicated. In practice, however, they're as easy as nodding off during a French New Wave film. Although there are several varieties of woven stitches, my personal favorite is *basic needleweaving*. Here's how it's done:

Basic needleweaving.

1. For the sake of example, pretend you'll be working a square, the outline of which has already been transferred to your fabric. To begin, start your thread in the bottom-left corner of the square.

2. Pass your needle back through the fabric from front to back at the top-left corner of the square. (Note that you could also work horizontally; I just went vertical here for shits and giggles.)

3. To the right of the spot through which your needle and thread passed in step 2, but leaving some space in between, draw your needle through the fabric from back to front.

4. Run the thread downward, parallel to the first stitch, passing your needle back through the fabric from front to back at the bottom of the square. Continue in this vein until the square is covered with long, vertical stitches. (I'll call these *warp threads* from here on out.)

5. Load a blunt needle with thread of any color—the same as or contrasting with the thread used in steps 1–4. You'll weave this thread into the stitches you just completed.

6. Start the new thread in the top-left corner of the square. Then, working *horizontally*, weave through the warp threads in an over-under fashion. When you reach the other side of the square, draw the needle back through the fabric from front to back.

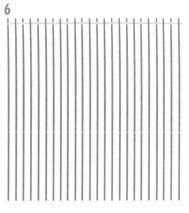

Weave through the warp threads in an over-under fashion.

7. Draw the needle back through the fabric from back to front just below the spot through which it passed in step 6. Then, weave back across the warp threads in an over-under fashion until you reach the other side of the square. As you do, alternate the "unders" and "overs" in this row with those in the previous one.

8. Repeat steps 6 and 7 as many times as necessary to complete the square.

Get to the Point: Needlepoint Stitches

Unlike cross-stitch and embroidery designs, which don't tend to cover every square inch of fabric, 99.999 percent of needlepoint designs do. That means that although some cross-stitch and embroidery stitches are sometimes used in needlepoint lacier and less substantial embroidery and cross-stitch stitches just won't work. The following are some popular types of needlepoint stitches:

- ◆ Tent stitches
- ◆ Gobelin stitches
- ◆ Scotch stitches

By the way, the stitches in this section are worked left to right, from top to bottom, just because I like to work that way. If you're just starting out, I suggest you do the same; if, however, you know your way around a canvas, don't hesitate to modify the steps as necessary to work right to left, bottom to top, or what have you.

Get Tent: Tent Stitches

Tent stitches are *the* needlepoint stitch. They're the ones that appear on just about every needlepoint piece *ever* in the history of the world. Ever wee, these stitches are ideal for the more detailed areas in a design. There are three types of tent stitches: *half-cross stitches, continental stitches,* and *basketweave stitches,* all of which look as identical as Jessica and Elizabeth Wakefield from *Sweet Valley High* from the front but differ wildly on the back.

The tent stitch: front view.

Back view of the tent stitch, from left to right: the half-cross version, the continental version, and the basketweave version.

If you're like me (and God help you if you are), you're probably thinking that if all three versions of the tent stitch look identical from the front, why bother learning more than one version? My answer: Because I told you to. That said, I often use the half-cross; of the three, it uses the least thread. Plus, you already know how to do it if you read the section "You Double-Crossing Stitch: Cross-Stitch Stitches." The only difference is that instead of crossing over a square in your fabric, as you do when cross stitching, you cross an intersection of the warp and weft threads in your canvas when needlepointing.

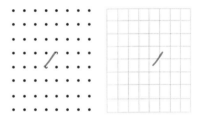

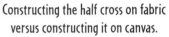

Constructing the half cross on fabric versus constructing it on canvas.

A caveat: the half-cross stitch works best on dual, rather than mono, canvas. Also, it tends to be a bit more fragile over time. If you're stitching a piece intended for use 500 years from now, you'll want to use a continental stitch or a basketweave stitch, as they're a bit hardier. (Note that you'll want to master the continental stitch in order to complete the project "British Invasion" in chapter 6, in which you needlepoint an iPod holder; because the continental stitch covers more of the back of the canvas, it will help protect your iPod's casing from scratches.)

To work a continental stitch, do the following:

1. Start your thread on the left side of the row you want to stitch.
2. Pass your thread through the hole (from front to back) that's diagonally one down and to the left of the hole in step 1.

3. In the hole next to the right of the one in step 1, draw your needle through the canvas from back to front.

4. Again moving down one hole and to the left, pass your needle through the canvas from front to back.

5. Continue stitching in this manner until the row is complete.

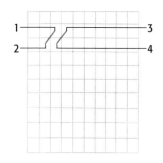

Work a continental stitch.

Like a continental stitch, the basketweave stitch covers a bit more of the back of the canvas. Unlike a continental stitch, however, a basketweave stitch works on the diagonal. Here's how it's done:

1. Start your thread in the upper-left corner of the area you want to stitch.

2. Pass your thread through the hole (from front to back) that's diagonally up and to the right of the hole in step 1.

3. Pass your thread through the hole (front back to front) that's two holes down from the one in step 2.

4. Pass your thread through the hole (from front to back) that's diagonally up and to the right of the hole in step 3.

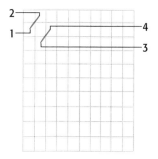

Work a basketweave stitch.

5. Continue in this vein until you've finished the diagonal row.

6. To start a new row, pass your thread through the hole (from back to front) that's immediately to the left of the hole through which the final stitch of the previous row was completed.

7. Pass your thread through the hole (from front to back) that's diagonally up and to the right of the hole in step 6.

8. Pass your thread through the hole (from back to front) that's two holes to the left from the one in step 7.

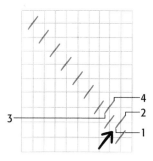

Start here and begin your next row of basketweave stitches.

9. Pass your thread through the hole (from front to back) that's diagonally up and to the right of the hole in step 8.

10. Continue in this vein until you've finished the second diagonal row. (Flip the canvas over to view its back side and note the basketweave pattern that has emerged.)

Go Go Gobelin: Gobelin Stitches

Gobelin stitches—named for the Gobelin family, who manufactured dyes and textiles beginning in the mid 1400s—cover a bit more ground than tent stitches do, making them ideal for larger blocks of color (think backgrounds). The Gobelin family of stitches (as opposed to the Gobelin family of dyers and weavers) include the *slanted Gobelin stitch*, the *encroaching slanted Gobelin stitch*, the *upright Gobelin stitch*, the *encroaching upright Gobelin stitch*, and the *Gobelin filling stitch*.

From left to right: the slanted Gobelin stitch, the encroaching slanted Gobelin stitch, the upright Gobelin stitch, the encroaching upright Gobelin stitch, and the Gobelin filling stitch.

Slant and Rave: The Slanted Gobelin and Encroaching Slanted Gobelin Stitches

Here's how the slanted Gobelin stitch works:

1. Start your thread, drawing your needle and thread through your canvas from back to front.

2. Moving up two holes and over one, pass your needle through the canvas from front to back. (Note that we moved one hole to the right, but you could just as easily move to the left to reverse the slant.)

3. Draw your needle and thread from back to front through the hole next to the one through which it passed in step 1 (here, the hole to the right).

4. Again moving up two holes and over one, pass your needle through the canvas from front to back.

5. Repeat steps 3 and 4 as many times as necessary to complete the row.

6. To start a new row, draw your needle through the canvas two holes below the one through which you passed to start the last stitch and work backward from right to left.

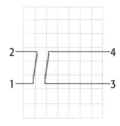

Work the slanted Gobelin stitch.

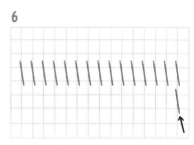

Start the next row here.

The encroaching slanted Gobelin stitch is nearly identical to the slanted Gobelin stitch. The difference? When starting a new row in step 6, you move down one hole instead of two.

Upright Citizens Brigade: The Upright Gobelin and Encroaching Upright Gobelin Stitches

To work an upright Gobelin stitch, do the following (note that you'll likely need more strands, in each length of thread for an upright stitch than for a slanted one):

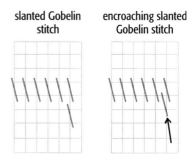

slanted Gobelin stitch   encroaching slanted Gobelin stitch

1. Start your thread, drawing your needle and thread through your canvas from back to front.
2. Move up two holes and pass your needle through the canvas from front to back.
3. Draw your needle and thread from back to front through the hole next to the one through which it passed in step 1.
4. Again moving up two holes, pass your needle through the canvas from front to back.
5. Repeat steps 3 and 4 as many times as necessary to complete the row.
6. To start a new row, draw your needle through the canvas two holes below the one through which you passed to start the last stitch in the preceding row and work backward, from right to left.

Starting a new row of encroaching slanted Gobelin stitches is only slightly different from starting a new row of regular slanted Gobelin stitches.

Surprise: The *encroaching upright Gobelin stitch* is worked almost identically to the regular upright Gobelin stitch. As you probably guessed, the only difference is that instead of moving down two holes when starting a new row, you move down only one. Note that for best results, try splitting the strands in the stitch above when completing an encroaching upright Gobelin stitch.

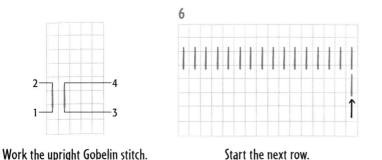

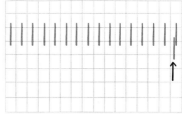

Work the upright Gobelin stitch.　　Start the next row.

Starting a new row of encroaching upright Gobelin stitches is only slightly different from starting a new row of regular upright Gobelin stitches.

Bargello of Blood

Similar to the Gobelin filling stitch is the *bargello stitch*, discussed in chapter 1, "Back Stitch to the Future." Rather than alternating between two starting planes, as the Gobelin filling stitch does, bargello stitches step their way up and down a zigzag pattern, creating peaks and valleys as they go. Bargello designs can be monochromatic, or the color can vary by row.

The bargello stitch.

To work a row of bargello stitches, first decide where the center of the row will be on your canvas. Then do the following:

1. Start your thread at the row's center point, drawing your needle and thread through your canvas from back to front.

2. Move up a few holes. Any single-digit number will do; for the sake of example, go with four. Then pass your needle through the canvas from front to back.

3. To begin the next stitch, move up anywhere from one to three holes from the one in step 1—in this case, I went with two. (The number of holes you move up should be less than the number of holes traveled by your first stitch. That is, if your first stitch traveled, say, six holes, the number of holes you move up should range from one to five. Note, too, that higher numbers here yield a sharper incline; for a more rolling effect, opt for a lower number.) Then draw your needle through the fabric from back to front.

4. Move up four holes and pass your needle through the canvas from front to back.

5. Repeat steps 2–4 as many times as necessary (here, twice) to complete the peak.

6. Move down two holes, draw your needle and thread through the canvas from back to front, and pass it back through four holes down.

7. Repeat step 6 as many times as necessary (here, twice) to complete the valley.

8. Continue in this manner, stitching peaks and valleys, until the right half of the row is complete.

9. Follow steps 2–7 to work the remaining half of the row, going in the opposite direction. When you're finished, the portion of the row to the left of the center stitch should contain the same number of stitches as the portion of the row to the right.

10. You worked the first row from the center outward so the left side would mirror the right side exactly. Subsequent rows, however, can be worked left to right. Simply stitch peaks and valleys following the same pattern as the preceding row, until the row is complete. (For a less regular design, try varying the length of your stitches from row to row. You can also vary the number of holes skipped in step 2 in the initial row.)

continued

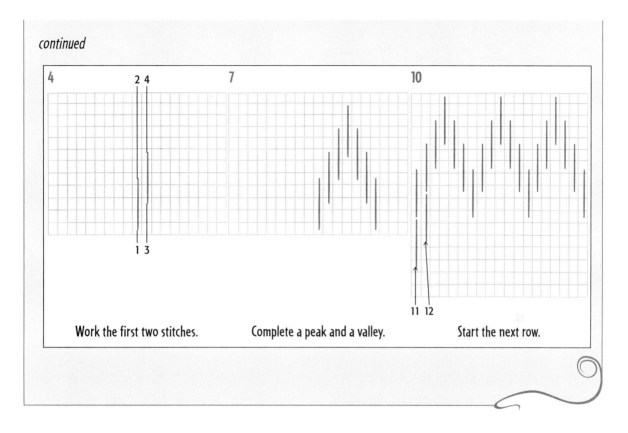

Work the first two stitches.

Complete a peak and a valley.

Start the next row.

Fill 'Er Up: The Gobelin Filling Stitch

The Gobelin filling stitch is an ideal stitch to use when you a) have a large area that needs stitching, and b) you have a short attention span. Here's how it works:

1. Start your thread, drawing your needle and thread through your canvas from back to front.
2. Move up an even number of holes—we'll do four— and pass your needle through the canvas from front to back.
3. Draw your needle and thread from back to front two holes over (in our case, two holes to the right) from the one through which it passed in step 1.
4. Again moving up four holes, pass your needle through the canvas from front to back.

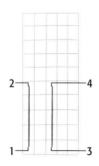
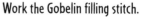

Work the Gobelin filling stitch.

5. Repeat steps 3 and 4 as many times as necessary to complete the row.

6. To start a new row, draw your needle through the canvas two holes down and one hole over (either to the right or the left) from the one through which you passed to start the last stitch in the preceding row. Then work backward, from right to left. (Note that you went down two holes here because your stitches are four holes tall. If your stitch had been six holes tall, you would have gone down three holes; an eight-hole stitch would have required you to move down four holes, and so on.)

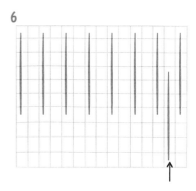

Start the next row.

Note: Use a long-and-short stitch to complete the top and bottom rows.

If It's Not Scottish, It's Crap: Scotch Stitches

Like the Gobelin stitch, the Scotch stitch is ideal for large blocks of color (again, think backgrounds). The result of the stitch is a delightfully Tetris-y effect. The Scotch stitch serves as a foundation for many other stitches, including the *checker stitch, Scottish squares, the condensed Scotch stitch,* and the *Moorish stitch.* In addition, reducing the number of stitches comprising each square yields a *mosaic stitch.* Finally, turning the Scotch stitch on its ear results in a *Hungarian diamond stitch.*

From top to bottom: the Scotch stitch, the checker stitch, Scottish squares, the condensed Scotch stitch, the Moorish stitch, the mosaic stitch, and the Hungarian diamond stitch.

Scotch on the Rocks: The Scotch Stitch

Here's how the Scotch stitch is done:

1. Start your thread, drawing your needle and thread through your canvas from back to front.

2. Moving down and to the right, complete a tent stitch.

3. Draw your needle from back to front through the hole directly above the one in step 1.

4. Pass your needle from front to back through the hole immediately to the right of the one in step 2.

5. Draw your needle from back to front through the hole directly above the one in step 3.

6. Pass your needle through the hole immediately to the right of the one in step 4.

7. Draw your needle from back to front through the hole immediately to the right of the one in step 5.

8. Pass your needle through the hole directly above the one in step 6.

9. Draw your needle from back to front through the hole immediately to the right of the one in step 7.

10. Pass your needle through the hole directly above the one in step 8.

11. To start the next stitch, move down one hole and draw your needle and thread through the canvas from back to front. (Note that this is the same hole through which the needle passed in step 8.) Then, moving down and to the right, complete a tent stitch.

12. Draw your needle through the hole directly above the one in step 11 and repeat steps 2–10 to complete the second stitch.

13. Continue stitching in this manner to complete the row. Then work the next row backward, from right to left.

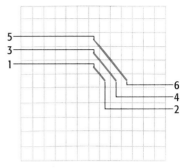

Start the Scotch stitch.

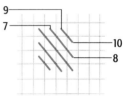

Complete the stitch.

Checkered Past: The Checker Stitch

To work a checker stitch, do the following:

1. Repeat steps 1–11 from the section "Scotch on the Rocks: The Scotch Stitch."

2. Moving left to right, complete two more tent stitches.

3. Moving upward, add two more rows of tent stitches, with three stitches in each row.

4. Move down one hole, work a second Scotch stitch, and then work another 3 × 3 block of tent stitches. Continue in this manner until the row is complete. Work the next row background, from right to left; make sure you alternate Scotch stitches and tent stitches as needed to create.

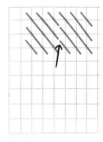

Starting here, work the second stitch.

Work a checker stitch.

Squares with Flair: Scottish Squares

Scottish squares involve stitching a grid to surround a series of Scotch stitches, the result being a nifty tile-and-grout effect. To work this stitch, you must first determine how large your grid should be by a) deciding how many Scotch stitches you want each row and column of the grid to contain and working from there, or b) evaluating how much room you have to work with to determine how many Scotch stitches will fit. Unfortunately, both involve math.

To figure out your grid size under the first scenario, in which you know how many Scotch stitches you want each row and column of your grid to include, do the following:

1. Decide how many Scotch stitches each row of your grid should contain. Let's pretend we want each row of our grid to contain 5 Scotch stitches. This tells you how many columns your grid will contain.

2. Multiply this number by 4—in our case, the result is 20.

3. Add 1—here, for a total of 21. This number represents the width of the grid: 21 stitches.

4. Decide how many Scotch stitches each *column* of your grid will contain. Let's say 6. This tells you how many rows your grid should contain.

5. Multiply this number by 4. In our case, the result is 24.

6. Add 1 to this number, for a total of 25. This tells you that your grid will be 25 stitches tall.

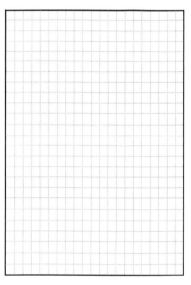

Here's how the grid should look.

7. You have the outer dimensions of the grid (i.e., the dimensions of the rectangle that envelops it): 21 × 25. Your next task is to establish how the lines separating the rows and columns should be spaced. I'll make this one easy for you: Each row should be separated from the next by 3 threads of your canvas; ditto the columns. Put another way, each square in your grid should be 4 holes by 4 holes with a stray column and row along the right side and bottom of the grid.

Figuring out your grid under the second scenario, in which you know how much room you have to work with on your canvas and want to determine how many Scotch stitches will fit, is trickier.

1. Count the number of holes in the area you want to work from left to right. For the sake of example, let's say the area is 42 holes wide.

2. Divide this number by 4. Here, the result is 10, with a remainder of 2.

3. Subtract the remainder (2) from the number of holes in the row (42) — here, the result is 40.
4. Add 1 to this number, for a total of 41. This tells you the number of stitches required for each row of your grid (41).
5. Subtract 1 from your remainder (here, leaving 1). This tells you how many blank holes you'll have left over on each row, outside the box containing your grid; these extra holes will need to be stitched using a technique other than Scottish squares, and may factor in your decision as to where, exactly, you'll begin stitching the Scottish squares.
6. Count the number of holes in the area you want to work from top to bottom. For the sake of example, let's say the area is 55 holes tall.
7. Divide this number by 4. Here, the result is 13, with a remainder of 3.
8. Subtract the remainder (3) from the number of holes in the column (53) — here, the result is 50.
9. Add 1 to this number, for a total of 51. This tells you the number of stitches required for each column of your grid (51).
10. Subtract 1 from your remainder (here, leaving 2). This tells you how many blank holes you'll have left over in each column, outside the box containing your grid. As in the case of the rows, these extra holes will need to be stitched using a technique other than Scottish squares, and may factor in your decision as to where, exactly, you'll begin stitching the Scottish squares.
11. You have the outer dimensions of the grid (i.e., the dimensions of the square that envelops it): 41 × 51. Your next task is to establish how the lines separating the rows and columns should be spaced. Again, I'll make this one easy for you: Each row should be separated from the next by 3 threads of your canvas; ditto the columns. Put another way, each square in your grid should be 4 holes by 4 holes.

Establishing the size of your grid is the tricky part. In contrast, actually *stitching* the Scottish squares is a snap. Working tent stitches, stitch the outline of your grid using the dimensions you just established. Then outline in the columns and rows, separating each with three canvas threads. Finally, starting in the top-left corner of the grid, cover the blank squares in the grid with Scotch stitches (for help, refer to the section "Scotch on the Rocks: The Scotch Stitch").

Condensed Ilk: The Condensed Scotch Stitch

Condensed Scotch stitches differ from regular Scotch stitches in a couple of significant ways. One, they're stitched diagonally. And two, rather than being discrete squares, each condensed Scotch stitch melds into the one before it. Here's how it's done:

1. Starting in the lower-left corner of the area you want to cover. Repeat steps 1–10 in the section "Scotch on the Rocks: The Scotch Stitch."

2. Rather than starting the next stitch by working a tent stitch, your next stitch will use the tent stitch you completed in steps 9 and 10 in the Scotch stitch section as its launching point. Your next move, then, is to draw your needle from back to front through the hole above the one in step 9 and then pass your needle through the hole to the right of the one in step 10.

3. Continue stitching in this manner, linking each new stitch to the one before it via the tent stitch, until the diagonal row is complete.

4. Rotate your canvas 180 degrees so your needle and thread are again in the bottom-left portion of your fabric. Then, starting three holes up and over one to the right from the hole in step 1, repeat steps 1–10 to complete the first Scotch stitch of the next row. Complete the row by repeating steps 2 and 3 in the Scotch stitch section.

2

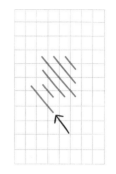

Start the second stitch here.

4

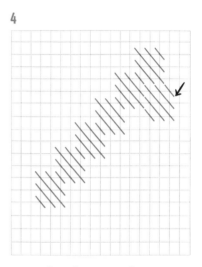

Start the next row here.

A Moor Perfect Union: The Moorish Stitch

Once you've mastered the condensed Scotch stitch, you're ready for the Moorish stitch. Here's how it works:

1. Work a diagonal row of condensed Scotch stitches as outlined in the preceding section, "Condensed Ilk: The Condensed Scotch Stitch."

2. Rotate your canvas 180 degrees to start the next diagonal row. Instead of stacking more condensed Scotch stitches on the existing ones, however, follow the top edge of the initial row using a tent stitch. To keep the vertical edge of the design area even, work the first tent stitch on the thread of your canvas that defines the left edge of the Scotch stitch below.

3. When you finish working tent stitches along the bottom of the initial row, again rotate your canvas 180 degrees. When you do, the line of tent stitches you just added will run along the bottom of the condensed Scotch stitches rather than along the top. Balance

the design by adding another row of tent stitches hugging what is now the top of the condensed Scotch stitches. Again, to keep the vertical edge of the design area even, work the first tent stitch on the thread of your canvas that defines the left edge of the Scotch stitch below.

4. When you finish working the second row of tent stitches, you're ready to work another row of condensed Scotch stitches above it. First, rotate your canvas 180 degrees. Then, beginning above the first tent stitch in the row, add two more tent stitches in an upward fashion; this will keep the vertical edge of your design even. Then work a diagonal row of condensed Scotch stitches as outlined in the section "Condensed Ilk: The Condensed Scotch Stitch."

5. When you finish working this row of condensed Scotch stitches, rotate your canvas 180 degrees yet again. When you do, the row of condensed Scotch stitches you just added will run along the bottom of the tent stitches rather than along the top. To balance the design, repeat step 4 to add another row of condensed Scotch stitches. Continue in this manner, alternating rows of tent stitches and condensed Scotch stitches.

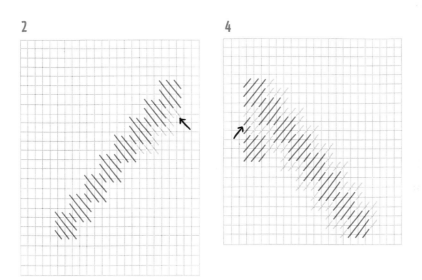

2	**4**
Starting here, trace the outline of the row of condensed Scotch stitches with tent stitches.	Start here to work the next row of condensed Scotch stitches, adding two tent stitches beforehand to keep the vertical edge of the design even.

Formulaic Mosaic: The Mosaic Stitch

The mosaic stitch is exactly like the Scotch stitch, except that instead of requiring five stitches to complete, only three are needed. Here's how it works:

1. Start your thread, drawing your needle and thread through your canvas from back to front.

2. Moving down and to the right, complete a tent stitch.

3. Draw your needle from back to front through the hole directly above the one in step 1.

4. Pass your needle through the hole immediately to the right of the one in step 2.

5. Draw your needle from back to front through the hole to the right of the one in step 3.

6. Pass your needle through the hole above the one in step 4.

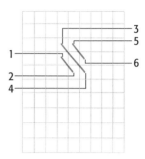

Work the mosaic stitch.

7. So far so good. Working the first mosaic stitch is nearly identical to working a Scotch stitch, except it's smaller and requires fewer stitches. Starting the *next* stitch, however, is a bit different. To begin, move *down* and to the *right* to the hole next to the one in step 4. Then draw your needle and thread through the canvas from back to front.

8. Moving *up* and to the *left*, pass your needle through the same hole as in step 6.

9. Moving up, draw your needle from back to front through the hole next to the one in step 5.

10. Now you're back to the regular pattern, moving from upper left to lower right. Pass your needle through the hole to the right of the one in step 7.

11. Draw your needle from back to front through the hole to the right of the one in step 9.

12. Pass your needle through the hole above the one in step 10.

13. Repeat steps 7–12 as many times as necessary to complete the row. Work the next row backward, from right to left.

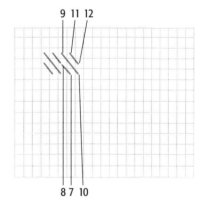

Complete the second stitch.

Hungarian Pangs: The Hungarian Diamond Stitch

The Hungarian diamond stitch is identical—identical!—to the Scotch stitch . . . almost. Rather than working the threads of the Hungarian diamond stitch diagonally, they're worked vertically; the result is a horizontal row of diamonds. Here's how it's done:

1. Start your thread, drawing your needle and thread through your canvas from back to front.

2. Moving up two holes, complete an upright straight stitch.

3. Move down three holes and over one (here, to the right), and draw your needle from back to front through the canvas.

4. Moving up four holes, complete an upright straight stitch.

5. Move down five holes and over one, and draw your needle from back to front through the canvas.

6. Moving up six holes, complete an upright straight stitch.

7. Move down five holes and over one, and draw your needle from back to front through the canvas.

8. Moving up four holes, complete an upright straight stitch.

9. Move down three holes and over one, and draw your needle from back to front through the canvas.

10. Moving up two holes, complete an upright straight stitch.

11. To start the next stitch, move down two holes and over two, draw your needle and thread through the canvas from back to front and move up two holes to complete an upright straight stitch. (Notice the gap between the first Hungarian stitch and this one; it'll be filled in when you complete the next row.)

12. Repeat steps 3–10 to work the next stitch; continue working stitches in this manner until the row is complete.

13. Begin the next row by completing a half diamond (this is to maintain an even vertical edge on the design). Start by moving down four holes and draw your needle from back to front through the canvas. Next, repeat steps 8–10 from right to left to complete the half diamond.

14. To work the next stitch—the first full diamond of the row—repeat steps 11–12. Continue in this manner, adding stitches and rows as needed.

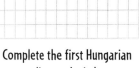
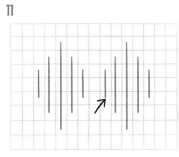

Complete the first Hungarian diamond stitch.

Start the second Hungarian diamond stitch here.

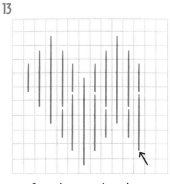

Start the second row here.

More Cushion for the Pushin'

Just as the mosaic stitch riffs off of the Scotch stitch—in its case, using three rather than five threads—so, too, does the cushion stitch. The *cushion stitch* differs from the mosaic stitch, however, in that it requires seven, nine, or more odd-numbered threads to complete.

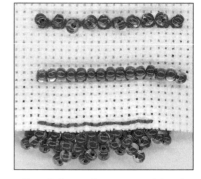

The cushion stitch.

But Wait! There's More: Other Needlework Techniques

Plain-old cross stitch, embroidery, and needlepoint aren't the only games in town. Other stitching techniques include (but, of course, are not limited to) the following:

♦ Bead work

♦ Punch needlework

The End All Bead All: Stitching with Beads

Look, beads are shiny—and what on this earth couldn't use a bit of added shine? Okay, alright, fine: my T-zone. You got me there. Still, incorporating beads into your stitching—whether it's cross stitch, embroidery, or needlepoint—is a great way to add a bit of sparkle to your pieces. Plus, it's way easy:

1. Thread two strands of cotton floss through a beading needle. (As you no doubt recall, the eye of a beading needle is as narrow as the shaft, allowing it to slip through the bead's hole more easily.) If you intend to add transparent beads to your design, opt for a

From left to right: cross-stitch bead work, couched bead work, and beaded fringe.

thread color that matches the background color; if you plan to work with opaque beads, match your thread color with the bead's color.

2. Start your thread as normal. Then, at the point in your fabric where you want to add a bead, draw the needle and thread through from back to front.

3. Slide the bead onto the needle and down the length of thread. (You might want to first make sure the beads are larger than the holes in your fabric; if they're not, they may slip through, thereby decorating the *back* of your piece, which, I'm guessing, is not the look you're after.)

4. Complete the first half of a cross stitch, pulling the thread taut, to attach the bead to the fabric.

5. Complete the second half of the cross stitch, splitting the strands of cotton so they fall on either side of the bead.

5

Split the difference with the strands of thread.

Beads can also be *couched* onto your fabric to great effect. To couch beads, first string a series of beads on your laying thread. Then follow the steps in the section titled "Couch Potato: Couching Stitches" to attach the beaded thread to your fabric, using the tying thread to add small stitches between each bead.

Finally, beads work beautifully for adding *fringe* around the edge of your fabric. Here's one way to do it:

1. In the bottom-left corner of your piece, on the edge of the fabric, start your thread. Then draw your needle through the fabric from back to front.

2. Work one running stitch, passing the needle and thread through the fabric from front to back.

3. Rather than working a second running stitch, thread some small beads on your needle.

4. Loop back up and pass your needle through the same hole as in step 2, from back to front.

5. Work a second running stitch. (Note that unlike a regular series of running stitches, which involve stitches with spaces in between, these running stitches will look more like a double running stitch or a back stitch.)

6. Repeat steps 3 and 4 to add the next loop of beads; continue in this manner to complete the fringe.

Punch Drunk: Punch Needlework

Like a manpanzee—half man, half chimpanzee—punch needlework is a hybrid craft of sorts: part embroidery and part latch hook. Simply put, *punch needlework* involves using a special, pencil-shaped needle (a.k.a. a *punch needle*) with a hollow core through which you feed your thread. You then punch your punch needle and thread through the back side of your fabric, leaving a tufted loop of yarn (think carpet pile) on the front.

To add a bit of dimension to the design, you can adjust the needle to lengthen or shorten the resulting loops. You can also use needles of different sizes, allowing for a broad range of thread types. As for fabric, avoid particularly tough material (think denim) in favor of looser weave (think linen or Aida)—although not *too* loose, or else the loops you make with the punch needle won't stay put. (If your heart is set on a very loosely woven fabric, iron a fusible interface onto the back.) Even better, go for fabric that's designed specifically for punch needle called, logically, "punch needle embroidery fabric."

Punch needlework.

To get the hang of punch needlework, try this:

1. Using whatever method you prefer, transfer your design to your fabric. Rather than transferring it to the front of the fabric, however, apply it to the back. (Note that if your design involves lettering, it need not appear backward, as would be the case if you were transferring a lettered design to be stitched with free embroidery.)

2. Place the fabric in a hoop, back side up, stretching the fabric until it's so taut you could bounce a quarter off it. The hoop should be as small as possible, but large enough for the entire design to fit within it.

3. Thread the needle. To do so, feed the loop end of the special threader that came with your punch needle through the needle's pointy end, stopping when the loop pokes out the other end. Then, pass your thread—start with three strands of cotton floss— through the loop, and draw the threaded loop back through the hollow shaft. (Unlike other types of needlework, where the recommended thread length is 15 to 18 inches, you can use lengths of thread that are 3 to 4 feet long for punch needle, which means you won't have to stop and rethread nearly as often. So you've got that going for you.)

4. With the thread in place, slide off the needle threader's loop; then adjust the length of the short end of the thread to about 2 inches. (You'll trim this bit from your fabric after you've finished stitching the design.)

5. Optionally, adjust the punch needle's depth gauge, keeping in mind that a shorter gauge results in tighter loops. (I left mine as is.) For guidance, see the instructions that came with your punch needle.

6. Hold the punch needle the same way you would a pencil. Then, with the needle perpendicular to the fabric, the bevel (angle) side of the needle facing the direction you plan to stitch, and the tip of the needle placed just inside your pattern line, punch

down through the fabric until the depth gauge engages (i.e., until it hits the fabric). Be sure that the thread flowing into the top of the needle can move freely.

7. Moving the needle straight up, slowly retract it from the fabric—but not so far that the tip of the needle totally loses contact with the fabric. (This ensures that you don't undo the loop you just made on the front side of the fabric.)

8. Following the line of the pattern, slide the needle over a wee bit (you'll want to travel just a couple-ish threads in your fabric), and repeat steps 6 and 7 to work the next stitch.

9. Continue in this fashion until the outline of the design is complete. As you work, avoid moving your fingers to the underside of the fabric; otherwise you might end up with an unexpected body piercing.

10. With the outline stitched, you're ready to fill in the center of your design using the colors of your choice. To do so, simply work rows of stitches, as you would a needle-point design. (Leave about a needle width between rows; start new rows by either rotating your fabric or by rotating the needle such that the bevel faces the proper direction.)

11. When you finish a length of thread, or if you're ready to switch to a different color, simply cut the thread in the needle as close to your work as possible. No knots are needed.

Hand Job: Hand-Sewing Stitches

Odds are when you finish a needlework design, you'll want to do something with it—say, sew it into a pillow or a purse. If you have a sewing machine and you're not afraid to use it, that's obviously the way to go—especially if you're all about immediate gratification. I suspect, however, that not all of you are so blessed. If you are a member of this unlucky group, you'll want to master some basic hand-sewing stitches. (Note that if you do plan to hand-sew your stitched pieces, you'll want to keep some sharps on hand, preferably in a variety of sizes. The needle you use for any given project should be adequately small so as to slide easily into the fabric, but not so small that it's prone to bend or break. As for thread, it's kind of six one, half a dozen the other, depending on the effect you want to achieve.)

Hand-sewing techniques typically involve stitching a seam or a hem; fortunately, this can be accomplished with many of the stitches you used earlier in this chapter—namely, the running stitch, double-running stitch, and back stitch. (Note that of the three, the back stitch is strongest; if your stitches need to hold over the long run, this is one way to go.) Likewise, the whipping technique you applied to several stitches will likely come into play. Rather than using it to embellish stitches, however, you'll use it along the raw edge of your fabric to prevent fraying. Beyond those, you'll likely make use of hem stitches, basting stitches, and slip stitches.

Incidentally, in hand sewing, the whip stitch is nearly identical to the *overhand stitch*; both are used to work the edge of a piece of fabric. The only difference is that overhand stitches tend to work diagonally, while whip stitches are typically straight up and down. Similar to the overhand stitch is the *lacing stitch*. It acts just like an overhand stitch, except that instead of stitching the edge of one piece of fabric, it is used to stitch two pieces of fabric together—a process called *binding*.

It's Us Against Hem: Hem Stitches

Hem stitches are used to work, er, *hems*—which are technically defined as an edge of fabric that is folded over and stitched. Working a hem stitch involves drawing your needle and thread through the folded fabric from back to front, and then back through from front to back. Typically diagonal or vertical, hem stitches should fine enough as to be near invisible from the front.

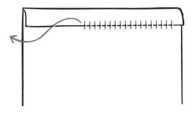

A vertical hem stitch.

Basting Away: Basting Stitches

Generally used as a temporary measure, basting stitches are a sort of pre-seam; that is, they hold pieces of fabric together and serve as a guide when the time comes to apply a stronger stitch to the fabric, after which basting stitches are generally removed. Basting stitches can be vertical, horizontal, or diagonal. Regardless of orientation, basting stitches are characterized as long and loose.

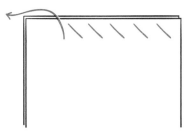

A diagonal basting stitch.

Slip Tease: Slip Stitches

A slip stitch, used to sew two folded edges together in such a way as to conceal the stitches, comes in especially handy when finishing pillows. Here's how it's done:

1. For the sake of example, let's say you've just stuffed a pillow, and you're ready to sew the area of the pillow through which the stuffing was, er, stuffed. To begin, situate the pillow such that the unsewn area is on the top.
2. Fold the raw edges of the pillow inward.
3. Start a 15 to 18-inch thread with a knotted tail on the left side of the unsewn area. To begin, draw the needle and thread through the short edge of the back fold, pulling it toward you from the inside of the fold.

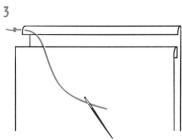

Start the slip stitch from inside the back fold.

4. Loop the needle around so that it faces away from you. Then, poke it all the way through the front fold, about ¼-inch below the crease of the fold.

5. Still drawing the needle away from you, poke it all the way through the back fold, again about ¼-inch below the fold's crease.

6. Loop the needle around and draw it through both folds, back and front.

7. Repeat step 6 as needed to finish closing the unsewn area.

5 and 6

crease of fold

Poke the needle all the way through the front fold, drawing the needle away from you, and then through the back fold.

Next!

Enough with the boring prelims! You're ready to start making actual, bona-fide pieces. In Part Two, "Projects," you'll learn how to make items ranging from embroidered pillows to needle-point wallets to cross-stitch cuffs and beyond.

◆ Part Two ◆

Projects

Chapter Five

◆◆◆

Wear Me Out: Stitching You Can Wear

Tie Me Up

Who says ties must connote conservatism? This project shows you how to embroider a tie to convey an altogether different message: silliness.

Tattoo You

Commitment-phobes, rejoice! No longer are you required to permanently alter your body just to sport a tattoo. Instead, stitch up this embroidered tattoo tank.

Hoodie Two Chews

Whether you think sushi is delicious or revolting (guilty!), it's undeniably easy on the eyes, making it a perfect embroidered embellishment—here, on a hoodie.

I Got My Eye on You

If you have trouble getting men to look you in the eye, try wearing this shirt. That way, when, inevitably, his gaze travels downward to check out your boobs, he'll still be looking you in the (embroidered) eye.

Tie Me Up

by Adam Moe

Recent research indicates several risks associated with wearing neckties. For example:

♦ Neckties can easily become entangled in machinery, thereby strangling the wearer.

♦ Because neckties are typically cleaned less frequently than other items of clothing, they are veritable breeding grounds for bacteria.

♦ When worn over a tight collar, vascular constriction can occur, resulting in a rise in intra-ocular pressure—especially dangerous for people with glaucoma or otherwise weakened retinas.

That can mean only one thing: Neckties are *hot*. I mean, what girl *isn't* turned on by a man who courts danger? That said, studies show that women rank "sense of humor" even higher than "sense of danger" on their list of attractive traits—which is what makes these ties so great. The fact that they're dangerous goes without saying; plus, they're designed to amuse.

Project Rating: Fling

Cost: $5 (More if you go for a super expensive tie)

Necessary Skills: Embroidery

Materials

♦ 1 tie (We used a vintage one.)

♦ Embroidery hoop, 4-in. (We like the oval-shaped ones for this project, but circular ones also work.)

♦ Transfer pencil

♦ Tracing paper

♦ Iron

♦ 1 skein cotton embroidery floss, white, DMC Blanc

♦ 1 skein cotton embroidery floss, mahogany, DMC 301

♦ 1 skein cotton embroidery floss, black, DMC 310

♦ 1 skein cotton embroidery floss, red, DMC 666

♦ 1 skein cotton embroidery floss, yellow beige, DMC 3045

♦ Embroidery scissors

♦ Embroidery needle, size 5

Prepare the Tie

1 **Iron** the back side of the tie either with low heat or high heat and steam. (If you opt for the latter, cover the tie with a layer or two of dishtowels to prevent melting or other type of damage.)

2 Using the tracing paper and the transfer pencil, **trace** the worm design supplied here.

Note: It appears in reverse here so that when you iron it on it comes out right.

3 Using the iron, **transfer** the traced design to the tie. Be careful—if the iron is too hot, the tie may warp, melt, or, well, catch on fire.

Note: If your tie is super dark or made of a particularly delicate fabric, your best bet may be to transfer the design using

carbon transfer paper and a ball-point pen. Alternatively, wing it, using tailor's chalk to draw it by hand.

4 Using your embroidery scissors, **cut** a 15–18-in. length of embroidery floss (any color will do) and **thread** it onto your needle.

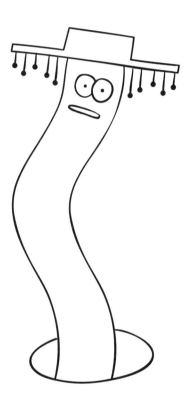

Trace this image for the worm tie.

5 **Apply** one stitch to the back of the tie, a few inches above where the design will appear on the front, and **tie** a knot on both ends of the stitch. This holds the back of the

tie together at the top, making it much easier to sew back together when you're finished embroidering.

6 If, on the back of the tie, there's a tag that spans the width of the tie, you won't be able to spread the tie out enough to embroider it. To rectify this, use your embroidery scissors to **cut** one side of the tag off. The tag should still be attached to the tie, but on one side only. (You'll reconnect that side of the tag after you finish embroidering the tie.)

7 Using embroidery scissors, carefully **snip** the seam on the back of the tie that joins the two sides of the tie together, starting at the bottom of the tie and stopping when you reach the stitch you added in step 4. (Don't cut the material itself, as you'll sew it back up later.)

8 **Situate** the tie in the hoop. If your tie has heavy interfacing inside it—and most do—be sure the interfacing is either perfectly flat in the hoop or hanging completely outside it. Trust us: When that stuff gets wrinkled, there's no fixing it. And there's nothing more frustrating than finishing your embroidery only to discover that the tie has a big bulge or wrinkle in it.

Stitch the Design

9 Using your embroidery scissors, **cut** a 15–18-in. length of mahogany embroidery floss (DMC 301), **strip** the floss, **recombine** three of the strands, and **thread** the three strands onto your needle.

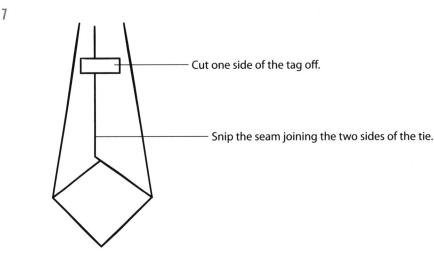

7

Cut one side of the tag off.

Snip the seam joining the two sides of the tie.

Separate one side of the tag from the back of the tie, and then carefully
snip the stitches that join the two sides of the tie together.

10 **Start** the thread using the method of your choice and, using a satin stitch, **fill in** the worm's body. Be sure to keep the stitches firm and the fabric tight—but not *too* tight, especially if your tie is constructed of a delicate fabric such as silk. Otherwise, you'll wind up with strange wrinkles and bunches on the tie, and believe you me: They're harder to fix than the Middle East. When you're finished, **tie off** and **snip** the excess thread.

Note: For best results, fill in the entire body—even the area where the eyes and lips will go. You can then layer the stitches needed to complete those parts of the design on top of the ones comprising the worm's body. This layered effect adds a certain dimensionality to the design, which rocks.

11 Using your embroidery scissors, **cut a** 15–18-in. length of red embroidery floss (DMC 666), **strip** the floss, **re-combine** three of the strands, and **thread** the three strands onto your needle.

12 **Start** the thread using the method of your choice and, using a satin stitch, **stitch** the worm's lips.

13 Still using the red thread, **add** the dangle balls to the hat. Starting on the left side of the hat, apply a single, vertical straight stitch, and then cross the very bottom of that stitch with a very small horizontal straight stitch. Repeat until you've added all the dangles. When you're finished, **tie off** and **snip** the excess thread.

14 Using your embroidery scissors, **cut** a 15–18-in. length of white embroidery floss (DMC Blanc), **strip** the floss, **re-combine** three of the strands, and **thread** the three strands onto your needle.

15 **Start** the thread using the method of your choice and, using a satin stitch, **fill in** the whites of the worm's eye. When you're finished, **tie off** and **snip** the excess thread.

16 Using your embroidery scissors, **cut a** 15–18-in. length of black embroidery floss (DMC 310), **strip** the floss, **re-combine** three of the strands, and **thread** the three strands onto your needle.

17 **Start** the thread using the method of your choice and, using a satin stitch, **fill in** the worm's hat and the hole from whence the worm emerges.

18 Still using the black thread, **stitch** the worm's pupils.

Stitch the Outline

19 Still using the black thread, **stitch** the outline of the worm's eyeballs using a double running stitch.

20 Still using the black thread, stitch the outline of the worm's hat as well as the outline of the hole from which the worm is emerging using a double running stitch. When you're finished, **tie off** and **snip** the excess thread.

21 Using your embroidery scissors, **cut a** 15–18-in. length of yellow-beige embroidery floss (DMC 3045), **strip** the floss, **re-combine** three of the strands, and **thread** the three strands onto your needle.

22 **Start** the thread using the method of your choice and, using a double running stitch, **stitch** the outline of the worm's body. When you're finished, **tie off** and **snip** the excess thread.

Wrap It Up, Missy

23 When you're finished embroidering, **remove** the tie from the hoop.

24 **Iron** the back of the tie to flatten it out. Again, keep the setting relatively low. Also, make sure the back of the tie overlaps the way it did when you first cut it open.

25 **Sew** the back of the tie back together, being careful to keep everything flat and straight. A double running stitch should do the trick. To make your life easier, put the tie face down on a flat surface for this step.

26 **Iron** the back of the tie yet again, still with a low setting. (This is the last time. We swear.)

27 **Face** the danger and **wear** the tie — or **give** it to someone who will.

Variation

Sticking It to the Man

by Adam Moe

Remember that "I'm #1" hat commercial on *Saturday Night Live?* Intended for "discriminating gentlemen" who are tired of *telling* people they're number one, this "fully adjustable rayon cap" proved the perfect accessory for trumpeting the wearer's #1 status. Likewise, the "The Man" tie can eliminate confusion about who's in charge. Simply prepare a tie as outlined above, use a double running stitch or a chain stitch to outline the letters, and apply a basic needleweaving stitch to fill them in.

Show 'em who's the man.

Tattoo You

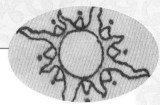

by Jenn Maruska

Tattoos. Sure, they're cool, but who wants to make that kind of commitment, especially given how topsy-turvy trends are? I mean, what's cool today will almost certainly be the kiss of death in a decade. That's why this tattooed tank is just the ticket, allowing you to look cool now—*and* look cool later.

Project Rating: Fling

Cost: $10

Necessary Skills: Embroidery

Materials

- 1 tank top (Ours was a C9 Champion tank from Target, which, conveniently, sells in packs of two.)
- Tape
- Transfer pencil
- Tracing paper
- Iron
- Pencil, #2
- Water-soluble fabric pen
- A few pins
- Embroidery scissors
- Embroidery hoop, 4 in.
- 1 skein cotton embroidery floss, red copper, DMC 919
- Embroidery needle, size 5

Preparing the Tank

1 **Wash** and **dry** the tank. This prevents it from shrinking later, after you've embroidered it. Afterward, iron it.

2 **Try on** the tank in front of a mirror to decide where to place your design. **Use** a small piece of tape to mark the area you've chosen.

3 Using the tracing paper and the transfer pencil, **trace** the tattoo design supplied here, but omit the letter "A" that appears near the top of the design, the arrow, and the plus sign in the middle. (These are simply guides for your use when you begin stitching the design.)

4 Using the water-soluble fabric pen, **mark** the tank with a small dot where you want the center of your tattoo to go. Then, make a similar dot on the back side of your tracing paper—that is, the side without the traced design. This will help you to position your tattoo.

5 **Lay** the tracing paper face down on the front of your tank (that is, with the marks made by the transfer pencil touching the tank), lining it up so the mark you made on the tracing paper in step 4 aligns with the mark made on the tank. Then, using the iron, **transfer** the traced design to the tank. (Placing a square of stiff cardboard under the fabric helps keep the fabric smooth when ironing.)

6 **Situate** the tank in the hoop.

Trace this tattoo.

Stitching the Design

7 Using your embroidery scissors, **cut** a 15–18-in. length of red-copper embroidery floss, **strip** the floss, **re-combine** all six of the strands, and **thread** the strands onto your needle.

8 Start the thread using the method of your choice at point "A" on the design and, using a back stitch, **embroider** the inner circle of the design. End with the circle complete and the needle inside the tank.

9 Again using a back stitch, **embroider** the sun's rays, but not the triangles with the dots above them. End with the sun's rays complete and the needle inside the tank.

10 Beginning at point "A," use a back stitch to **embroider** the first small triangular point around the sun, applying two back stitches for each side of the triangle (you'll make four stitches in all). Make sure that each side of the triangle meets the embroidery line of the sun's rays so that the triangle is closed on all three sides. Finish with your needle inside the tank.

11 From inside the tank, bring the thread through the fabric where the dot is drawn above the triangle and **make** a tight French knot. End with your thread back inside the tank.

12 Use your needle to **pull** the thread through the loops of your previous stitches inside the tank until you reach the next triangle.

13 **Repeat** steps 10–12 until the eight triangles have been completed. When you're finished, **tie off** and **snip** any excess thread.

Variation

Bull's-eye

by Jenn Maruska

Remember that scene in *Wedding Crashers* when Vince Vaughan's character spots some chick with a tattoo on her lower back? "Might as well be a bull's-eye," he says. Why? Because a tattoo on the back is dead sexy! But what if the idea of some gigantic bald guy named "Bullet" putting a needle in *your* back makes you want to vomit? In that case, simply follow the steps in the preceding project, but position the tattoo on the lower-back portion of your tank. When you're ready to start stitching, try using the following design for a bit of variety.

This design will look great as a lower-back tattoo.

continued

continued

1. Beginning at point "A," use a back stitch to embroider the outline of the tattoo in a clockwise direction. For now, avoid the four triangles on the top half of the tattoo, the curved lines in the inner portion of the tattoo (labeled "C"), and the areas on each side (labeled "D").

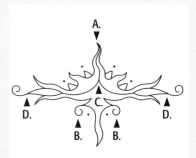

Use this as a guide.

2. When you come to the right point labeled "B," bring the thread through the fabric from the inside of the tank out where the dot is drawn and make a tight French knot. Repeat with the left point labeled "B."

3. Continue embroidering the outline of the tattoo. When you reach the "A" point, use a back stitch to embroider the curved lines in the inner portion of the tattoo labeled "C". After you complete one curved line, draw your needle through your previous stitches on the back of the fabric to secure them, and then stitch the other curved line. When you're finished, the needle should be coming out of the inside of the tank.

4. Stitch through the loops of your previous stitches inside the tank fabric to situate your needle at one of the flourishes labeled "D."

5. Using a back stitch, embroider the flourish. Then draw your needle through the previous stitches on the inside of the tank to situate your needle at the other flourish ("D") and embroider it.

6. Draw your needle through the loops of the previous stitches inside the tank to situate your needle at the closest triangle.

7. Use a back stitch to embroider the triangle, applying two back stitches for each side of the triangle (you'll make four stitches in all). End with your needle thread inside the tank.

8. From inside the tank, bring the thread through the fabric where the dot is drawn above the triangle and make a tight French knot. End with your thread back inside the tank.

9. Repeat steps 6–8 until the four triangles have been completed. When you're finished, tie off and snip any excess thread.

Hoodie Two Chews

by Jenn Maruska

Among the staples of any wardrobe is at least one hoodie—which explains why everyone and their brother have one. To set yours apart, embellish it with embroidery!

Project Rating: Flirtation
Cost: $25
Necessary Skills: Embroidery

Materials

- 1 hoodie (Ours was a Pro Spirit hoodie from Target.)
- Tape
- Transfer pencil
- Tracing paper
- Iron
- Pencil, #2
- Water-soluble fabric marker, fine-point
- A few pins
- Embroidery hoop, 4-in.
- Embroidery scissors
- 1 skein cotton embroidery floss, white, DMC Blanc
- 1 skein cotton embroidery floss, black, DMC 310
- 1 skein cotton embroidery floss, dark navy blue, DMC 919
- 1 skein cotton embroidery floss, light pumpkin, DMC 970
- 1 skein cotton embroidery floss, light moss green, DMC 3819
- Embroidery needle, size 5

Preparing the Hoodie

1. **Wash** and **dry** the hoodie. This prevents it from shrinking later, after you've embroidered it. Afterward, iron it.

2. **Try on** the hoodie in front of a mirror to decide where to place your design. **Use** a small piece of tape to mark the area you've chosen.

3. Using the tracing paper and the transfer pencil, **trace** the sushi design shown here.

Note: It appears in reverse here so that when you iron it on it comes out right.

4. Using the water-soluble fabric pen, **mark** the hoodie with a small dot where you want the center of your sushi design to go. Then, make a similar dot on the back side of your tracing paper—that is, the side without the traced design. This will help you to position your sushi design.

5. **Lay** the tracing paper face down on the front of your hoodie (that is, with the marks made by the transfer pencil touching the hoodie), lining it up so the mark you made on the tracing paper in step 4 aligns with the mark made on the hoodie. Then, using the iron, **transfer** the traced design to

Trace this sushi design. (Note that the top portion of the design is the salmon, the middle part is the wasabi, and the bottom part is the rice.)

the hoodie. (Placing a square of stiff cardboard under the fabric helps keep the fabric smooth when ironing.)

6 **Situate** the hoodie in the hoop.

Stitching the Salmon

7 Using your embroidery scissors, **cut** a 15–18-in. length of light-pumpkin embroidery floss (DMC 970), **strip** the floss, **re-combine** all six of the strands, and **thread** the strands onto your needle.

8 **Start** your thread using the method of your choice and, using a split stitch, **outline** the left-most segment of salmon. Go completely around the segment.

9 **Remove** the needle from the light-pumpkin thread, leaving the thread hanging from the back of the piece.

10 Using your embroidery scissors, **cut** a 15–18-in. length of white embroidery floss (DMC Blanc), **strip** the floss, **re-combine** all six of the strands, and **thread** the strands onto your needle.

11 **Start** your thread using the method of your choice. Then use a split stitch to **stitch** a white line from bottom to top against the right side of the light-pumpkin line that separates the first segment of the salmon from the next segment. Take care to avoid tangling the white thread with the light-pumpkin thread.

12 **Remove** the needle from the white thread, leaving the thread hanging from the back of the piece.

13 **Thread** the needle onto the light-pumpkin thread hanging from the back of the piece.

14 **Repeat** steps 8–13 until you've outlined all the segments of the salmon and added the white highlights. To situate the needle correctly when starting a new segment, pull the needle through the loops of previous stitches on the back of the piece. When you're finished, **tie off** and **snip** any excess thread.

15 Using your embroidery scissors, **cut** a new 15–18-in. length of light-pumpkin embroidery floss, **strip** the floss, **re-combine** all six of the strands, and **thread** the strands onto your needle.

16 **Start** your thread using the method of your choice and, using a satin stitch, **fill in** each segment of the salmon. When you're finished, **tie off** and **snip** any excess thread.

Stitching the Wasabi

17 Using your embroidery scissors, **cut** a 15–18-in. length of light moss green embroidery floss (DMC 3819), **strip** the floss, **re-combine** all six of the strands, and **thread** the strands onto your needle.

18 **Start** your thread using the method of your choice and **complete** two rows of split stitches in the area between the salmon

and the rice, following the contours of the sushi. When you're finished, **tie off** and **snip** any excess thread.

Stitching the Rice

19 Using your embroidery scissors, **cut** a new 15–18-in. length of white embroidery floss, **strip** the floss, **re-combine** all six of the strands, and **thread** the strands onto your needle.

20 **Start** your thread using the method of your choice and, using French knots, **fill in** the rice area, underneath the wasabi. When you're finished, **tie off** and **snip** any excess thread.

Finishing the Sushi

21 Using your embroidery scissors, **cut** a 15–18-in. length of dark navy blue embroidery floss (DMC 919), **strip** the floss, **re-combine** all six of the strands, and **thread** the strands onto your needle.

22 **Start** your thread using the method of your choice and, using a back stitch, **outline** the top portion of the sushi to make it stand out from the background. When you're finished, **tie off** and **snip** any excess thread.

Stitching the Letters

23 Using your embroidery scissors, **cut** a 15–18-in. length of black embroidery floss (DMC 310), **strip** the floss, **re-combine** all six of the strands, and **thread** the strands onto your needle.

24 **Start** your thread using the method of your choice and, using small back stitches, **stitch** the letters. When you're finished, **tie off** and **snip** any excess thread.

Stitching the Circular Border

25 Using your embroidery scissors, **cut** a new 15–18-in. length of dark navy blue floss, **strip** the floss, **re-combine** all six of the strands, and **thread** the strands onto your needle.

26 **Start** your thread using the method of your choice and, using a split stitch, **stitch** the large outer circle around the sushi. When you're finished, **tie off** and **snip** any excess thread.

27 Using your embroidery scissors, **cut** a new 15–18-in. length of light moss green embroidery floss, **strip** the floss,

re-combine all six of the strands, and **thread** the strands onto your needle.

28 **Start** your thread using the method of your choice and, using a split stitch, **stitch** a smaller circle inside the dark navy blue one. When you're finished, **tie off** and **snip** any excess thread.

I Fought the Raw and the Raw Won.

This sushi design would make a great patch, which you could then sew onto, say, the back pocket of your jeans. For help, follow the patch-specific steps in the project titled "The Diet of Worms" in chapter 6.

I Got My Eye on You

by Lindsay Evans

Has this ever happened to you? You meet a guy. He strikes up a conversation. Suddenly you realize, rather than looking you in the eye, he's gazing at your breasts. Solution? Wear this T-shirt. That way, he can do *both*.

Project Rating: Fling

Cost: $15

Necessary Skills: Embroidery

Materials

* 1 cotton T-shirt (Ours is a white, ribbed, long-sleeved baddie, purchased at Wal-Mart.)
* 8 × 10-in. piece of cut-away interfacing (We used the kind that you iron on.)
* Transfer pencil
* Tracing paper
* Iron
* Embroidery hoop, 8-in.
* 1 skein cotton embroidery floss, white, Anchor 1
* 1 skein cotton embroidery floss, bright red, Anchor 46
* 1 skein cotton embroidery floss, medium Delft blue, Anchor 136
* 1 skein cotton embroidery floss, royal blue, Anchor 139
* 1 skein cotton embroidery floss, sky blue, Anchor 160
* 1 skein cotton embroidery floss, kelly green, Anchor 226
* 1 skein cotton embroidery floss, very dark emerald green, Anchor 230
* 1 skein cotton embroidery floss, light beige, Anchor 336
* 1 skein cotton embroidery floss, ultra dark coffee brown, Anchor 381
* 1 skein cotton embroidery floss, cream, Anchor 387
* 1 skein cotton embroidery floss, black, Anchor 403
* Embroidery scissors
* Embroidery needle, size 7
* Shears

Preparing the Shirt

1. **Wash** and **dry** the T-shirt to prevent it from shrinking later, after you've embroidered it. Afterward, iron it.

2. **Cut** the piece of fusible interfacing to fit the eyeball design.

3. Following the instructions that came with the fusible interfacing, use a hot iron to **iron** the interfacing onto the inside of the front of the T-shirt.

4. Using the tracing paper and the transfer pencil, **trace** the eyeball plant design supplied here.

5. **Turn** the T-shirt right side out and, using the iron, **transfer** the traced design to the shirt.

Trace the eyeball plant image.

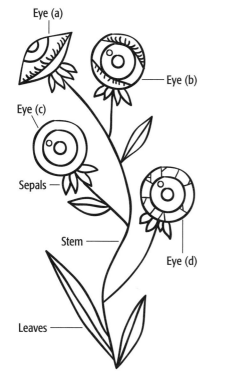

Use this image as a reference guide as you stitch.

6 **Situate** the portion of the front of the T-shirt on which the design appears in the hoop, right side out.

Stitching the Stem

7 Using your embroidery scissors, **cut** a 15–18-in. length of very dark emerald green embroidery floss (Anchor 230), **strip** the floss, **re-combine** two of the strands, and **thread** the two strands onto your needle.

8 **Start** the thread using the method of your choice and, using a double-running stitch, **embroider** the stem. When you're finished, **tie off** and **snip** the excess thread.

9 Using your embroidery scissors, **cut** a 15–18-in. length of kelly green embroidery floss (Anchor 226), **strip** the floss, **re-combine** two of the strands, and **thread** the two strands onto your needle.

10 **Start** the thread using the method of your choice and **whip** the double-running stitches you applied in step 8.

11 Still with the kelly green thread, **stitch** the leaves using a satin stitch starting at the tip of the leaves and working your way toward the stem. When you're finished, **tie off** and **snip** the excess thread.

12 **Re-combine** two of the four remaining strands of very dark emerald green embroidery floss (Anchor 230) and **thread** the two strands onto your needle.

13 **Start** the thread using the method of your choice and, using a back stitch, **outline** the leaves you stitched in step 11. When you're finished, **tie off** and **snip** the excess thread.

14 Using your embroidery scissors, **cut** a 15–18-in. length of very dark emerald green embroidery floss (Anchor 230), **strip** the floss, **re-combine** three of the strands, and **thread** the three strands onto your needle.

15 **Start** the thread using the method of your choice and, using a satin stitch, **stitch** the sepals under each eyeball. When you're finished, **tie off** and **snip** the excess thread.

Stitching the Eyes

16 Using your embroidery scissors, **cut** a 15–18-in. length of black embroidery floss (Anchor 403), **strip** the floss, **re-combine** three of the strands, and **thread** the three strands onto your needle.

17 **Start** the thread using the method of your choice and, using a satin stitch, **stitch** the pupils of each eye. When you're finished, **tie off** and **snip** the excess thread.

18 Using your embroidery scissors, **cut** a 15–18-in. length of kelly green embroidery floss (Anchor 226), **strip** the floss, **re-combine** two of the strands, and **thread** the two strands onto your needle.

19 **Start** the thread using the method of your choice and, using a satin stitch, **embroider** the iris of "eye a." To maintain the correct angle of satin stitches around the iris, it might help to add straight-stitch "spokes" around the iris before filling in with satin stitches. When you're finished, **tie off** and **snip** the excess thread.

20 Using your embroidery scissors, **cut** a 15–18-in. length of royal blue embroidery floss (Anchor 226), **strip** the floss, **re-combine** three of the strands, and **thread** the three strands onto your needle.

21 **Start** the thread using the method of your choice and, using a satin stitch, **embroider** the iris of "eye b." Again, to maintain the correct angle of satin stitches around the iris, it may help to add straight-stitch "spokes" around the iris before filling

in with satin stitches. Note that you should cover the entire iris with stitches—even the small circle near the pupil. When you're finished, **tie off** and **snip** the excess thread.

22 Using your embroidery scissors, **cut** a 15–18-in. length of ultra dark coffee brown embroidery floss (Anchor 381), **strip** the floss, **re-combine** three of the strands, and **thread** the three strands onto your needle.

23 **Start** the thread using the method of your choice and, using a satin stitch, **embroider** the iris of "eye c," beginning by adding straight-stitch spokes. Again, fill in the entire iris, including the small circle near the pupil. When you're finished, **tie off** and **snip** the excess thread.

24 Using your embroidery scissors, **cut** a 15–18-in. length of medium Delft blue embroidery floss (Anchor 136), **strip** the floss, **re-combine** three of the strands, and **thread** the three strands onto your needle.

25 **Start** the thread using the method of your choice and, using a long-and-short satin stitch of randomly varying lengths, **embroider** the inner portion of the iris of "eye d." When you're finished, **tie off** and **snip** the excess thread.

26 Using your embroidery scissors, **cut** a 15–18-in. length of sky blue embroidery floss (Anchor 160), **strip** the floss, **re-combine** three of the strands, and **thread** the three strands onto your needle.

27 **Start** the thread using the method of your choice and, using a long-and-short satin stitch, **fill in** the rest of the iris of "eye d." When you're finished, **tie off** and **snip** the excess thread.

28 Using your embroidery scissors, **cut** a 15–18-in. length of white embroidery floss (Anchor 1), **strip** the floss, **re-combine** three of the strands, and **thread** the three strands onto your needle.

29 **Start** the thread using the method of your choice and, using a satin stitch, **fill in** the white areas around the irises of all four eyeballs. Again, you may want to begin by adding straight-stitch spokes.

30 Still using the white thread, **apply** a French knot on the iris of "eye b" to create a highlight. Repeat for "eye c" and "eye d." When you're finished, **tie off** and **snip** the excess thread.

31 Using your embroidery scissors, **cut** a 15–18-in. length of bright red embroidery floss (Anchor 46), **strip** the floss, and **thread** one strand through your needle.

32 **Start** the thread using the method of your choice and, using a back stitch, **apply** the blood vessels on "eye d." When you're finished, **tie off** and **snip** the excess thread.

33 Using your embroidery scissors, **cut** a 15–18-in. length of light beige embroidery floss (Anchor 336), **strip** the floss, **re-combine** three of the strands, and **thread** the three strands onto your needle.

34 **Start** the thread using the method of your choice and, using a satin stitch, fill in the eyelids of "eye a" and "eye b." When you're finished, **tie off** and **snip** the excess.

35 Using your embroidery scissors, **cut** a 15–18-in. length of black embroidery floss (Anchor 403), **strip** the floss, **re-combine** two of the strands, and **thread** the two strands onto your needle.

36 **Start** the thread using the method of your choice and, using a back stitch, **stitch** a border around the pupil, iris, eyeball, and eyelid of "eye a."

37 Repeat step 36 on "eye b."

38 Still using the black thread, **outline** the pupil, iris, and eyeball of "eye c."

39 **Repeat** step 38 on "eye d." When you're finished, **tie off** and **snip** the excess.

40 Using your embroidery scissors, **cut** a 15–18-in. length of black embroidery floss, **strip** the floss, and **thread** one strand through your needle.

41 **Start** the thread using the method of your choice and **stitch** the eyelashes on "eye a" and "eye b." For a more realistic look, you'll want the base of the eyelashes to appear thicker than the tip. You'll also want the lashes to curve a bit. To begin, **pull** the needle from the inside of the T-shirt at point 1 (see the following diagram) and poke it through the front of the T-shirt at point 2.

Use this guide when stitching the eyelashes.

42 **Pull** the needle from the inside of the T-shirt at point 3, draw the thread underneath the stitch you made in step 41, and **poke** the needle back through point 1. This creates a curve in the first stitch and the appearance of a thicker base than tip.

43 Repeat steps 41–42 for the remaining eyelashes. When you're finished, **tie off** and **snip** the excess thread.

44 Use your shears to **cut away** the excess stabilizer around the design inside the T-shirt.

Variation

The Eyes Have It

This design would look equally spectacular on the back of a T-shirt or even a hoodie. Although the eyes wouldn't be "in the back of your head," they would nonetheless be backward-facing—handy if small, gullible children are in your charge.

Chapter Six

◆◆

Yarn and Floss Accoutrements: Gussy Up Your Look with Stitching

You're So Money

With this Gucci-inspired needlepoint wallet, you'll be so money—and you'll *know* it.

I'll Stop the World and Belt with You

Belts. Are they in? Are they out? Who knows—and who cares? With this embroidered ribbon belt, you'll *always* be stylish.

Hip Code

The next time your moron boss asks you the dumbest question you've ever heard, flash him this cuff. Embroidered with the Morse code for a question mark and embellished with beads, it's a perfect non-verbal response to any office speak/just plain ridiculousness you encounter during your day.

Felt Up

Adopt a new skill—felting—using the result as your ground fabric to embroider a fantastic pendant.

Chuck Berries

Look, Chuck Taylors are plenty cool as is. But what pair of shoes wouldn't look better with some stitching applied? This project shows you how to use embroidery to make your tennies *tight*.

British Invasion

iPods: They're everywhere. So how do you tell yours apart from your three roommates'? With this kick-ass needlepoint Union Jack iPod holder, *that's* how. In addition to setting it apart, this cool caddy also protects your iPod.

Germ Warfare

I know, hankies have gone the way of sock suspenders. That just means they're ripe for a comeback. To help spread the fever, stitch up this embroidered germkerchief.

The Diet of Worms

Late risers among you: Celebrate! Thanks to this embroidered bird and worm patch, smug morning people no longer corner the market on invertebrates.

Laptop Dance

No more boring, black nylon laptop bags for you. This project shows you how to stitch up a kick-ass needlepoint carry-on.

You're So Money

by Amy Holbrook

Girl, you're so money, and you don't even know it. Or maybe you do. Either way, you'll love this incredible Gucci-inspired needlepoint wallet.

Project Rating: Flirtation

Cost: $5

Necessary Skills: Needlepoint

Materials

- Tapestry needle, size 22
- 1 sheet 14-count plastic canvas with round, rather than square, holes (We used Darice brand.)
- 1 skein pearl cotton thread, size 5, red, DMC 321
- 1 skein pearl cotton thread, size 5, dark green, DMC 890
- 1 skein pearl cotton thread, size 5, chocolate brown, DMC 938
- 2 skeins pearl cotton thread, size 5, ecru
- Shears
- X-Acto knife
- Embroidery scissors
- Optional (for lining the inside of the wallet): 1 square ft. thin cotton fabric, dark brown
- Optional (for lining the inside of the wallet): Heavy-duty sewing thread in a color to match the dark brown fabric
- Optional (for lining the inside of the wallet): 1 size 6 (or thereabouts) sharp

Cut the Canvas

1 Using your shears, **cut** a rectangular piece of plastic canvas that is 94 × 78 holes. This will be the body of your wallet. (Note that cutting canvas with round holes is trickier than cutting square-holed canvas because the edges of the hole don't define a clear grid; for this project, you'll want to cut on the *next* set of holes all the way around and then trim the canvas down to create a straight line on all four sides.)

2 Using the following diagram as a guide, use your shears to **cut** a second piece of plastic canvas. The main portion of the shape you cut should be 94 × 18 holes, with a long piece that extends from the center of the bottom edge that is 16 holes long and 10 holes wide. This will be the front flap of the wallet.

3 Use your shears to **cut** one more piece of plastic canvas, this one 24 × 13 holes. This will become the buckle.

4 Following the diagram shown, use an X-Acto knife to **cut** out two rows of holes in the top half of the buckle and two more rows in the bottom half.

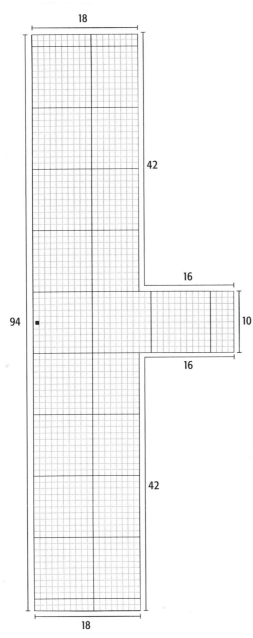

Cut the front flap of the wallet.

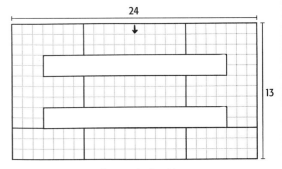

Create the buckle.

Needlepoint the Body

5 Using the next diagram as a guide, you'll needlepoint the body of the wallet, starting with the chocolate-brown border. To begin, use your embroidery scissors to **cut** a 15–18-in. length of chocolate brown pearl cotton thread (DMC 938) and **thread** it onto your needle.

6 **Situate** the body of the wallet longside up.

7 **Start** the thread using the method of your choice, then **draw** it from back to front through the hole just below the one in the top-left corner of the canvas.

8 Moving diagonally up and to the right, **complete** a tent stitch.

9 **Draw** your thread from back to front through the hole beneath the one in step 7.

10 Moving up and to the right, **pass** your thread through the hole to the right of the one in step 8.

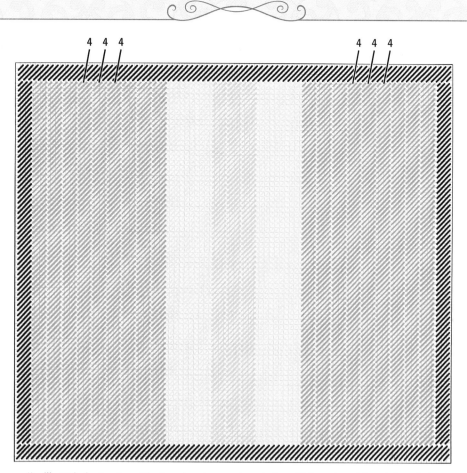

4 4 4   4 4 4

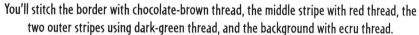

You'll stitch the border with chocolate-brown thread, the middle stripe with red thread, the two outer stripes using dark-green thread, and the background with ecru thread.

11 Draw your thread from back to front through the hole beneath the one in step 9.

12 Moving up and to the right, **pass** your thread through the hole to the right of the one in step 10.

13 If you're feeling a sense of *déjà vu*, it's because you just worked the first three stitches of a Scotch stitch. Instead of completing the Scotch stitch, however, **repeat** a stitch like the one you worked in steps 11 and 12, crossing three intersections in your canvas.

14 Repeat step 13 as many times as needed to reach the end of the row. When you run out of room to stitch across three intersections, "finish" the Scotch stitch by next stitching across two intersections, then by one. When you're finished, **tie off** and **snip** the excess thread.

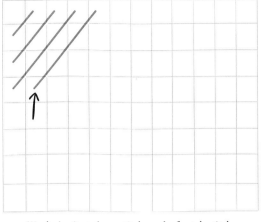

Work the first three stitches of a Scotch stitch; then, rather than completing the Scotch stitch, repeat the third stitch.

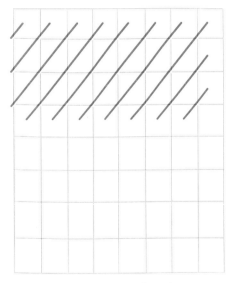

"Finish" the Scotch stitch.

15 Rotate the canvas 180 degrees, so the other long edge faces upward. Then, **repeat** steps 5–14, but don't tie off.

16 **Rotate** the canvas 90 degrees to the left, so the needle and thread are again in the upper-left area of the wallet.

17 Pretend the "half" Scotch stitch currently on the far-left end of the row is a full Scotch stitch, and that you're about to start another one. To begin, **draw** the needle through from back to front as shown.

18 **Repeat** steps 8–12, but in the opposite direction. That is, rather than moving up and to the right to complete each stitch, move *down* and to the right.

19 You've finished the half Scotch stitch. As before, instead of working the other half of the Scotch stitch, instead **repeat** the last stitch you made, crossing three intersections in your canvas.

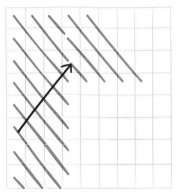

Start here to work the side edge, pointing each stitch downward and to the right, to complete half of a Scotch stitch. Then, instead of completing the Scotch stitch, repeat the longest stitch, crossing three intersections in your canvas.

Repeat step 19 as many times as needed to reach the end of the row. When you run out of room to stitch across three intersections, "finish" the Scotch stitch by next stitching across two intersections, then by one. When you're finished, **tie off** and **snip** the excess thread.

Rotate the canvas 180 degrees, so the other short edge faces upward. Then, **repeat** steps 17–20 to complete the border. When you're finished, **tie off** and **snip** the excess thread.

Using your embroidery scissors, **cut** a 15–18-in. length of ecru pearl cotton thread and **thread** it onto your needle.

With the same edge of the canvas facing up as in step 21, **start** the ecru thread using the method of your choice, drawing it from back to front three holes below the hole where the tent stitch in the preceding row started.

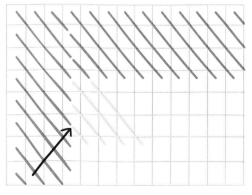

Start the first ecru row here, then continue with the row as normal.

Repeat steps 18–20, again moving down and to the right to complete each stitch, but don't tie off.

Add two more rows of ecru stitches, rotating the canvas 180 degrees after completing each row to return the needle and thread to the left side.

So far, the rows you've stitched have been composed primarily of stitches that cross three intersections in your canvas. For a bit of variety, work your next row of ecru stitches to cross four intersections. To begin the row, move down four holes from the one where the tent stitch in the preceding row started. Then **draw** your needle and thread through the canvas from back to front.

Still completing each stitch by working down and to the right, **complete** half of a Scotch stitch as before. Instead of copying the third stitch the rest of the way across the row, however, **add** a fourth stitch that spans four intersections to complete half of a *cushion stitch*. (If you recall from chapter 4, "Stitch Hitter: Your Guide to Cross-Stitch, Embroidery, and Needlepoint Stitches," cushion stitches are really just Scotch stitches whose middle threads cross four or more intersections rather than three.)

Repeat the fourth stitch, crossing four intersections in your canvas, as many times as necessary to complete the row. When you run out of room to stitch across four intersections, taper the remaining stitches as needed.

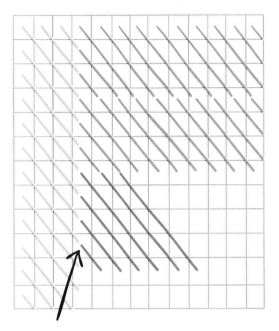

Start here to begin a row of stitches that cross four intersections in your canvas.

29 Still using ecru thread, **add** two more rows of stitches that cross four intersections.

30 Continuing with the ecru thread, **add** three more rows of stitches that cross only three intersections. When you finish the third row, **tie off.**

31 **Thread** your needle with dark-green thread (DMC 890) and **add** three rows of stitches that cross only three intersections. When you finish the third row, **tie off.**

32 **Thread** your needle with red thread (DMC 321) and **add** three rows of stitches that cross only three intersections. When you finish the third row, **tie off.**

33 Again **thread** your needle with dark-green thread and **add** three rows of stitches that cross only three intersections. When you finish the third row, **tie off.**

34 Switch to ecru thread and **stitch** three more rows of stitches that cross only three intersections.

35 Still using ecru thread, **add** three rows of stitches that cross four intersections.

36 Continuing with the ecru thread, **stitch** three more rows of stitches that cross only three intersections. When you finish the last row, **tie off** and **snip** the excess thread. You've finished stitching the body of the wallet.

Stitch the Flap

37 Using this diagram as a guide, you'll needlepoint the wallet's flap. To begin, use your embroidery scissors to **cut** a 15–18-in. length of chocolate brown pearl cotton thread and **thread** it onto your needle.

38 **Position** the flap short edge up, with the bit that extends out to the side pointing to the right.

39 **Start** the thread using the method of your choice, and, **draw** it from back to front through the hole that's three holes down from the top-left corner of the canvas.

40 **Repeat** steps 18–36, moving down and to the right to complete each stitch. (Note that the piece that sticks out to the side should be an extension of the red stripe on the body of the wallet.)

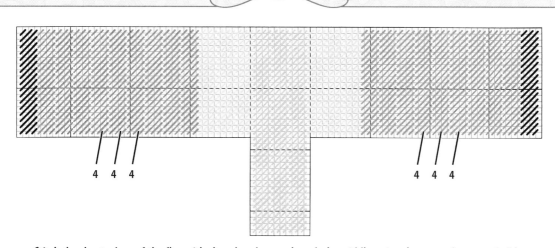

4 4 4   4 4 4

Stitch the short edges of the flap with chocolate-brown thread, the middle stripe that extends outward with red thread, the two outer stripes using dark-green thread, and the background with ecru thread.

41 **Add** one more row—this one a chocolate brown one whose stitches cross three intersections on your canvas. When you finish the row, **tie off** and **snip** the excess thread. You've finished the flap!

Needlepoint the Buckle

42 Using your embroidery scissors, **cut** a 15–18-in. length of chocolate brown pearl cotton thread and **thread** it onto your needle.

43 Using a continental stitch, **stitch** the buckle in the areas shown. Notice that two rows of nine holes in the middle of the buckle—moving left to right, holes 8–16—should remain unstitched.

44 Still using the chocolate-brown thread, use an overhand stitch to **cover** the raw edges on the buckle—even the ones whose adjacent holes were left blank in step 43. When you're finished, **tie off** and **snip** the excess thread.

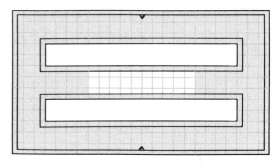

Stitch these dark areas of the buckle.

Note: To prevent the plastic canvas from peeking through your overhand stitch, try first **covering** the entire length of the edging you're about to stitch with a length of your thread. Then, stitching in the opposite direction (i.e., along the path of the thread covering the edging), **work** your overhand stitch over the thread and the edging at the same time. In addition to obscuring the plastic canvas, this extra thread also gives the edges a bit of padding. The same goes for the lacing stitch you'll use in a moment to bind the pieces of the wallet together.

Bind the Body to the Flap

45 On the wallet flap, use an overhand stitch to **cover** the raw edges on the two short sides and on the side with the extending red stripe. (Leave the top edge raw for now.) Take care to match the color of your thread on the edges with the corresponding stitches on the canvas—that is, if a row is, say, ecru, then the overhand stitch at the end of the row should be, too.

46 **Lay** the wallet flap and the body of your wallet face down on your work surface, positioning the flap so the raw edge points downward. Then, lining up the stripes on the wallet flap and the wallet body, **align** the wallet body with the raw edge of the wallet flap, making sure the holes match up exactly.

47 Using your embroidery scissors, **cut** a 15–18-in. length of chocolate brown pearl cotton thread, **thread** it onto your needle, and **knot** the tail end.

48 **Weave** the needle and thread through a few stitches on the back panel of the body of the wallet until it reaches the upper-left corner. Then, using a lacing stitch, **bind** the flap to the body of the wallet. (Remember, a lacing stitch is just like an overhand stitch, except that instead of finishing an edge, it binds two edges together.) When you're finished, **tie off** and **snip** the excess thread. To prevent the binding from unraveling later, be sure when tying off to first run the thread under several rows of stitches.

Affix the Buckle

49 Your next move is to affix the buckle to the body of the wallet. To begin, use your embroidery scissors to **cut** a 15–18-in. length of chocolate brown pearl cotton thread, **thread** it onto your needle, and **knot** the tail end.

50 **Weave** the needle and thread through a few stitches on the back panel of the body of the wallet, stopping somewhere near the middle.

51 **Flip** the wallet so it's finished side up, with the flap of the wallet on top.

52 Starting at the hole through which the bottom-left stitch on the red stripe began, **count** up the holes; then **draw** your needle and thread through the 15th hole from back to front.

53 Next, **draw** your thread through the bottom-left unstitched hole in the middle of your buckle.

54 Moving up and to the right, **complete** a tent stitch, passing the needle and thread back down through the buckle *and* the body of the wallet.

55 Using a continental stitch, **stitch** the remaining empty holes in the buckle, passing the needle and thread through both the body of the wallet and the buckle each time. When you're finished, **tie off** and **snip** the excess thread.

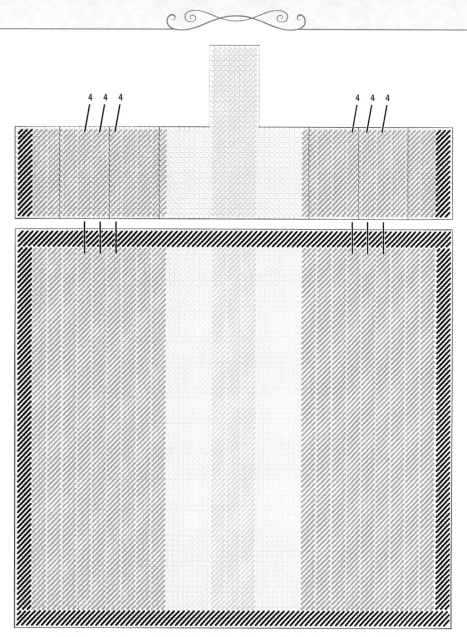

4 4 4   4 4 4

Position the flap and body like this, facedown, aligning the raw edge of the flap with the body, using the stripes on both pieces for guidance.

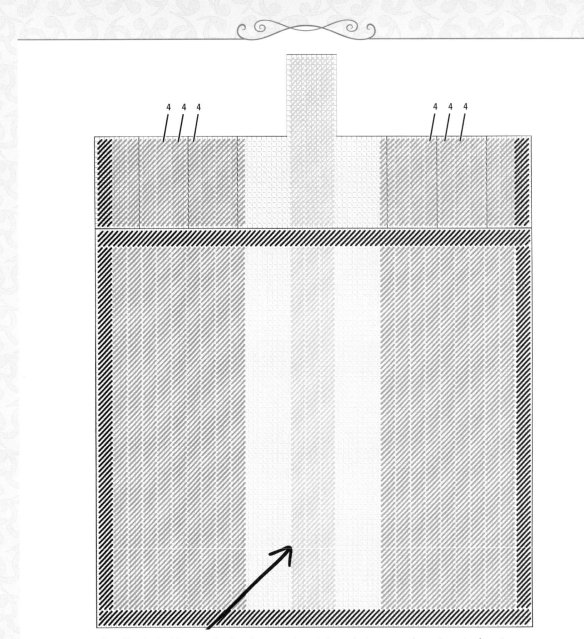

To affix the buckle, start by drawing your thread through the canvas here, from back to front.

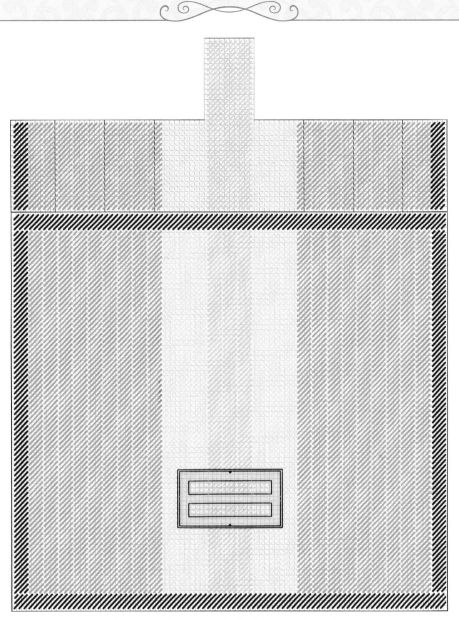

Use continental stitches to affix the buckle to the front of the wallet.

Finish the Bottom Edge

56 Use your embroidery scissors to cut a 15–18-in. length of chocolate brown pearl cotton thread, **thread** it onto your needle, and **knot** the tail end.

57 **Weave** the needle and thread through a few stitches on the back panel of the body of the wallet, stopping when you reach the bottom-left corner.

58 Use an overhand stitch to **cover** the raw, bottom edge of the body of the wallet. When you're finished, **tie off** and **snip** the excess thread.

Optional: Line the Wallet

59 If you want to line your wallet, **cut** a piece of the thin, brown fabric that's ¼-in. larger than the body of the wallet on all four sides.

60 **Thread** a sharp needle with a length of heavy-duty sewing thread.

61 **Lay** the wallet flat on your work surface with the back side facing up.

62 **Fold** the top edge of the brown fabric under a wee bit and **sew** it to the top edge of the body of your wallet. Rather than sewing it directly onto the canvas, however, sew it onto the threads comprising the chocolate-brown border. (Otherwise you'll be able to see the stitches on the front side of the canvas.)

63 **Repeat** step 62 for the remaining three sides of the wallet body.

Assemble the Wallet

64 Use your embroidery scissors to cut a 15–18-in. length of chocolate brown pearl cotton thread, **thread** it onto your needle, and **knot** the tail end.

65 Still with the wallet face down, with the flap at the top, **weave** the needle and thread through a few stitches on the back side of the body of the wallet, stopping near the center point of the left edge.

66 **Fold** the body of the wallet almost—but not quite—in half. (This is so the flap will close more easily.) **Align** the row of holes formerly along the bottom edge of the wallet body with the third row of holes from the top. (You'll probably want to use the raw side edges of the wallet to line things up, as the holes will be more visible there.)

67 Using chocolate-brown thread, **work** a length of lacing stitches from bottom to top to join the front and back of the wallet on the left side. When you're finished, **tie off** and **snip** the excess thread. (Be sure you finish off your threads carefully so they don't come undone later, when your wallet is bursting with cash. Or not.)

68 **Repeat** steps 63–66 on the right side of the wallet.

Variation

All Business

by Amy Holbrook

If you have some thread and plastic canvas left over after you finish stitching your wallet, put it to use by making a matching business-card holder. Here's what to do:

1. Use your shears to cut a rectangular piece of plastic canvas that is 58 × 35 holes. This will be the front.

2. Cut a second piece that is 58 × 36 holes to serve as the back.

3. Create a T-shaped piece to serve as the flap. The top of the T-shaped piece should be 28 × 13 holes, with a base of 22 × 10 holes.

4. Create a buckle that is identical to the one you made for the wallet. Start with a piece of canvas that is 24 × 13 holes. Then, using an X-Acto knife, cut out the two sections to form the buckle following the same diagram as before.

5. Using the chocolate-brown thread, stitch the top and bottom borders of the "front" piece. (These borders go on the longer edges of the canvas.) As you did with the wallet, use a modified Scotch stitch that covers three thread intersections.

6. Rotate the front piece 90° and, starting from top to bottom, use a modified Scotch stitch to complete rows in the following order:

   ◆ One row of chocolate-brown stitches over three thread intersections

   ◆ Three rows of ecru stitches over four thread intersections

   ◆ Three rows of dark green stitches over three thread intersections

   ◆ Three rows of red stitches over three thread intersections

   ◆ Three rows of dark green stitches over three thread intersections

   ◆ Three rows of ecru stitches over four thread intersections

   ◆ One row of chocolate-brown stitches over three thread intersections

7. Repeat steps 5 and 6 to complete the back of the card holder. (Note that the back piece of the card holder is one row longer than the front piece. If you're a super-perfectionist type and want the front and back patterns of your card holder to match up exactly, you might want to make the top row of chocolate-brown stitches across four thread intersections rather than three.)

continued

continued

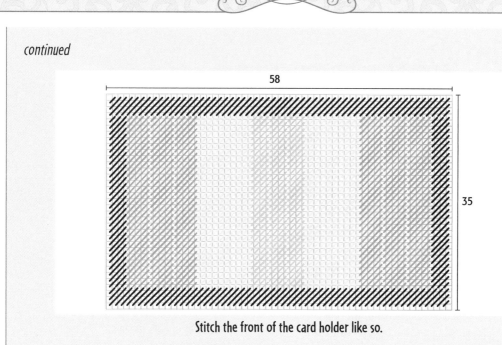

Stitch the front of the card holder like so.

8. Situate to T-shaped flap so the long part of the T is pointing to the right. Then stitch the T-shaped flap using this pattern:

- Three rows of dark green stitches over three thread intersections

- Three rows of red stitches over three thread intersections (these will extend across the longest section of the T)

- Three rows of dark green stitches over three thread intersections

9. Using continental stitches with chocolate-brown thread, stitch the buckle as before–again leaving holes 8-16 in the middle of the buckle unstitched.

10. Using an overhand stitch, cover the raw edges on the buckle–even the ones whose adjacent holes were left unstitched in step 9.

11. On the card-holder's flap, use an overhand stitch to cover all the raw edges (except the top edge). Take care to match the color of your thread on the edges with the corresponding stitches on the canvas–that is, if a row is, say, ecru, then the over-hand stitch at the end of the row should be ecru too. (Remember that to better hide the plastic canvas, you may want to first cover the area with a piece of thread and then stitch over it.)

12. Center the T-shaped flap on the top edge of the back panel (the larger piece of canvas). Then, using chocolate-brown thread, attach the flap with a lacing stitch.

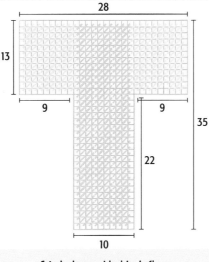

28

13

9   9

35

22

10

Stitch the card holder's flap.

13. Still using chocolate-brown thread, use an overhand stitch to finish the raw edges on the top edge of the back panel on either side of the flap.

14. Follow the steps in the section "Affix the Buckle" to attach the buckle to the front panel of the card holder. Center it such that there are 17 holes both to the left and right of the buckle and it is 9 holes down from the top of the panel.

15. Using an overhand stitch with chocolate-brown thread, finish the top edge of the front panel.

16. Still using chocolate-brown thread, use a lacing stitch to attach the front and back panels together along both sides and the bottom. Align the bottoms of each panel, ensuring that the front panel is one row shorter than the back one. (This will enable the flap to close more easily.)

I'll Stop the World and Belt with You

by Roxane Cerda

Belts. Are they in? Are they out? Who knows—and who cares? With this stitched ribbon belt, replete with leaf motifs, you'll *always* be stylish.

Project Rating: Flirtation

Cost: $25

Necessary Skills: Embroidery

Materials

- 3 yd. spool of 1½-in. olive green grosgrain ribbon
- 1½-in. belt buckle (This measurement reflects the opening where the belt goes through, not the whole buckle.)
- Tailor's chalk
- Embroidery hoop, 6-in.
- 1 skein pearl cotton thread, size 5, blue, DMC 800
- 1 skein pearl cotton thread size 5, red, DMC 900
- 1 skein pearl cotton thread size 5, orange, DMC 922
- 1 skein pearl cotton thread size 5, light green, DMC 734
- Embroidery needle, size 5
- Tape measure
- Embroidery scissors
- Shears
- Iron
- Heavy-duty sewing thread in a color to match the ribbon
- 1 package double-sided fusible stabilizers (We used Steam-A-Seam 2 Double-Stick Fusible Web.)

1 Using a tape measure, **measure** your waist. Then, add 14 in., and double the sum. This is the amount of ribbon you will need for your belt.

2 Using your shears, **cut** this amount of ribbon from your spool.

3 **Fold** the ribbon in half. For example, if your ribbon is 84-in. long, you'll fold it such that it's 42-in. long. Then, using your tailor's chalk, **draw** a line where the middle of the ribbon falls. Half the ribbon will become the outside of your belt, which we'll call the *facing side*. The other half of the ribbon will be fused to the back of the facing side, becoming the inside of the belt.

4 **Select** your motifs from the ones provided—you'll want six in all. Alternatively, make a look entirely your own by creating your own motifs.

5 After you unfold your ribbon, use tailor's chalk to **sketch** the motifs onto the facing-side half of your ribbon. Space them evenly, making sure to leave an extra inch or so at each end of the half to accommodate the buckle and the hem.

Orange   Light green   Red   Light green

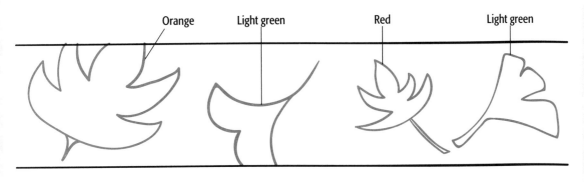

Light green   Light blue

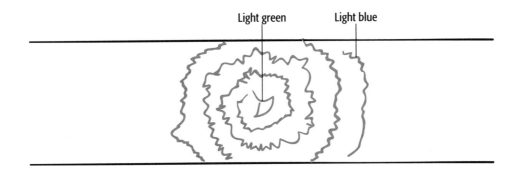

Light green

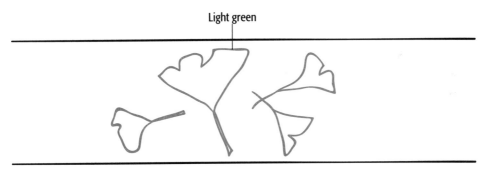

Orange

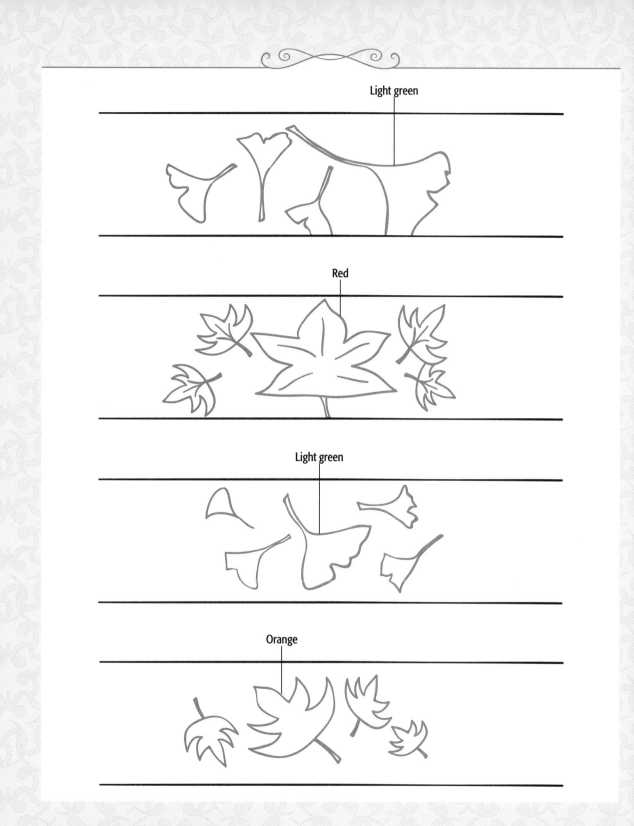

Light green

Red

Light green

Orange

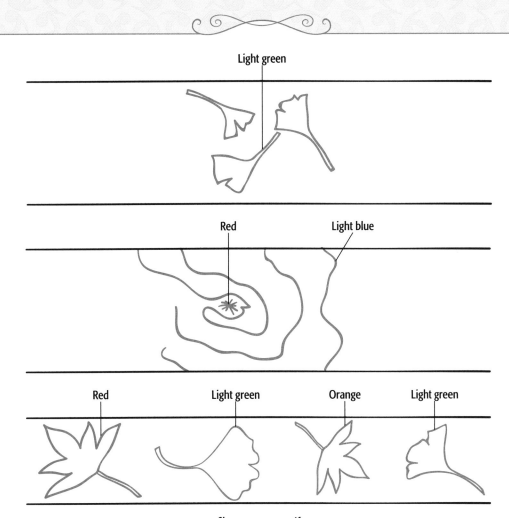

Light green

Red   Light blue

Red   Light green   Orange   Light green

Choose your motifs.

Mount the left-most portion of the facing-side half of the ribbon in your embroidery hoop.

Using your embroidery scissors, **cut** a 15–18-in. length of thread and **thread** it onto your needle. (The color you use depends on which motif you're working on; refer to the motif patterns for details.)

Start the thread using the method of your choice and, using a whipped running stitch, **embroider** your first motif onto the facing-side half of the ribbon. When you're finished, **tie off**. (You will **snip** the excess thread a little later in the process.)

Repeat steps 6–8, hooping the next segment of the ribbon as needed, until all the motifs have been stitched onto the ribbon.

10 **Turn** the ribbon over and **cut** all thread ends down to ¼-in.

11 **String** the buckle onto the ribbon, and **fold** the ribbon in half.

12 Following the instructions on your package of fusible webbing, **adhere** the facing side half of the ribbon onto the other half of the ribbon, leaving just under 1 in. unfused at either end. Be sure that the two halves of the ribbon are securely fused; if there are any loose portions, **repeat** this step, following the instructions on the package until the sides are securely fused.

13 On the end of the belt opposite the buckle, **fold** the ends of the ribbon so that both halves are tucked under, **line up** the folded ends, and **iron.**

14 **Cut** a small piece of fusible webbing to fit into each fold, and one more to fit the space between the two folded ends. Then, following the directions on your package of fusible webbing, **adhere** the ends.

Variation

All Choked Up

The techniques in these project instructions are easily adaptable. For example, rather than making a belt, you can follow these instructions to make a swell choker. Just use ribbon that's ¾-in. or narrower and, instead of a belt buckle, use a heavy-duty snap closure (just follow the directions on the closure's packaging to work it onto the ribbon).

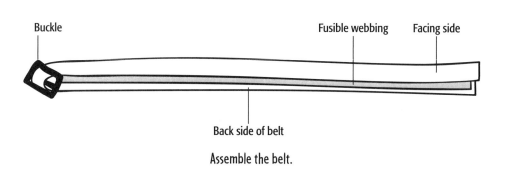

Buckle   Fusible webbing   Facing side

Back side of belt

Assemble the belt.

Felt Up

by Roxane Cerda

You may have noticed that *felting*—i.e., the process of matting wool yarn into felt—is all the rage among crafty types. But why stop there? Felt is a fabric, after all—which means you can stitch on it. Start small, though—like with the necklace pendant described here. (By the way, if, during the course of completing this project, you catch the felting fever—it is apparently quite viral—check out *Not Your Mama's Felting* to learn more.)

Project Rating: Flirtation

Cost: $20

Necessary Skills: Felting (don't panic; we'll step you through it), embroidery

Materials

- 100% wool roving (For those of you who have no idea what *wool roving* is, it's raw wool that's been washed, cleaned, and carded and is ready to be spun into yarn; it can be bought online or at many yarn stores. We chose a variegated brown.)
- Crock pot or large bowl
- Dishwashing liquid
- Kitchen towel
- Tongs
- Shears
- Embroidery scissors
- Pencil
- 1 skein cotton embroidery floss, very dark mocha brown, DMC 3031
- 1 skein cotton embroidery floss, ecru, DMC Ecru
- Embroidery needle, size 5
- Felting needle (This is a long, barbed needle that has a handle of sorts and can be found at just about any store that sells yarn.)
- Beading needle, size 10

- Foam block (You'll use this to support your piece during the part of the felting process that involves stabbing the felt over and over and over, like Norman Bates.)
- Approximately 12 size 11 delica seed beads in colors that complement embroidery floss
- 24 in. of 3mm faux suede cord
- 1 sterling silver jump ring, soldered closed, 6mm
- 2 large-bore bone beads, 8mm
- 2 large-bore bone disk-shaped beads, 4mm
- 2 large-bore wooden beads, 2mm

Felt the Wool

1 **Fill** your crock pot halfway with water and add a teaspoon of dishwashing liquid. Then turn the pot on to the High setting. (If you don't have a crock pot, or just don't feel like extracting yours from the deep recesses of your kitchen cabinetry, heat some water on the stove and then pour it in a bowl with a teaspoon or so of dish-washing liquid. Add more hot water as needed to maintain a hot bath.)

2 While the pot is heating, **pull** tufts of fleece from your roving. **Spread** the fleece out on your work surface, laying it in

a thin, even layer that is approximately the size of your hand. Over this layer, lay a new layer—this time lying in the opposite direction. Continue adding layers until you have four or five.

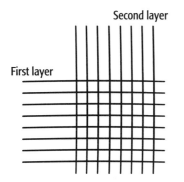

Layer your fleece in opposite directions.

3 Carefully pick up your fleece layers and gently **rub** them between your palms just enough to lightly mat them, but taking care to ensure they don't roll.

4 **Dunk** the mat into your hot water bath for a few seconds.

5 Using tongs, **pull** the mat back out of the pot. (Don't be concerned if, at this point, it resembles your Uncle Ernie's toupé more than it does felt.) Let some of the hot water drain off and, making sure not to burn yourself, rub the mat once more between your palms. If it gets all sudsy, rinse it in warm water.

6 **Repeat** steps 4 and 5 until you have an even and thin—but sturdy—layer of felt, approximately the size of your palm.

7 **Lay** the felt on a kitchen towel and let it dry overnight.

Create the Pendant

8 **Trace** the shape provided here onto a piece of paper and cut it out. You'll use it as a template to construct the pendant for your necklace.

Trace this shape for the pendant.

9 Using the template, **cut** two identical pieces of the felt you made. (If you'd rather use a different shape, have at it! Just make sure you wind up with two identical pieces of felt.)

10 Using your embroidery scissors, **cut** a 15–18-in. length of ecru embroidery floss (DMC Ecru), **strip** the floss, **recombine** two of the strands, and **thread** the two strands onto your needle.

11 **Start** the thread using the method of your choice and, using a straight satin stitch, **stitch** the design provided here on one piece of the felt. Be sure to leave a ¼-in. margin of unstitched felt around the

perimeter of the pendant. When you're finished, **tie off** and **snip** the excess.

Stitch the design with ivory thread.

12 Using your embroidery scissors, **cut** a 15–18-in. length of very dark mocha brown embroidery floss (DMC 3031), **strip** the floss, and **thread** one strand onto your needle.

13 **Start** the thread using the method of your choice and, where indicated, use small half-cross stitches to stitch on beads. When you're finished, **tie off** and **snip** the excess.

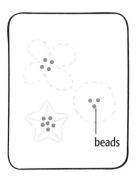

Add the beads.

14 **Lay** the unstitched piece of felt on your foam block and cover it with the stitched piece, face up.

15 Using your felting needle, carefully **stab** the unstitched portions of the pendant. Take care to avoid the areas with the stitched motif. Move the needle in a straight-up-and-down fashion, making sure you manage to repeatedly shove it through both layers of felt. Note that you're not sewing here, just piercing the felt; stabbing the two pieces in this manner will fuse them together.

16 When the two layers of the pendant have been joined, use your felting needle to repeatedly **pierce** any portions that aren't smooth. The up and down motion of the felting needle will meld the fibers together more tightly and will smooth the area.

17 **Thread** one strand of very dark mocha brown embroidery floss (DMC 3031) on your needle.

18 **Push** the needle into the side of the pendant, then up through the center of the top. Draw the needle and thread through the pendant until about 3 in. of the thread's tail is sticking out the side of the pendant.

19 **Capture** the jump ring, **thread** it onto the pendant, and **tie** a knot.

20 **Loop** your thread through the jump ring and the pendant several more times; then tie one more knot.

21 **Push** your needle back through the piece from the top near the jump ring out the opposite side of your piece from where you started.

22 **Cut** the excess thread on both sides of the pendant to conceal both the starting end of the thread and the tail.

String the Necklace

23 **Tie** a knot at the end of your suede cord.

24 **String,** in this order, a 2mm bead, an 8mm bead, and a 4mm bead.

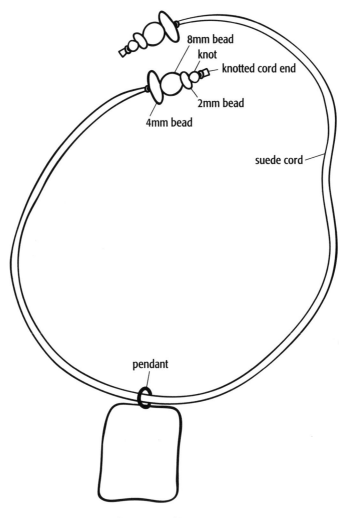

Making the necklace.

25 **Tie** a second knot just above the 4mm bead to secure the three beads you just added to the end of the cord.

26 **Slide** the pendant onto the necklace using the jump ring at the top of the pendant.

27 Tie a third knot approximately 2 in. from the opposite end of the suede cord; then string a 4mm bead, an 8mm bead, and the remaining 2mm bead.

28 **Tie** a final knot on the very end of the cord to secure this second set of beads and **cut** the end of the cord to match the opposite end. The result is a leather strand with some beads at each end and a pendant in the middle.

29 Tie the cord jauntily around your neck. A necklace you have!

Variation
Double or Nothing
by Roxane Cerda

You can use this same technique to make fabulous earrings. To do so, just follow the preceding steps—except use a slightly smaller shape (or a different one entirely) and cut out 4 pieces of felt this time, two fronts, and two backs. (We used a penny as a template.) Carefully stitch your design, staying at least $1/4$-in. away from all edges, and then stitch on your delica beads the same way you did in the main project. After using your felting needle to meld the fronts to the backs, attach the closed jump rings (5mm size for earrings) to the top of your felt pieces. Attach these rings to ear wires; now you have a set!

Chuck Berries

Obviously, Chuck Taylors are plenty cool on their own. But embellished with a bit of simple embroidery they can be *even cooler.*

Project Rating: Flirtation
Cost: $40
Necessary Skills: Embroidery

Materials

- 1 pair Chuck Taylor All-Star high tops (ours are black)
- 1 skein embroidery floss, bright red, DMC 666
- 1 skein embroidery floss, chartreuse, DMC 703
- 1 skein embroidery floss, medium old gold, DMC 729
- 1 skein embroidery floss, very dark coral red, DMC 817
- 1 skein jewel effects floss, red ruby, DMC E321
- 1 skein jewel effects floss, light green emerald, DMC E703
- 1 skein jewel effects floss, green emerald, DMC 5269 or E699
- Embroidery scissors
- Embroidery needle, size 7
- Beading needle, size 10
- Approximately 24 size 10 seed beads, gold-colored
- Ballpoint pen
- Carbon transfer paper (Ours was white, since our shoes were black.)

1 Using the ballpoint pen and carbon transfer paper, **trace** the design shown here on the outside of either shoe, on the fabric comprising the shoe's high top. (Don't worry about drawing in the seeds; you can use the drawing here for reference when it's time to add those.)

2 Using your embroidery scissors, **cut a 15–18-in.** length of chartreuse floss (DMC 703) and a 15–18-in length of light green emerald jewel effects floss (DMC E703), **strip** both lengths of thread, **combine** two strands of the chartreuse floss with one strand of the light green emerald floss, and **thread** all three strands onto your embroidery needle.

3 **Start** the thread using the method of your choice and, using a satin stitch, **fill in** the green leafy thingies on top of the strawberry. When you're finished, **tie off** and **snip** the excess.

4 Using your embroidery scissors, **cut a 15–18-in.** length of bright red floss (DMC 666) and a 15–18-in. length of very dark coral red floss (DMC 817), **strip** both lengths of thread, **combine** two strands of the bright red floss with one strand of the very dark coral red floss, and **thread** all three strands onto your embroidery needle.

5 **Start** the thread using the method of your choice and, using a satin stitch, **fill**

in the berry portion of the design. When you're finished, **tie off** and **snip** the excess.

Use this design as your guide.

6 Using your embroidery scissors, **cut** a 15–18-in. length of light green emerald jewel effects floss (DMC E703) and a 15–18-in. length of green emerald jewel effects floss (DMC 5269 or E699), **strip** both lengths of thread, **combine** two strands of the light green emerald floss with one strand of the green emerald floss, and **thread** all three strands onto your embroidery needle.

7 **Start** the thread using the method of your choice and, using a back stitch, **outline** the leafy area. When you're finished, **tie off** and **snip** the excess.

8 Using your embroidery scissors, **cut** a 15–18-in. length of red ruby jewel effects floss (DMC E321), **strip** the thread, **re-combine** three of the strands, and **thread** the three strands onto your embroidery needle.

9 **Start** the thread using the method of your choice and, using a back stitch, **stitch** the outline of the strawberry. When you're finished, **tie off** and **snip** the excess.

10 Using your embroidery scissors, **cut** a 15–18-in. length of bright red floss (DMC 666), **strip** the thread, **re-combine** two of the strands, and **thread** the two strands onto your beading needle.

11 **Start** the thread using the method of your choice and add several gold-colored seed beads to the berry, scattered randomly. These represent the seeds. When you're finished, **tie off** and **snip** the excess thread. (If you don't have any beads handy, try applying French knots to the shoe using gold-colored thread instead.)

12 Optional: **Repeat** steps 1–11 on the remaining shoe. Or, if you're a half-asser like I am, just do one and call it a "statement."

Variation

China Girl

You aren't limited to stitching on your Chucks. Why not try a few designs on those nifty cotton shoes you buy in Chinatown?

British Invasion

by Amy Holbrook

It's a sad fact: Everybody has an iPod—which means you need some *new* way to convey your supreme coolness. This Brit-inspired iPod holder is *just* the ticket. Simply stitch it up, slip it on, and enjoy your restored cool status!

Project Rating: Flirtation
Cost: $10
Necessary Skills: Needlepoint

Materials

- Tapestry needle, size 22
- 1 sheet 10-count clear plastic canvas (We used Uniek brand.)
- 1 skein tapestry wool, white, Anchor 8000
- 1 skein tapestry wool, cherry red, Anchor 8218
- 1 skein tapestry wool, China blue, Anchor 8636
- Shears
- X-Acto knife
- Embroidery scissors

Cut the Canvas

1 Using your shears, **cut** two rectangular pieces of plastic canvas, both 25 × 41 holes. These will serve as the front and the back of the iPod holder.

2 **Cut** two more rectangular pieces of plastic canvas, this time making both 6 × 41 holes. These rectangles will be the holder's sides.

3 **Cut** one piece of rectangular canvas that's 25 × 6 holes. This will be the bottom of the holder.

4 **Trim** any stubby plastic bits from the edges of each piece of plastic canvas.

5 **Cut** the window for the iPod's screen into one of the rectangles you cut in step 1. To begin, count down three holes from the top and over five holes from the left. Starting at the intersecting hole, use your X-Acto knife to excise a piece of canvas that is 17 × 14 holes. (See the template that follows for additional guidance.)

6 Using the template that follows for guidance, use your X-Acto knife to **cut** out a circle beneath the rectangle. This will be the window through which the iPod's dial is visible.

Needlepoint the Canvas

7 Using a continental stitch, **needlepoint** the Union Jack design provided on the back panel of the iPod holder, tying off when you're finished. The stitches in this panel should be framed by the plastic outline of your canvas.

8 Again using a continental stitch, **needlepoint** the side and bottom panels of the holder using the blue thread. When you're finished, tie off.

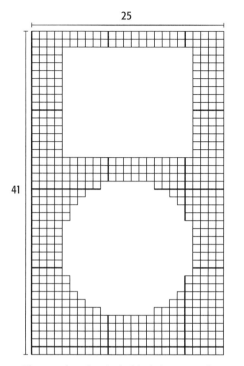

25

41

The template for the holder's front panel.

9 **Stitch** the front of the holder still using blue thread.

10 To **stitch** the edges of the canvas that frame the circular dial opening and the rectangular window first, **thread** your needle with red thread and, on the back side of the canvas, **start** the thread by pulling it through some existing stitches to secure it.

11 Beginning somewhere in the middle of the row above the rectangular window, **draw** the needle and thread through a hole adjacent to the opening, **bring** it around the plastic edge of the canvas, and **pass** it back through the canvas in the next hole. (In case you didn't recognize it from the section on hand-sewing techniques, this is an *overhand stitch.*)

The Union Jack chart. Note that the square shapes represent blue stitches, the diamonds represent red stitches, and the blank areas represent white stitches.

12 **Repeat** step 11, working your way around the edges framing the window.

Note: To prevent the plastic canvas from peeking through your overhand stitch, try first covering the entire segment of the edging you're about to stitch with a segment of thread the same color. Then, stitching in the opposite direction (i.e., along the path of the thread covering the edging), work your overhand stitch over the thread and the edging at the same time. In addition to obscuring the plastic canvas, this extra thread also gives the edges a bit of padding. The same goes for the *lacing stitch* you'll use in a moment to bind the pieces of the holder together.

13 **Repeat** steps 10 and 11 to stitch the edge around the dial opening. (In order to ensure that the plastic in each corner is completely covered, you may have to stitch each hole more than once.) When you're finished, **tie off.**

Construct the Holder

14 Your next move is to stitch the pieces of your holder together. To begin, **spread** the pieces of the holder out on your workspace, face down.

15 **Align** the back panel with the bottom panel, lining up the holes so they match.

16 Using your embroidery scissors, **cut** a 15–18-in. length of red tapestry wool and knot the end.

17 **Thread** the needle with the red thread and weave through a few stitches on the back panel to start the thread. When you're finished, your thread should come from the bottom edge of the back panel, toward the middle.

18 **Work** a lacing stitch from left to right, attaching half of the back panel to the bottom panel.

19 **Align** the right side panel with the bottom panel, lining up the holes so they match.

20 **Repeat** step 18 to attach the side panel to the bottom panel. Take care to fully cover each corner with thread; this may require multiple stitches.

21 **Align** the front panel with the bottom panel, ensuring that the dial opening is closer to the bottom panel than the rectangular window opening.

22 **Repeat** step 18 to attach the front panel to the bottom panel. Again, make sure you cover each corner with thread.

23 **Align** the remaining side panel with the bottom panel, lining up the holes so they match.

24 **Repeat** step 18 to stitch the side panel to the bottom panel. Again, make sure you cover each corner with thread.

25 Rounding the corner, **repeat** step 18 to stitch the remaining half of the back panel to the bottom panel. When you're finished, **tie off** and **snip** the excess.

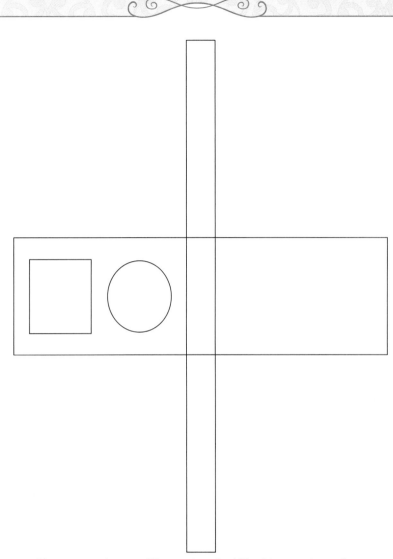

After you complete step 25, your piece should be this approximate shape.

26 Your next step is to join the side panels with the front and back panels; let's begin with the back panel. **Start** a new 15–18-in. length of red tapestry wool where the bottom panel meets the back panel and either side panel. Then work a lacing stitch to join the back and side. **Stitch** all the way to the top of the holder, making sure that the two panels are lined up correctly and are stitched snugly together.

27 **Work** an overhand stitch across the top of the side panel to cover the edge of the plastic canvas.

28 When you complete the top edge of the side panel, **align** the front panel of the holder with this side panel and **repeat** step 18—stitching downward, toward the bottom panel. When you're finished, **tie off** and snip the excess.

29 **Start** two 15–18-in. lengths of red tapestry wool, each on its own needle, on the two remaining corners of the bottom panel.

30 **Align** the remaining side panel with the back panel and, using one of the two threads you just started, use a lacing stitch to join the two. When you reach the top, **work** an overhand stitch, stopping halfway across the top edge of the side panel.

31 With the second thread, **repeat** step 30, joining the front panel to the side panel. When you reach the top, **work** an overhand stitch across the top edge of the side panel until you meet the stitches from the other thread.

32 **Tie off** both threads and **snip** the excess.

33 **Start** a new 15–18-in. length of red tapestry wool and use an overhand stitch to **finish** the top edge of the front panel.

34 Your last step is to finish the top edge of the back panel. **Pass** the needle and red thread through some stitches on the inside of the side panel to **position** your needle properly; then **work** an overhand stitch to finish the top edge of the back panel. When you're finished, **tie off** and **snip** the excess.

Variation

Mini Me

by Amy Holbrook

If your iPod of choice is an iPod nano, don't despair! You can still stitch up a holder for it—or any other type of music player, for that matter. (Note that unfortunately, a Union Jack won't fit on a holder for an iPod shuffle because the holder will be too long and skinny. Other flags, however, work well—think Italy, France, Ireland, the Netherlands, etc.) To determine how large the various panels should be, lay the player on a sheet of plastic canvas and trace it.

Germ Warfare

by Jennifer Beeman

You're coughing. You're sneezing. Your nose is running. You are in a very bad mood. Face it: You have a cold. Of course, taking medicine can assuage your physical symptoms, but fixing your frame of mind is another matter. You just won't feel like yourself until the microbe that made you sick suffers in kind. Unfortunately, however, germs are wee, making it difficult to pin one down and physically punish it. Moreover, even if you *could* physically punish a germ, it wouldn't feel it, what with it lacking a brain and nerves and all. That means you'll need to take your revenge symbolically. What better way than blowing your nose into this germ hankie?

Project Rating: Fling

Cost: $5

Necessary Skills: Embroidery

Materials

- 1 white handkerchief
- Transfer pencil
- Tracing paper
- Iron
- Embroidery hoop, 4 in.
- 1 skein cotton embroidery floss, garnet medium, DMC 815
- 1 skein cotton embroidery floss, medium parrot green, DMC 906
- 1 skein cotton embroidery floss, turquoise ultra very dark, DMC 3038
- 1 skein cotton embroidery floss, dark straw, DMC 3820
- 1 skein cotton embroidery floss, straw, DMC 3821
- Embroidery scissors
- Embroidery needle, size 5
- Thin towel

Preparing the Fabric

1. Using the tracing paper and the transfer pencil, **trace** the germ design supplied here.

2. Using the iron, **transfer** the traced design to the hankie.

3. **Mount** the hankie in the hoop.

Stitching the Germ

4. Using your embroidery scissors, **cut a** 15–18-in. length of dark straw embroidery floss (DMC 3820), **strip** the floss, **re-combine** all six strands, and **thread** the strands onto your needle.

5. **Start** the thread using the method of your choice and, beginning at the base of the *flagellum* (for those of you who failed Biology, that's the part of the germ that looks like a tail, labeled "6" in the diagram) and working in a clockwise direction, use a stem stitch to **stitch** half of the germ capsule (line 1 in the diagram).

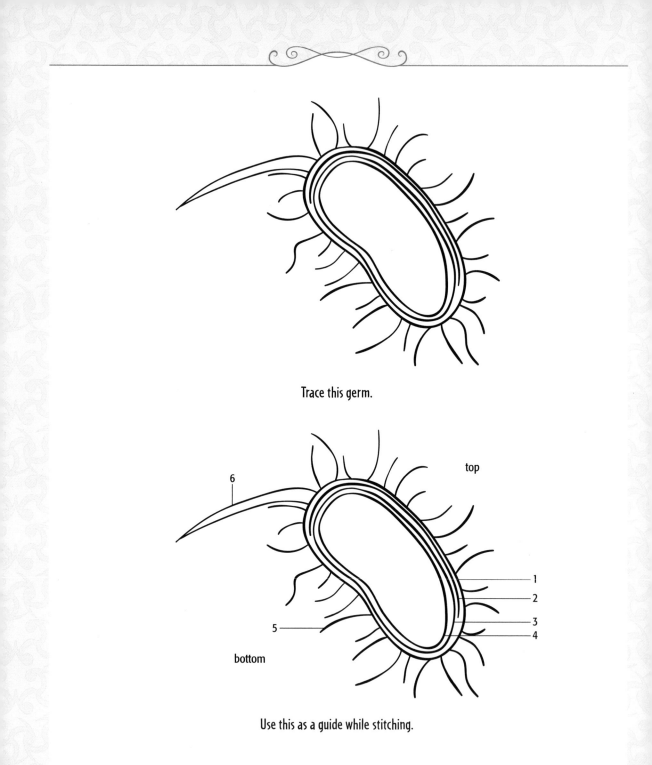

Trace this germ.

top

6

bottom

5

1
2
3
4

Use this as a guide while stitching.

6 **Remove** the needle from the dark straw thread, leaving the remaining thread hanging from the back of the piece.

7 Using your embroidery scissors, **cut** another 15–18-in. length of dark straw embroidery floss, **strip** the floss, but this time **re-combine** just three of the strands and **thread** them onto your needle.

8 **Start** the thread using the method of your choice and, using a stem stitch, **stitch** the remaining half of the germ capsule (line 1), stopping when you reach the flagellum. When you're finished, **tie off** and **snip** the excess thread.

9 Using your embroidery scissors, **cut** a 15–18-in. length of straw embroidery floss (DMC 3821), **strip** the floss, **re-combine** all six strands, and **thread** them onto your needle.

10 **Start** the thread using the method of your choice and, again beginning at the base of the flagellum and working in a clockwise fashion, use a stem stitch to **stitch** line 2 on the diagram, snuggling up against the stitches you made in step 5. (Notice that, like the stitches you made in step 5, these stitches should traverse only half of the capsule.) When you're finished, **tie off** and **snip** the excess thread.

11 Using your embroidery scissors, **cut** a 15–18-in. length of medium parrot green embroidery floss (DMC 906), **strip** the floss, **re-combine** three of the strands, and **thread** the three strands onto your needle.

12 **Start** the thread using the method of your choice and, again beginning at the base of the flagellum and working in a clockwise fashion, use a stem stitch to **stitch** the cell wall (line 3 on the diagram). As before, snuggle up against the stitches you've already made, but this time go all the way around the cell wall instead of stopping at the halfway point. When you're finished, **tie off** and **snip** the excess thread.

13 Using your embroidery scissors, **cut** a 15–18-in. length of turquoise ultra very dark embroidery floss (DMC 3038), **strip** the floss, **re-combine** three of the strands, and **thread** them onto your needle.

14 **Start** the thread using the method of your choice and, again beginning at the base of the flagellum and working in a clockwise fashion, use a stem stitch to **stitch** the cytoplasmic membrane (line 4 on the diagram). As before, snuggle up against the stitches you've already made, going all the way around the cell wall instead of stopping at the halfway point.

15 **Remove** the needle from the turquoise ultra very dark thread, leaving the remaining thread hanging from the back of the piece.

16 **Thread** the needle onto the dark straw thread hanging from the back of the piece, left over from step 6.

17 Using a chain stitch, **form** the pili (that's the part that looks like hair, labeled "5" on the diagram). Make sure the pili are plenty wiggly so your germ can get

around easily. When you're finished, **tie off** and **snip** the excess thread.

18 Using your embroidery scissors, **cut** a 15–18-in. length of garnet medium embroidery floss (DMC 815), **strip** the floss, **re-combine** all six strands, and **thread** them onto your needle.

19 **Start** the thread using the method of your choice and, using short satin stitches, **fill in** the flagellum. When you're finished, **tie off** and **snip** the excess thread.

20 Using your embroidery scissors, **cut** another 15–18-in. length of garnet medium embroidery floss, **strip** the floss, but this time **re-combine** only three of the strands and **thread** them onto your needle.

21 **Start** the thread using the method of your choice and, using a stem stitch, **outline** the flagellum for a nice, clean line. When you're finished, **tie off** and **snip** the excess.

22 Obviously, a germ just isn't a germ without ribosomes. To add them, first **thread** the needle onto the turquoise ultra very dark thread hanging from the back of the piece, left over from step 15.

23 Using a basic running stitch, haphazardly **add** a few stitches along the inside of the cytoplasmic membrane to serve as the ribosomes. Then **add** a few more rows of these random stitches in the top half of the cell, rounding each row slightly to match the curve comprising the top half of the germ. When you're finished, **tie off** and **snip** any excess.

Variation

Get Well Soon

This design makes for a swell "get well" card. Just follow the instructions for adding a stitched piece to a card in the project "Sweet Emoticon" in chapter 8.

The Diet of Worms

by Adam Moe

In 1521, Holy Roman Emperor Charles V launched the Diet of Worms, which:

A. demanded that monks who broke the vow of silence eat worms as penance.

B. suggested a new weight-loss strategy, along the lines of the tapeworm diet, for the overfed cardinals in the church.

C. was a treatise that described in detail the eating habits of birds.

D. was the name of the assembly convened to question Martin Luther after he posted his *95 Theses*.

If you answered D, you're correct—the Diet of Worms was, in fact, an assembly (hence the *diet* part, which, supposedly, is sometimes used to mean "assembly") conducted in the German town of Worms to question Martin Luther on his heretical views. However, using embroidery to depict such an event would require more than we're willing to give, hence our decision to portray option C in this nifty patch.

Project Rating: Fling

Cost: $5

Necessary Skills: Embroidery

Materials

- 1 sq. ft. sturdy fabric (We used a cotton canvas fabric. Denim is also good. Whatever you choose, just make sure it's not stretchy, and it isn't *too* hard to stitch. Also, if you opt for a darker fabric, use a lighter-colored thread when stitching the frame around the design to make it pop a bit more.)
- Transfer pencil
- Tracing paper
- Iron
- Embroidery hoop, 4 in.
- 1 skein cotton embroidery floss, white, DMC Blanc
- 1 skein cotton embroidery floss, black, DMC 310
- 1 skein cotton embroidery floss, very light avocado green, DMC 471
- 1 skein cotton embroidery floss, bright chartreuse, DMC 704
- 1 skein cotton embroidery floss, medium tangerine, DMC 741
- 1 skein cotton embroidery floss, very dark blue, DMC 824
- 1 skein cotton embroidery floss, dark beige brown, DMC 839
- 1 skein cotton embroidery floss, medium electric blue, DMC 996
- 1 skein cotton embroidery floss, medium wedgewood, DMC 3760
- 1 skein cotton embroidery floss, golden brown, DMC 3826

- 1 skein cotton embroidery floss, light lavender blue, DMC 3840
- Embroidery scissors
- 2 embroidery needles, size 5 (If you have only one handy, that's fine–having two just makes a few steps go a bit more quickly.)
- 1 sq. ft. felt
- 2 sheets iron-on adhesive (We used HeatnBond.)
- Optional: No-fray fabric glue (Try Fray Check.)
- Shears

Prepare the Fabric

1 Using the tracing paper and the transfer pencil, **trace** the patch design supplied here.

Trace this image for the patch.

2 Using the iron, **transfer** the traced design to the fabric on which you want to stitch (i.e., not the felt).

3 **Situate** the fabric in the hoop.

Stitch the Patch

4 Using your embroidery scissors, **cut** a 15–18-in. length of very light avocado green embroidery floss (DMC 471), **strip** the floss, **re-combine** three of the strands, and **thread** the strands onto your needle.

5 **Start** the thread using the method of your choice and, using a nice, tight satin stitch, **stitch** the square that frames the design. When you're finished, **tie off** and **snip** the excess thread.

6 Using your embroidery scissors, **cut** a 15–18-in. length of golden brown embroidery floss (DMC 3826), **strip** the floss, **re-combine** three of the strands, and **thread** the three strands onto your needle.

7 Using a straight satin stitch, **fill in** the worm's body. When you're finished, **tie off** and **snip** the excess thread.

8 Using your embroidery scissors, **cut** a 15–18-in. length of dark beige brown embroidery floss, **strip** the floss, **re-combine** three of the strands, and **thread** the strands onto your needle.

9 **Start** the thread using the method of your choice and, using a double running stitch, **outline** the worm's body. When you're finished, **tie off** and **snip** the excess thread.

10 Using your embroidery scissors, **cut** a 15–18-in. length of bright chartreuse embroidery floss (DMC 704), **strip** the floss, **re-combine** three of the strands, and **thread** the strands onto your needle.

11 **Start** the thread using the method of your choice and, using a double running stitch, **outline** the left, bottom, and right edges of the grassy area.

12 Still with the bright chartreuse embroidery floss, use satin stitches of varying lengths in an up-and-down pattern to **fill in** the grassy area. When you're finished, **tie off** and **snip** the excess thread.

13 Using your embroidery scissors, **cut a** 15–18-in. length of medium tangerine embroidery floss (DMC 741), **strip** the floss, **re-combine** three of the strands, and **thread** the strands onto your needle.

14 **Start** the thread using the method of your choice and, using a satin stitch, **fill in** the bird's legs.

15 Still with the medium tangerine thread, using a long-and-short satin stitch, **fill in** the bird's beak. When you're finished, **tie off** and **snip** the excess thread.

16 Using your embroidery scissors, **cut a** 15–18-in. length of medium wedgewood embroidery floss (DMC 3760), **strip** the floss, **re-combine** three of the strands, and **thread** the strands onto your needle.

17 **Start** the thread using the method of your choice and, using a satin stitch, **fill in** the tip of the bird's wing. When you're finished, **tie off** and **snip** the excess thread.

18 Using your embroidery scissors, **cut a** 15–18-in. length of very dark blue embroidery floss (DMC 824), **strip** the

floss, **re-combine** three of the strands, and **thread** the strands onto your needle.

19 **Start** the thread using the method of your choice and, using a satin stitch, **fill in** the bird's neck, breast, and tail feather. Also **fill in** the bird's head, even the part where the eyeball will appear. (When you eventually stitch the eyeball, you'll do it as a layer on top of the stitches covering the bird's head in order to create a bit of dimension.)

20 Still with the very dark blue floss, using a long-and-short satin stitch, **fill in** the rest of the bird's body, including its wing. When you're finished, **tie off** and **snip** the excess thread.

21 Using your embroidery scissors, **cut a** 15–18-in. length of white embroidery floss (DMC Blanc), **strip** the floss, **re-combine** three of the strands, and **thread** the strands onto your needle.

22 **Start** the thread using the method of your choice and using a satin stitch, **fill in** the bird's eyeball—even the part where the pupil will go. (You'll complete that in a bit.) When you're finished, **tie off** and **snip** the excess thread.

23 Using your embroidery scissors, **cut** a 15–18-in. length of the medium electric blue embroidery floss (DMC 996) and a 15–18-in. length of the light lavender blue embroidery floss (DMC 3840), **strip** both lengths of thread, **combine** two strands of the medium electric blue thread with one strand of the light lavender blue thread, and **thread** the three strands onto your needle.

24 **Start** the thread using the method of your choice and, using satin stitches of varying lengths in an up-and-down fashion, **fill in** the area just above the grass. (Note that you'll use varying lengths to accommodate the staggered grass. The tops of each stitch, however, should be level.)

25 **Still** with the medium electric blue and light lavender blue thread, using a double running stitch, **outline** the sky.

26 **Still** with the medium electric blue and light lavender blue thread, **add** two more columns of double running stitches in a staggered fashion along the left side of the sky.

27 **Still** with the medium electric blue and light lavender blue thread, **add** two more columns of double running stitches in staggered fashion along the right side of the sky.

28 **Still** with the medium electric blue and light lavender blue thread, using a horizontal long-and-short satin stitch, **fill in** the remaining sky. When you're finished, **tie off** and **snip** the excess thread.

29 **Using** your embroidery scissors, **cut** a 15–18-in. length of black embroidery floss, **strip** the floss, **re-combine** three of the strands, and **thread** them onto your needle.

30 **Start** the thread using the method of your choice and, using a satin stitch, **fill in** the bird's pupil.

31 **Still** with the black thread, using a double running stitch, **outline** the bird's pupil.

32 **Still** with the black thread, using a double running stitch, **outline** the bird's eyeball. When you're finished, **tie off** and **snip** the excess thread.

33 **Using** your embroidery scissors, **cut** another 15–18-in. length of black embroidery floss, **strip** the floss, **re-combine** three of the strands, and **thread** the strands onto your needle.

34 **Start** the thread using the method of your choice and, using a satin stitch, **fill in** the wormhole.

35 **Still** with the black thread, using a double running stitch, **outline** the wormhole.

36 **Still** with the black thread, using a double running stitch, **outline** the bird's body. When you're finished, **tie off** and **snip** the excess.

Applying Finishing Touches

37 **Remove** the stitched fabric from the hoop.

38 **Using** a high setting—with steam, if available—**iron** the back side stitched fabric.

39 Using your shears, **cut** a piece of felt the size of your stitched design plus a 1-in. margin all the way around.

40 Following the instructions that came with your iron-on adhesive, **iron** one iron-on adhesive sheet onto the felt.

41 **Iron** one iron-on adhesive sheet onto the *back side* of your stitched design. Make sure you iron onto the *back* side! (Did we mention you should iron onto the BACK SIDE?)

42 **Peel** the protective paper from the iron-on adhesive sheets on the felt and on your stitched fabric.

43 **Press** the adhesive side of the felt onto the adhesive side of the stitched design.

44 With the felt side facing up, **iron** the patch.

45 After the patch cools, use your shears to **cut** it to size.

46 If you suspect the edges of the patch will fray, try ironing it a second time, or apply some liquid fray-blocking fabric glue to the edges.

47 To attach your patch onto, say, your Girl Scout uniform, sew it, glue it, or use the iron-on glue adhesive.

Variation

Bomb Squad

by Adam Moe with Ari Bakke

Any design that can be stitched into a patch, including this excellent bomb pattern, can likewise be made into a magnet. Simply make the patch as you normally would, but instead of sewing it onto something when you're finished, apply yet *another* iron-on adhesive sheet to the felt on the back of the patch. Then, get your hands on a printable magnet sheet–Avery makes one. Peel the protective paper from the iron-on adhesive and press the glue side of the patch onto the "paper" side of the printable magnet sheet. Finally, use your shears to cut the excess iron-on adhesive sheet and printable magnet sheet away.

continued

continued

Try this design for your magnet.

Laptop Dance

by KB VanHorn

This project is a perfect marriage of modernity and tradition: a laptop bag that showcases a killer piece of hand-stitched needlepoint on the outside but has special pockets for your mouse and cables inside. We used some vintage mod material for the body of our bag, but part of the fun of this project is mixing up your own palette of fabrics.

Project Rating: Love o' Your Life

Cost: $25

Necessary Skills: Needlepoint, sewing

Materials

- 1 12 × 18-in. piece 10-count interlock single canvas
- 3 8-yd. strands black/charcoal wool yarn, Paternayan 220
- 3 8-yd. strands white/cream wool yarn, Paternayan 260
- 2 8-yd. strands sunny yellow wool yarn, Paternayan 771
- Tapestry needle, size 18
- Embroidery scissors
- Shears
- ½ yd. novelty fabric to frame the needlepoint (We used some yellow "fur.")
- 1½ yd. fabric for the body of the bag (Ours is a vintage brocade mod block material.)
- 1½ yd. fabric for the front stripes and the straps (We used black cotton.)
- 1½ yd. fabric for the interior of the bag (We used a yellow squiggly print cotton material.)
- 1 yd. fleece (Any color will do, as this will serve as batting and won't be visible.)
- 7½ in. Velcro

- Sewing machine (If you don't have one, you can stitch by hand.)
- Sewing needle
- Sewing thread to match the front of the bag (Ours is black.)
- Sewing thread to match the bag's interior (Ours is yellow.)
- Loop turner (This indispensable sewing tool, composed of a long wire with a tiny latch hook on one end, allows you to turn tubes of sewn fabric inside out and vice versa; find one in the sewing section of your local craft store.)

Stitch the Needlepoint Design

1 Using tent stitches that point diagonally up and to the right, **complete** the portion of the needlepoint design shown here. (Note that squares containing the number 6 should be stitched with yellow yarn; squares with the number 7 should be stitched with black yarn; and squares with the number 8 should be stitched with white yarn. By the way, we used all three strands of the Paternayan thread when stitching this piece except where noted.) When you're finished, **tie off** and **snip** any remaining thread.

Work this portion of the design.

3 Along the top of the design, above the yellow border, **work** one row of single upright stitches, alternating between black and white. (Think of these as half upright Gobelin stitches; rather than crossing two threads of your canvas, as is the case with the upright Gobelin stitch, cross only one.) When you're finished, **tie off** and **snip** any remaining thread.

4 Counting from the hole where the first yellow stitch in the upper-left corner of the border began, **move up** two and over two to the left.

5 **Complete** a Scotch stitch with white yarn, with the components of the stitch moving up and to the left.

6 **Modify** the Scotch stitch by crossing it once. We'll call the resulting stitch a "cross Scotch stitch."

7 **Repeat** steps 5 and 6 with black yarn, but work the components of the Scotch stitch up and to the *right* rather than up and to the left.

8 Skip one canvas thread; then **repeat** steps 5–7 to create a second block of two cross Scotch stitches, one white and one black.

9 **Continue** adding blocks in this manner, skipping a thread between each block, until you reach the end of the row. You should finish with a black cross Scotch stitch.

2 Using a bargello stitch, **cover** the two strips across the work with yellow and black yarn in a Charlie Brown–shirt design. When you're finished, **tie off** and **snip** any remaining thread.

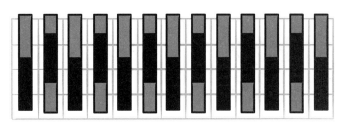

Use this Charlie Brown bargello stitch across the strips as described in step 2.

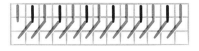

Add one row of alternating upright stitches.

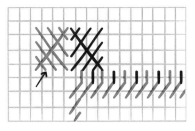

Start here to work a Scotch stitch; then modify the stitch, crossing it once, for extra coolness.

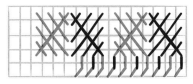

Skip one thread before starting the next block of two Scotch stitches.

10 **Rotate** your canvas 90 degrees so your needle is again in the top-left corner of the piece. Then, without skipping a thread, **add** one white cross Scotch stitch and one black one, stitching left to right.

This results in an L-shaped series of cross Scotch stitches with no blank threads in between.

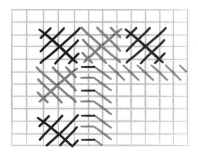

Turn the corner and start the next row.

11 Skip one canvas thread; then **repeat** steps 5–7 to create a second block of two cross Scotch stitches.

12 **Continue** adding blocks in this manner, skipping a thread between each block, until you reach the end of the row. You should finish with a white cross Scotch stitch.

13 **Rotate** your canvas 90 degrees so your needle is again in the top-left corner of the piece. Then, this time skipping a thread, **add** one white cross Scotch stitch and one black one (stitching left to right).

Turn the next corner and start the next row.

14 **Repeat** steps 8–12 to complete the remaining two cross Scotch stitch borders. When you're finished, **tie off** and **snip** any remaining black or white thread.

15 Start a new yellow thread in the top-right corner of the design and, moving your needle diagonally up and to the right, **work** a tent stitch all the way around the piece, filling in spaces between your blocks of cross Scotch stitches along the way. When you're finished, **tie off.**

16 **Wash** and **press** the needlepoint piece as outlined in chapter 3 in the section "The Final Cut: Finishing Your Piece," also blocking it if necessary.

Cut Your Fabric

17 Using your shears on your novelty fabric, **cut** two 10- × 3-in. pieces. These will border the long sides of the needlepoint piece.
Note: Set aside all the pieces of fabric you cut in this section until it's time to construct the bag.

18 Using your shears on your novelty fabric, **cut** two 9- × 3-in. pieces. These will border the short sides of the needle-point piece.

19 Using your shears on the fabric meant for the body of your bag, **cut** one 19- × 15-in. panel. This will become the back of your bag.

20 **Repeat** step 19 twice on the fabric you chose for the interior of your bag, resulting in two 19- × 15-in. panels.

21 **Repeat** step 19 twice on the fleece fabric, resulting in two 19- × 15-in. panels. These will act as batting inside the bag.

22 Using your shears, **cut** a 9- × 12-in. piece of the interior fabric. This will be the outside of the pocket in the bag's interior.

23 Using your shears, **cut** a 9- × 12-in. piece of fleece. This will line the pocket in the bag's interior.

24 Using your shears, **cut** a 5- × 11-in. piece of the same fabric as in step 19; this is for the outside of the flap that closes the bag.

25 **Repeat** step 24, but on the interior fabric.

26 Using your shears on the fabric meant for the body of your bag, **cut** two 15- × 3-in. pieces. This will be sewn on the outer edges of the front of the bag.

27 **Cut** one 13- × 5-in. strip of the same fabric. This will border the novelty fabric along the top of the needlework design.

28 Still using the same fabric, **cut** one 13- × 4-in. strip. This will border the novelty fabric along bottom of the needle-work design.

29 Using your shears on the fabric meant for the stripes and straps, **cut** two 24- × 4-in. pieces. These will become vertical stripes on the front of the bag.

30 On the same fabric as in step 29, use your shears to **cut** two 40- × 4-in. pieces. These will become the straps.

Sew the Bag's Front

Note: If you're using a sewing machine, a regular straight stitch will suffice for the steps in this project unless otherwise indicated. If you're sewing by hand, use a back stitch.

31 **Sew** the strips of novelty fabric you cut in step 17 onto the long edges, i.e., the top and bottom, of your needlepoint piece. (If your novelty fabric is faux fur like ours, smooth the fur pile away from the path of your stitches. Then use a zigzag stitch if you're using a sewing machine or a lacing stitch if you're stitching by hand to sew the fur onto the needlepoint.)

32 **Sew** the strips of novelty fabric you cut in step 18 onto the sides of your needlepoint piece, also joining them with the novelty fabric bordering the needlepoint's top and bottom edges, as shown here.

33 **Sew** the piece of 13- × 5-in. fabric you cut in step 27 to the top of your

novelty fabric. (The top strip of novelty fabric should now be 1½-in. wide-ish.)

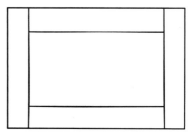

Frame your needlework piece with the novelty fabric.

34 **Sew** the piece of 13- × 4-in. fabric you cut in step 28 to the bottom of your novelty fabric. (Like the top strip of novelty fabric, the bottom strip of novelty fabric should also be 1½-in. wide, give or take.)

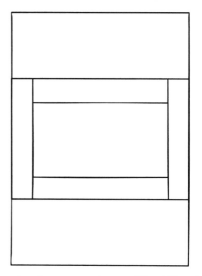

Sew the pieces you cut in steps 27 and 28 to the top and bottom of the novelty fabric.

35 **Sew** one piece of 24- × 4-in fabric you cut in step 29 to the left side of your novelty fabric and the body fabric above and below your needlepoint. (Like the top and bottom strips, the left strip of novelty fabric should be about 1½-in. wide.)

36 **Repeat** step 35 to attach the remaining piece of 24- × 4-in. fabric to the right side of the novelty fabric.

37 **Sew** one piece of 15- × 3-in. fabric you cut in step 26 to the left side of the left stripe sewn in step 35. The stripe should now be roughly 1½-in. wide.

38 **Repeat** step 37 with the remaining piece of 15- × 3-in. fabric on the right side of the bag.

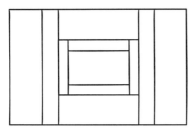

Add the stripes, then attach the remaining front panels (steps 35–38).

Construct the Bag

39 **Place** the front of the bag (the panel containing your needlepoint) and the bag's back panel (the piece you cut in step 19) with their right sides together. Then, **stitch** the sides and bottom of the front and back panels together.

40 **Place** the 9- × 12-in. piece of interior fabric you cut in step 22 with the fleece you cut in step 23 (also 9- × 12-in.), with their right sides together. Then, **stitch** the top, sides, and bottom together, but leave an opening in the bottom that's large enough to allow you to turn the pieces right-side out. This piece will become the pocket.

41 Using the opening you left in step 40, **turn** the pocket right-side out. Then, use a needle and thread to **hand-stitch** the opening closed. (A slip stitch will do the trick.) When you're finished, set the pocket aside for now.

42 **Situate** the interior pocket in the desired spot on one of the 19- × 15-in. panels of interior fabric you cut in step 20, with both pocket and panel right-side up. We placed ours in the center of the panel, about 4 in. from the top. Then, using a zigzag stitch (machine users) or a back stitch (hand-stitchers), **sew** the sides and bottom of the pocket to the panel. Finally, **add** one more line of stitches down the middle of the pocket to create two separate compartments.

43 **Place** the other interior panel on top of the one with the pocket, right sides together, with the two 19- ×15-in. fleece panels you cut in step 21 on the outside. Then **sew** the sides and bottom of the interior panels together, leaving a 5-in. opening in the bottom. (You'll use this later to turn the bag right-side out.) When you're finished, lay the interior of the bag aside.

44 **Construct** the flap. To do so, lay the 5- × 11-in. piece of interior fabric

you cut in step 25 face up. Then, lay the 5- × 11-in. piece of body fabric you cut in step 24 on top of it, face down. **Stitch** the top and sides of the two pieces of fabric to join them. When you're finished, turn it right-side out. Then set it aside for the time being.

45 **Fold** one of the 40- × 4-in. pieces of strap fabric that you cut in step 30 in half lengthwise and **sew** a line of stitches down the middle as shown. Notice how a tube is created on the side of the strap where the fold is.

46 Using your loop turner, **turn** the strap you just sewed inside out so the "edge" side is inside the "tube" side. (To use the loop turner, **insert** the long wire through the fabric tube, **hook** onto the end of the fabric, **close** the latch, and **pull** the hooked end through the tube to the other side.)

47 **Iron** the strap flat. Then, again **sew a** line of stitches down the middle.

48 **Repeat** steps 45–47 with the remaining 40- × 4-in. piece of strap fabric. When you're finished, set both straps aside.

49 **Place** the lining of bag inside the bag, with the right sides facing each other. That is, the raw edges of each piece should be exposed.

50 **Lay** the bag flat on your work surface. Then **slide** the flap and one strap inside the bag, between the interior and the exterior of the bag's back panel. The raw edge of the flap and the edges of the strap should align with the raw edges along the top of the bag. Make sure the flap is facing the correct direction (i.e., the interior fabric on the flap is facing the interior

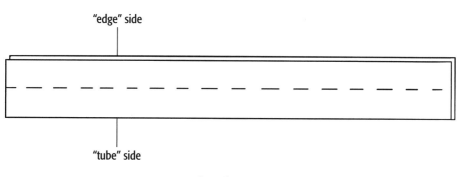

Start the strap.

fabric in the back panel) and that your strap is not twisted, and then pin everything in place.

51 **Slide** the remaining strap inside the bag between the interior and the exterior of the bag's front panel, aligning the raw edges, making sure the strap isn't twisted and that its position mirrors that of the other strap.

52 **Sew** all the way around the top of the bag, securing the flap and straps in place.

53 Using the 5-in. opening you left along the bottom of the bag's interior, **turn** the bag right-side out. Then, use a needle and thread to **hand-stitch** the opening closed. (A split stitch will do the trick.)

54 **Sew** the fuzzy half of the Velcro strip onto the inner part of the flap and the rough half onto the front panel, where the flap will attach.

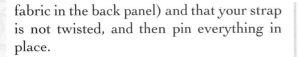

Variation

Rescue Me

by KB Van Horn

It breaks our hearts to find needlepoint pieces at yard sales, thrift stores, or flea markets—often priced at 25¢ or less. We can't help but feel for the poor person who made it. We imagine her stitching while watching TV (*M.A.S.H.? Matlock? Murder, She Wrote?*), or on a family vacation in a station wagon full of screaming kids, or maybe just whiling away an afternoon on her front porch. We imagine her stopping every so often to rest her fingers and examine her progress. But 25¢ is a deal to say the least, so we snatch it up knowing we can stitch it up into a kick-ass retro bag. Now, armed with the skills you learned in this project, you too can rescue a piece of needlework that has been thoughtlessly cast aside by strangers.

Chapter Seven

◆◆

Canvas the Area: Needlework for the Home

You Bore Me

Face it: Art is for the rich—unless the art you're talking about is this fantastic needlepoint pillow, adapted from a painting by contemporary artist Paul Moschell.

Cue the Violins

If you're a whine magnet, this cross-stitch sign is for you. Use it to convey your disgust *without ever saying a word*.

We Got Spirits, Yes We Do!

It's the eternal dilemma: trying how to remember how to concoct a Wildberry Kamihuzi while already three sheets to the wind. Enter this drinks recipe box: It keeps all your favorite drink recipes in one easy-to-find spot.

Wash Your Damn Hands!

These cross-stitched hand towels cut to the chase, reminding your party guests that if they're planning on diving into the tortilla chips you set out, a little personal hygiene can go a long way.

Case in Point

Obviously, not every drawing your kid does is a masterpiece. But every so often, one deserves to be preserved somewhere other than your refrigerator. Why not stitch it for posterity? This project adapts my kid's scribbles into a fantastic pillowcase.

Coffee, Tea, or Me?

Even if, like me, you think the tea lobby has conspired for millennia to convince people that tea is good when in fact it's really just hot water with a trace of disgusting flavor, you can still enjoy tea *towels*—like this embroidered one.

The 25,000-Calorie Pyramid

Sure, that food pyramid thingie the USDA puts out is a good guide to what I *should* eat, but doesn't reflect what I *do* eat. This embroidered napkin, however, does.

You Bore Me

by Paul Moschell

I'll be straight with you: You could conceivably gestate a baby in the time it takes to stitch this design, derived from a wee painting by kicky contemporary artist Paul Moschell. Hell, you'd be in your second trimester by the time you actually gathered together all the necessary floss. (On that topic: May I also suggest that a) you purchase enough project cards to house your thread so as to keep track of which thread color is which, and b) you stock up on the necessary thread the next time your local crafts store puts its stock of embroidery floss on sale?) But I swear that the results are well worth it.

Project Rating: Love o' Your Life

Cost: $30

Necessary Skills: Needlepoint, sewing

Materials

- 1 10 × 18-in. piece 14-count canvas (Ours is interlocking.)
- Scroll frame
- Tapestry needle, size 22
- Embroidery scissors
- Shears
- 1 skein each cotton embroidery floss in the following colors:
    - medium dark blue violet, DMC 155
    - dark blue, DMC 158
    - dark lavender, DMC 209
    - medium baby blue, DMC 334
    - rose, DMC 335
    - light blue violet, DMC 341
    - very dark salmon, DMC 347
    - dark coral, DMC 349
    - medium coral, DMC 350
    - coral, DMC 351
    - light pistachio green, DMC 368
    - light mustard, DMC 372
    - very light mahogany, DMC 402
    - dark desert sand, DMC 407
    - light brown, DMC 434
    - tan, DMC 436
    - dark shell gray, DMC 451
    - light shell gray, DMC 453
    - very light avocado green, DMC 471
    - sky blue, DMC 519
    - moss green, DMC 581
    - light turquoise, DMC 598
    - light drab brown, DMC 612
    - dark beige gray, DMC 642
    - medium beige gray, DMC 644
    - dark beaver gray, DMC 646
    - light old gold, DMC 676
    - very light old gold, DMC 677
    - kelly green, DMC 702
    - chartreuse, DMC 703
    - light orange spice, DMC 722
    - light salmon, DMC 761
    - dark cornflower blue, DMC 792
    - medium Delft blue, DMC 799
    - light blue, DMC 813
    - light beige gray, DMC 822

- ◆ medium blue, DMC 826
- ◆ medium golden olive, DMC 831
- ◆ very dark beige brown, DMC 838
- ◆ very light beige brown, DMC 842
- ◆ medium rose, DMC 899
- ◆ dark parrot green, DMC 905
- ◆ medium parrot green, DMC 906
- ◆ dark antique blue, DMC 930
- ◆ tawny, DMC 945
- ◆ dark dusty rose, DMC 961
- ◆ very dark forest green, DMC 986
- ◆ medium forest green, DMC 988
- ◆ medium khaki green, DMC 3012
- ◆ light khaki green, DMC 3013
- ◆ very light mocha brown, DMC 3033
- ◆ light antique violet, DMC 3042
- ◆ medium yellow beige, DMC 3046
- ◆ light yellow beige, DMC 3047
- ◆ medium yellow green, DMC 3347
- ◆ ultra dark dusty rose, DMC 3350
- ◆ pine green, DMC 3364
- ◆ black brown, DMC 3371
- ◆ mauve, DMC 3687
- ◆ medium mauve, DMC 3688
- ◆ dark melon, DMC 3705
- ◆ medium salmon, DMC 3712
- ◆ medium shell pink, DMC 3722
- ◆ dark antique mauve, DMC 3726
- ◆ light antique mauve, DMC 3727
- ◆ dusty rose, DMC 3733
- ◆ medium wedgewood, DMC 3760
- ◆ medium desert sand, DMC 3773
- ◆ light terra cotta, DMC 3778
- ◆ dark brown gray, DMC 3787

- ◆ pale golden brown, DMC 3827
- ◆ light raspberry, DMC 3833
- ◆ light grape, DMC 3836
- ◆ light rosewood, DMC 3859
- ◆ 2 skeins cotton embroidery floss in the following colors:
    - ◆ medium lavender, DMC 210
    - ◆ light desert sand, DMC 950
    - ◆ light tawny, DMC 951
- ◆ ½-yd. piece decorative fabric (Ours is a medium-weight, olive-green duck cloth. Whatever you choose, go for something that will pick up one or more colors in the needlework design. In fact, you might want to hold up on buying this fabric until after you finish stitching the design. That way, you can bring the finished piece with you.)
- ◆ Sewing machine (if you don't have one, you can stitch by hand using a sewing needle)
- ◆ Sewing needle
- ◆ Sewing thread to match your fabric (ours is olive green)
- ◆ 1 12-oz. package fiberloft stuffing

Stitch the Needlepoint Design

1 **Mount** your canvas onto your scroll frame.

2 Using your tapestry needle to work tent stitches that point diagonally up and to the right, **complete** the needlework design using the charts and color key supplied on the following pages. (Use all six strands of the floss when stitching this piece.)

```
1  1  1  1  1  1  1  1  1  1  1  1  1  1  1  1  1  1  1  1  1  1  1  1  1  1  1  1  1  1  1  30 30 30 1  30 30 1  1  1  1  1  1  1  1
1  1  1  66 66 1  22 30 30 30 30 30 1  1  30 1  30 30 30 30 30 30 1  1  1  22 30 30 30 22 1  1  1  1  1  1  1  1  1  1  1
1  1  1  73 73 73 73 70 70 70 70 70 70 70 70 70 75 75 70 70 70 70 73 20 72 73 69 69 72 42 70 75 75 75 70 70 75 75 75
1  1  1  72 47 42 73 73 70 70 70 70 70 70 75 75 75 75 70 70 70 70 42 72 72 19 47 72 68 75 75 75 75 75 75 75 75 75
1  1  1  72 47 65 73 73 70 70 75 70 70 70 75 75 75 70 70 70 70 70 42 47 72 72 72 42 70 75 75 75 75 70 70 70 70
1  1  1  65 19 47 47 73 70 70 70 70 70 75 75 75 70 70 70 70 70 70 42 71 65 42 70 70 70 70 70 70 70 70 70 70 70
1  1  30 19 19 47 47 73 70 70 75 75 70 70 70 70 70 70 70 70 70 70 70 70 70 70 70 70 70 70 70 70 70 70 70 70 70
1  1  30 19 47 47 47 73 70 70 70 70 70 70 70 70 70 70 70 70 70 70 70 70 70 70 76 45 51 79 12 12 12 12 12 12
1  30 30 69 65 47 73 73 73 42 70 70 70 70 70 70 70 70 70 70 70 70 70 70 70 70 70 51 51 79 12 12 12 12 12 12
1  30 30 20 47 47 47 47 47 47 42 73 41 70 70 70 70 70 70 70 70 70 70 70 70 50 51 79 79 12 12 12 12 12 12 12
1  1  1  69 69 73 47 65 65 65 65 47 42 76 70 70 70 70 70 70 70 70 70 70 70 51 79 79 12 12 12 12 12 12 12 12
1  1  30 69 69 69 69 69 69 19 65 47 42 42 70 70 70 70 70 70 70 70 70 45 79 12 12 12 12 12 12 12 12 12 12 12
1  30 30 69 69 19 69 69 47 47 65 47 73 42 70 70 70 70 70 70 70 70 76 41 79 12 12 12 12 12 12 12 12 12 12 12
1  30 30 69 69 69 69 47 47 47 47 47 73 73 70 70 70 70 70 70 70 59 79 79 12 12 12 12 12 12 12 12 12 12 12
1  30 30 20 47 47 47 47 47 47 42 73 73 70 70 70 70 70 70 70 59 79 79 12 79 79 79 79 79 79 12 12 12 12 12
1  30 30 69 47 65 73 73 73 73 42 70 70 70 70 70 52 79 79 79 79 79 79 79 79 79 79 79 79 12 79 79 79
1  30 30 69 69 47 47 73 42 42 70 70 70 70 70 70 62 79 79 79 12 79 79 79 79 79 79 79 79 79 79 79 79
30 30 30 69 19 20 65 42 62 70 70 70 70 70 70 70 41 79 79 79 79 79 79 79 79 79 79 79 79 79 79 79 79
30 30 30 19 69 69 65 65 73 70 70 70 70 70 70 37 79 79 79 79 79 79 79 79 79 79 79 79 79 79 79 79 79
30 30 30 47 69 69 65 65 73 70 70 70 70 70 49 79 79 79 79 79 79 79 79 79 79 79 79 79 79 79 79 79 79
30 30 30 47 47 65 65 47 73 62 70 70 70 70 71 79 79 79 79 79 79 79 79 79 79 79 79 79 79 79 79 79 79
30 30 30 20 47 47 73 73 62 70 70 70 76 79 79 79 79 79 79 79 79 79 79 79 79 79 79 79 79 79 79 79 79
30 30 30 73 73 73 73 73 19 70 70 79 79 79 79 79 79 79 79 79 79 79 79 79 79 79 79 79 79 79 79 79 79
30 30 30 73 73 73 73 68 70 70 70 79 79 79 79 79 79 79 79 79 79 79 79 79 79 79 79 79 79 79 79 79 79
30 30 30 62 73 73 42 70 70 70 70 76 53 79 79 79 79 79 12 12 12 12 12 12 12 79 79 79 79 79 79 79 79
30 30 30 70 36 70 70 70 70 70 70 79 53 79 79 79 79 79 12 12 12 12 12 12 79 79 79 12 12 12 12 12 12
30 30 30 70 50 50 70 70 70 70 70 76 56 79 79 79 79 12 79 12 12 12 79 79 79 79 79 79 79 79 79 12
30 30 30 70 50 50 70 70 70 70 70 52 79 79 79 79 79 12 12 12 12 12 12 12 12 12 18 18 18 18 18 18 12
30 30 30 70 70 70 70 70 70 70 62 79 79 79 79 12 21 12 12 79 79 12 28 54 78 78 78 78 78 78 78 78 78
30 30 30 70 70 70 70 70 70 62 79 79 79 79 12 12 79 79 28 54 78 78 78 78 78 78 78 78 78 78 78 78 78
30 30 30 70 70 70 70 70 62 49 79 12 12 12 12 28 78 78 78 78 78 78 78 78 78 78 78 78 78 78 78 78 78
30 30 30 30 70 70 70 70 62 79 12 12 12 78 78 78 78 78 78 78 78 78 78 78 78 78 78 78 78 78 78 78 78
30 30 30 70 70 70 70 70 45 79 54 78 78 78 78 78 78 78 78 78 78 78 78 78 78 78 78 78 78 78 78 78 78
30 30 30 70 70 70 70 47 78 78 78 78 78 78 78 78 78 78 78 78 78 78 78 78 78 78 78 74 74 74 74 74 74
30 30 30 70 70 70 70 78 78 78 78 78 78 78 78 78 78 78 78 78 78 78 46 58 74 74 74 74 74 74 74 74
30 30 30 70 70 70 70 76 78 78 78 78 78 78 78 78 78 78 78 78 25 74 74 74 74 74 16 74 74 74 80 80 80
30 30 30 70 70 70 70 62 78 78 78 78 78 78 78 78 78 78 78 51 74 74 74 74 74 74 58 64 74 80 80 80 80 80 80
30 30 1  70 70 70 70 49 78 78 78 78 78 78 78 78 74 74 74 74 74 74 74 80 36 55 80 80 80 80 80 80 80
30 30 1  70 70 70 70 49 78 78 78 78 78 78 78 74 74 74 74 74 74 80 80 80 80 51 51 80 80 80 80 80 80
30 30 1  70 70 70 70 49 78 78 78 78 78 78 56 74 74 74 74 74 74 80 80 80 80 80 36 51 80 80 80 80 80 80
30 30 1  70 70 70 70 49 78 78 78 78 78 74 74 74 74 74 74 80 80 80 80 80 80 80 55 80 80 80 80 80 80
30 30 1  70 70 70 70 47 78 78 78 78 74 74 74 74 74 74 80 80 80 80 80 80 80 80 16 80 80 80 80 80 80
30 30 1  70 70 70 70 71 78 78 78 78 59 59 77 16 80 74 80 80 80 80 80 80 80 80 46 80 80 80 80 80 80
15 30 1  70 70 70 70 71 78 78 78 78 78 77 25 74 74 80 80 80 80 80 80 80 80 80 80 77 80 80 80 80 80 80
22 30 1  70 70 70 70 71 78 78 78 77 77 25 74 74 74 80 80 80 80 80 80 80 80 80 80 77 80 80 80 80 80 80
22 30 1  70 70 70 70 71 78 78 77 77 77 36 74 80 80 80 80 80 80 80 80 80 80 80 77 80 80 80 80 80 80
1  30 1  70 70 14 70 70 72 78 60 77 77 77 59 80 74 80 80 80 80 80 80 80 80 80 59 80 80 80 80 80 80
1  1  1  70 70 70 70 70 70 55 60 46 77 77 16 74 80 80 80 80 80 80 80 80 80 80 80 25 80 80 80 80 80
1  1  1  70 70 70 70 70 70 70 71 77 77 77 80 80 80 80 80 80 80 80 80 80 80 80 46 80 80 80 80 80 80
1  1  30 75 75 70 70 70 70 70 70 77 77 77 74 74 80 80 80 80 80 80 80 80 80 77 80 80 80 80 80 80
1  1  30 75 75 70 70 70 70 70 77 77 77 54 79 14 75 6  6  80 80 80 80 80 80 80 80 80 58 80 80 80 80 80
1  1  30 75 75 70 70 70 70 70 46 77 77 54 54 54 54 45 70 74 74 80 80 80 80 80 80 80 64 80 80 80 80 80
1  1  30 75 75 75 70 70 70 70 70 45 77 77 54 54 54 54 28 9  49 70 80 80 80 80 80 80 80 64 80 80 80 80 80
```

The top-left portion of the design.

```
1  1  1  1  1  1  1  1  1  30 30 1  30 1  1  1  1  1  1  1  1  1  1  1  1  1  1  1  1  1  1  1  1  1  1  1  1  1  1  1  1  1  1
1  30 1  30 30 1  1  1  1  1  1  1  1  30 1  1  1  1  1  1  1  1  1  1  1  1  1  1  1  1  1  1  1  1  1  1  1  1  1  1  1  1  1
75 70 70 75 75 75 75 70 75 70 14 14 14 76 62 71 71 71 71 71 71 65 65 65 76 76 65 71 37 19 19 19 68 37 42 42 1  1  1
75 75 75 75 75 75 75 75 75 14 14 14 14 76 62 62 62 71 71 71 71 65 76 76 76 65 71 37 68 68 68 68 68 37 1  1  1
70 70 70 70 70 70 70 75 75 75 14 14 17 17 44 62 71 71 71 71 65 76 76 76 76 65 71 37 68 68 68 68 68 1  1  1
70 70 70 70 70 70 70 75 75 75 75 14 14 17 17 17 44 71 71 71 65 65 76 76 76 76 76 71 71 44 68 68 68 1  1  1
12 12 51 36 70 70 70 70 70 70 70 75 75 75 75 70 17 17 76 44 71 71 65 76 76 76 76 76 76 44 44 44 68 19 1  1  1
12 12 12 12 12 12 12 45 70 70 70 70 70 75 75 14 17 17 17 44 44 71 71 44 65 76 76 76 76 71 44 44 42 1  1  1
12 12 12 12 12 12 12 12 45 70 70 70 70 70 75 75 14 17 17 17 44 71 71 44 44 65 76 76 76 76 44 44 44 71 1  1  1
12 12 12 12 12 12 12 12 12 12 45 70 70 70 70 75 75 14 17 17 17 44 71 71 44 76 76 76 76 76 65 44 62 1  1  1
12 12 12 12 12 12 12 12 12 12 12 70 70 70 70 70 75 14 14 17 17 44 71 71 44 76 76 76 76 76 65 71 1  1  1
12 12 12 12 12 12 12 12 12 12 12 12 70 70 70 70 70 75 14 14 17 17 44 71 71 44 76 76 76 76 76 65 71 1  1  1
12 12 12 12 12 12 12 12 12 12 12 12 70 70 70 70 70 75 14 17 17 17 44 44 44 76 76 76 76 71 1  1  1
12 12 12 12 12 12 12 12 12 12 12 12 70 70 70 70 75 75 75 17 17 17 44 44 44 76 76 76 76 76 1  1  1
79 12 12 12 12 12 12 12 12 12 12 12 12 70 70 70 75 75 75 75 17 17 17 44 44 76 76 76 76 76 1  1  1
79 79 79 12 12 12 12 12 12 12 12 12 12 39 12 49 70 70 70 75 75 75 75 17 17 44 65 76 76 76 76 1  1  1
79 79 79 79 79 12 12 12 12 12 12 12 12 64 12 38 41 70 70 70 75 75 75 75 17 17 76 76 76 76 76 1  1  1
79 79 79 79 79 12 12 12 12 12 12 12 8  12 11 12 7  7  70 70 70 75 75 75 75 17 17 76 76 76 76 1  1  1
79 79 79 79 79 79 79 12 12 12 12 12 12 79 2  2  24 38 49 70 70 75 75 75 75 14 17 17 76 76 76 1  1  1
79 79 79 79 79 79 79 79 12 12 12 12 12 31 31 12 38 26 42 7  70 70 75 75 75 75 75 17 17 76 76 76 1  1  1
79 79 79 79 79 79 79 79 12 12 12 12 12 12 38 42 7  40 47 70 70 75 75 75 75 75 17 17 76 76 76 1  1  1
79 79 79 79 79 79 79 79 12 12 12 12 12 12 24 35 26 7  70 70 75 75 75 75 75 14 17 76 76 1  1  1
79 79 79 79 79 79 79 79 12 12 12 12 12 12 79 26 7  71 70 75 75 75 75 75 75 14 17 76 76 1  1  1
12 79 12 79 79 79 79 79 79 12 12 12 12 12 51 12 12 12 38 38 23 70 75 75 75 75 75 17 17 76 1  1  1
12 12 12 12 12 12 12 12 12 12 12 12 12 38 38 12 12 12 12 70 70 75 75 75 75 75 75 17 17 1  1  1
12 79 12 79 12 12 12 12 12 12 12 12 12 79 12 26 52 35 38 56 12 62 70 75 75 75 75 75 75 14 17 1  1  1
78 54 28 79 12 12 12 12 12 12 12 12 12 2  42 40 69 42 26 38 12 70 70 75 75 75 75 75 75 17 1  1  1
78 78 78 78 78 78 54 28 79 79 79 10 79 51 38 26 58 7  7  38 12 12 79 70 75 75 75 75 75 75 1  1  1
78 78 78 78 78 78 78 78 78 78 53 79 79 38 26 47 40 27 7  38 24 12 70 75 75 75 75 75 75 1  1  1
78 78 78 78 78 78 78 78 78 78 28 79 35 38 26 20 20 42 42 38 12 12 72 70 75 75 75 75 75 75 1  1  1
78 78 78 78 78 78 78 78 78 78 78 28 53 60 26 26 56 38 34 55 79 62 70 75 75 75 75 75 75 75 1  1  1
74 74 48 25 74 74 24 78 78 78 78 78 78 78 78 28 79 55 2  8  8  79 70 75 75 75 75 75 75 75 1  1  1
74 74 74 16 74 74 80 74 74 58 54 78 78 78 78 78 78 78 28 79 2  79 79 70 75 75 75 75 75 75 1  1  1
80 80 80 77 80 80 80 80 80 80 80 58 78 78 78 78 78 78 78 54 79 79 79 70 75 75 75 75 75 75 1  1  1
80 80 80 77 80 80 80 80 80 80 80 80 80 24 78 78 78 78 78 78 78 28 79 65 70 75 75 75 75 75 1  1  1
80 80 80 46 80 80 80 80 80 80 80 80 80 80 45 78 78 78 78 78 54 71 70 70 75 75 75 75 75 1  1  1
80 80 80 80 80 80 80 80 80 80 80 80 80 80 80 51 78 78 78 78 78 71 70 70 75 75 75 75 75 1  1  1
80 80 80 16 80 80 80 80 80 80 80 80 80 80 80 80 74 78 78 78 78 78 70 75 75 75 75 75 75 1  1  1
80 80 80 80 80 80 80 80 80 80 80 80 80 80 80 80 74 77 78 78 78 78 70 75 75 75 75 75 75 1  1  1
80 80 80 16 80 80 80 80 80 80 80 80 80 80 80 74 64 80 77 77 46 78 78 70 75 75 75 75 75 1  1  1
80 80 80 46 80 80 80 80 80 80 80 80 80 80 58 80 80 80 77 77 46 60 78 70 75 75 75 75 75 1  1  1
80 80 80 55 80 80 80 80 80 80 80 80 80 80 80 80 80 77 77 46 60 72 75 75 75 75 75 75 75 1  1  1
80 80 80 80 80 80 80 80 80 80 80 80 80 80 80 74 77 33 65 70 75 75 75 75 75 75 75 1  1  1
80 80 80 80 80 80 80 80 80 80 80 80 80 80 6  14 77 49 70 70 75 75 75 75 75 75 1  1  1
80 80 16 80 80 80 80 80 80 80 80 80 80 80 6  75 14 51 77 71 70 70 75 75 75 75 75 75 1  1  1
80 80 80 80 80 80 80 80 80 80 80 80 80 80 6  75 14 56 54 77 65 70 75 75 75 75 75 75 1  1  1
80 80 80 80 80 80 80 80 80 80 80 80 80 80 6  14 51 54 54 54 77 70 70 75 75 75 75 75 75 1  1  1
80 80 80 80 80 80 80 80 80 80 80 80 80 80 14 59 54 54 54 78 77 70 70 75 75 75 75 75 75 1  1  1
80 80 80 80 80 80 80 80 80 80 80 80 80 75 55 9  54 79 4  32 77 70 70 75 75 75 75 75 75 1  1  1
80 80 80 80 80 80 80 80 80 80 80 80 6  59 32 4  63 63 63 46 77 23 70 70 75 75 75 75 75 1  1  1
80 80 80 80 80 80 80 80 80 80 80 80 80 36 67 48 63 63 63 63 77 77 47 70 70 70 70 75 75 75 75 75 75 1  1  1
```

The top-right portion of the design.

```
1  1  30 75 75 75 70 70 70 75 70 70 70 77 77 32 32 9  9  32 32 32 32 49 74 80 80 80 80 80 80 80 80 80 74 80 80 80 80
1  1  30 75 75 70 70 70 75 70 70 70 77 77 77 31 63 63 63 43 48 48 38 75 80 80 80 80 80 80 80 80 80 80 77 80 80 80 80
1  1  30 75 75 75 75 75 75 75 70 70 70 70 62 77 77 4  63 63 63 25 48 48 73 74 80 80 80 80 80 80 80 80 80 80 80 80 80
1  1  30 75 75 75 75 75 75 70 70 70 70 70 77 77 4  63 63 63 48 48 36 74 80 80 80 80 80 80 80 80 80 80 46 80 80 80 80
1  1  30 75 75 75 75 75 75 75 70 70 70 70 77 77 77 63 63 43 48 36 6  25 80 80 80 80 80 80 80 80 80 80 80 80 80 80 80
1  30 30 75 75 75 75 75 75 75 70 70 70 36 77 77 63 43 59 70 6  74 74 80 80 80 80 80 80 80 80 80 80 80 80 25 80 80
1  1  30 75 75 75 75 75 75 75 75 70 70 70 77 77 77 47 75 6  6  80 80 80 80 80 80 80 80 80 80 80 80 80 80 80 80 80
1  1  30 75 75 75 75 75 75 75 70 70 70 36 77 36 74 74 80 80 80 80 80 80 80 80 80 80 80 80 80 80 80 80 80 80 80
1  1  30 75 75 75 75 75 75 75 70 70 70 74 74 74 74 80 80 80 80 80 80 80 80 80 80 80 80 80 80 80 80 80 80 80 80
1  1  22 70 75 75 75 75 75 70 70 70 70 74 6  6  24 51 80 80 80 80 80 80 80 80 80 80 80 80 80 80 80 80 80 80 80 80
1  1  22 75 75 75 75 75 75 70 70 70 70 74 6  56 16 77 74 80 80 80 80 80 80 80 80 80 80 80 80 80 80 80 80 80 80 80
1  1  22 75 75 75 75 75 75 70 70 70 70 6  6  56 56 77 77 74 80 80 80 80 80 80 80 80 80 80 80 80 80 80 80 80 80 80
1  1  22 75 75 75 75 75 75 75 70 70 70 70 6  45 56 56 46 56 74 80 80 80 80 80 80 80 80 80 80 80 80 80 80 80 80 80
1  1  30 75 75 75 75 75 75 75 70 70 70 70 6  6  75 56 56 74 51 80 80 80 80 80 80 80 80 80 80 80 80 80 80 80 77 80
1  1  22 75 75 75 75 75 75 70 75 75 70 70 70 70 6  6  6  6  58 36 80 80 80 80 80 80 80 80 80 80 80 80 80 80 80 80
1  1  22 75 75 75 75 75 75 75 75 75 75 70 70 70 70 65 6  6  77 77 58 80 80 80 80 80 80 80 80 80 80 80 80 80 6  80
1  1  1  75 75 75 75 75 75 75 75 75 75 75 75 70 70 70 70 70 55 77 77 74 80 80 80 80 80 80 80 80 80 80 80 25 43
1  1  22 75 75 75 75 75 75 75 75 75 75 75 75 70 70 70 70 70 70 77 77 25 80 80 80 80 80 80 80 80 80 74 43 43
1  1  1  75 75 75 75 75 75 75 75 75 75 75 75 75 75 70 70 70 70 70 70 77 77 46 74 80 80 80 80 80 80 80 43 31 31
1  1  1  75 75 75 75 75 75 75 75 75 75 75 75 75 75 75 75 70 70 70 70 70 7  77 77 59 80 80 80 80 80 80 74 25 11
1  1  1  75 75 75 75 75 75 75 75 75 75 75 75 75 75 75 75 70 70 70 70 70 36 77 77 16 80 74 80 80 80 80 74 74
1  1  1  75 75 75 75 75 75 75 75 75 75 75 75 75 75 70 70 70 70 70 72 72 70 70 70 77 77 46 74 74 74 74 74
1  1  1  75 75 75 75 75 75 75 75 75 75 75 75 75 75 70 70 70 70 70 72 72 47 41 56 77 77 77 77 77 46 58 74
1  1  1  75 75 75 75 75 75 75 75 75 75 75 75 75 75 70 70 70 70 70 62 56 33 34 77 77 77 77 77 77 16 53
1  1  1  75 75 75 75 75 75 75 75 75 75 75 75 75 75 70 70 70 70 62 16 29 34 77 77 77 77 77 77 77 77 74
1  1  1  75 75 75 75 75 75 75 75 75 75 75 75 75 75 70 70 70 62 16 56 41 47 77 77 77 77 77 77 77 46 74
1  1  1  75 75 75 75 75 75 75 75 75 75 75 75 75 14 14 14 70 70 41 77 41 46 46 77 77 77 77 77 77 64 74
1  1  1  75 75 75 75 75 75 75 75 75 75 75 75 75 14 14 14 70 41 77 23 62 47 77 77 77 77 77 77 77 51 74
1  1  30 75 75 75 75 75 75 75 70 75 70 70 70 70 14 70 70 41 70 41 24 47 77 77 77 77 77 77 77 74 74
1  1  30 75 75 75 75 75 75 70 70 70 70 70 70 70 70 62 77 70 41 23 47 46 77 77 77 77 77 77 77 74 74
30 1  1  14 14 75 70 75 75 75 75 75 75 75 70 70 70 70 70 41 70 16 62 70 72 24 77 77 77 77 77 61 74 74
30 30 30 17 76 14 70 70 75 75 75 75 75 75 75 75 70 70 62 29 70 16 76 70 72 62 77 77 77 77 58 18 74 74
30 30 30 17 17 17 14 70 70 75 70 70 70 70 70 70 75 75 70 70 76 70 70 70 46 62 77 77 77 46 74 18 74 74
30 30 30 62 17 17 17 17 70 70 70 70 70 70 70 70 70 75 75 70 70 75 70 70 77 76 51 77 77 77 74 25 74 74
30 30 30 62 62 17 17 17 17 70 70 70 70 70 70 70 70 70 75 75 75 70 70 77 76 70 77 77 77 74 74 28 74
30 30 30 62 62 62 62 17 17 17 70 70 70 70 70 70 70 70 75 75 75 75 70 70 77 76 34 77 77 77 74 58 61 61
30 30 1  62 62 62 62 62 17 17 17 70 70 70 70 70 70 70 75 75 75 70 70 56 17 70 70 16 77 25 67 61 61
30 30 30 62 76 62 62 62 62 17 17 17 17 70 70 70 70 70 70 70 75 75 75 75 75 70 17 70 70 70 74 46 55 61 61 61
30 30 30 62 76 76 76 62 62 62 17 17 17 17 70 70 70 70 70 70 70 75 75 75 75 70 17 70 70 70 59 61 61 61
30 30 30 62 76 76 76 76 76 17 17 17 17 17 17 17 70 70 70 70 70 70 75 75 75 75 70 70 72 61 61 61
30 30 30 62 62 62 76 76 76 76 76 76 76 76 17 17 17 17 14 70 70 70 70 70 70 70 70 70 45 39 39 9
30 30 30 62 62 62 76 76 76 76 76 76 76 17 17 17 17 17 70 70 70 70 70 70 70 70 70 70 66 67 9  39
30 30 30 62 62 62 62 76 76 76 76 76 17 17 17 17 17 17 17 14 70 70 70 70 70 70 70 70 67 67 67 28
30 30 30 42 62 62 62 62 76 76 37 19 68 44 17 17 17 17 17 17 17 17 70 70 70 70 70 70 67 53 53 28
30 30 30 19 62 76 76 62 62 73 65 65 65 65 44 76 76 76 17 17 17 17 70 75 75 75 70 70 67 67 53 53
30 30 30 19 19 19 37 76 76 68 47 65 19 65 65 19 76 76 76 76 76 76 17 17 17 70 75 75 75 70 70 52 67 61 67 53
30 30 30 19 19 68 19 19 76 42 65 19 69 19 65 68 76 76 76 76 76 76 17 17 14 70 75 70 70 70 67 61 61 61 67
30 30 1  16 16 16 16 35 35 23 16 16 34 23 23 23 23 55 23 23 24 56 56 33 24 49 52 24 52 52 45 62 9  9  9  9
1  1  1  1  1  1  1  1  1  1  30 1  1  1  1  1  1  1  1  1  1  1  1  1  1  1  1  1  1  1  1  1  22 22 22
1  1  1  1  1  1  1  1  30 30 30 15 30 30 30 30 30 30 30 30 30 30 30 30 30 30 1  1  1  1  1  1  1  1  1
1  1  15 15 15 15 15 30 15 15 15 15 15 15 15 15 15 15 15 30 30 30 1  30 30 30 30 1  1  1  1  1  1  1  1
```

The bottom-left portion of the design.

```
80 80 80 80 80 80 80 80 80 80 80 80  6 62 67 68 43 63 63 63 77 77 70 70 70 70 70 75 75 75 75 75 75 75 70  1  1  1
80 80 80 80 80 80 80 80 80 80 80 80  6 58 49 48 50 63 63 77 77 70 70 70 70 14 75 75 75 75 75 75 75 70  1  1  1
80 80 80 80 80 80 80 80 80 80 80 80 80 51  6 70 40 48 77 77 23 70 70 70 14 70 75 75 75 75 75 75 75 70  1  1  1
80 80 80 80 80 80 80 80 80 80 80 80 80 80  6 14 45 77 77 71 70 70 70 14 70 14 75 75 75 75 75 75 75 70  1  1  1
80 80 80 80 80 80 80 80 80 80 80 80 80 80  6 14 77 46 46 71 70 70 70 14 70 75 75 75 75 75 75 75 70  1  1  1
80 80 80 80 80 80 80 80 80 80 80 80 80 80 80 58  6  6  6 58 70 70 70 14 14 14 75 75 75 75 75 75 70  1  1  1
80 80 80 80 80 80 80 80 80 80 80 80 80 80 80 56 56 56  6  6 70 70 70 14 14 14 75 75 75 75 75 75 70  1  1  1
80 80 80 80 80 80 80 80 80 80 80 80 80 80 59 77 56 56  6 70 70 70 14 14 14 75 75 75 75 75 75 70  1  1  1
80 80 80 80 80 80 80 80 80 80 80 80 80 80 77 77 56 45  6 70 70 70 14 14 14 75 75 75 75 75 75 36  1  1  1
80 80 80 80 80 80 80 80 80 80 80 80 80 52 77 56 56  6 70 70 70 14 14 75 75 75 75 75 75 36  1  1  1
80 80 80 80 80 80 80 80 80 80 80 80 80 14 56 56 75 70 70 70 70 14 14 75 75 75 75 75 75 36  1  1  1
80 80 80 80 80 80 80 80 80 80 80 80 80 51 74  6  6 75 70 70 70 14 14 14 75 75 75 75 75 75 36  1  1  1
80 80 80 80 80 80 80 80 80 80 80 80 74 77 25 25 76 70 70 70 14 14 14 14 75 75 75 75 75 75 36  1  1  1
80 80 46 80 80 80 80 80 80 80 80 80 77 77 77 70 70 70 14 14 14 14 75 75 75 75 75 75 75 51  1  1  1
80 80 80 80 80 80 80 80 80 80 80 80 77 77 77 70 70 70 14 14 14 14 75 75 75 75 75 75 75 51  1  1  1
80 80  6 80 80 80 80 80 80 80 80 77 77 77 70 14 14 14 14 14 75 14 14 75 75 75 75 75 75 51  1  1  1
43 43  4 80 80 80 80 80 80 80 77 77 16 70 70 14 14 14 14 75 75 75 14 14 75 75 75 75 75 75 51  1  1  1
43 43 43  6 80 80 80 80 80 46 77 70 70 70 14 75 75 75 14 14 14 14 75 75 75 75 75 75 75 51  1  1  1
31 31 50 25 80 80 80 80 77 77 70 70 70 70 75 75 75 75 14 75 14 14 14 14 14 14 14 19 19 68 14 51  1  1  1
31 11 25 80 80 80 74 77 49 14 70 70 70 75 75 75 75 75 75 75 14 14 14 14 14 14 14 41 19 19 73 19 49  1  1  1
74 74 80 80 80 80 36 77 77 56 44 44 70 70 75 75 14 75 75 14 14 14 14 14 14 14 14 19 47 47 47 73 73  1  1  1
80 80 80 74 77 77 77 77 46 56 16 29 44 14 14 14 14 14 14 14 14 14 14 14 14 14 14 19 47 65 65 65 26  1  1  1
74 25 77 77 77 77 77 77 51 16 49 24 33 44 14 14 14 14 14 14 14 14 14 14 14 14 14 19 65 19 19 65 47  1  1  1
79 51 77 77 77 77 77 77 77 62 77 70 36 44 14 14 14 14 14 14 14 14 14 14 14 19 65 47 69 69 47  1  1  1
74 74 77 77 77 77 77 77 77 62 33 78 70 62 70 14 14 14 14 14 14 14 14 14 14 14 19 47 65 69 69 69  1  1  1
74 74 77 77 77 77 77 77 77 77 29 46 70 46 76 14 14 14 14 14 14 14 14 14 14 14 70 19 65 19 69 38  1  1  1
74 74 77 77 77 77 77 77 77 77 70 24 70 70 44 14 14 14 14 14 14 14 14 14 14 62 19 19 19 71 65 69 38  1  1  1
74 74 77 77 77 77 77 77 77 77 47 41 70 70 44 14 14 14 14 14 14 14 14 14 19 19 19 71 65 65 47 71 38  1  1  1
74 74 56 77 77 77 77 77 77 77 76 70 70 70 17 14 14 14 14 14 14 14 14 14 19 19 47 65 65 65 19 69 69 38  1  1  1
74 74 77 77 77 77 77 77 77 77 76 70 70 70 14 14 14 14 14 14 14 14 14 14 19 47 65 65 65 65 69 69 69 26  1  1  1
74 74 74 67 77 77 77 77 77 49 46 76 70 70 70 14 14 14 14 14 14 14 14 19 47 47 65 65 71 19 69 69 69 49  1  1  1
74 74 74 58 77 77 77 77 77 71 77 44 70 70 14 14 14 14 14 14 14 14 19 19 47 65 65 65 65 47 65 47 69  1  1  1
74 74 25 58 46 77 77 77 77 70 52 41 70 70 14 14 14 14 14 14 14 14 19 19 42 71 71 42 42 65 65 69  1  1  1
74 74 53 74 46 77 77 77 46 70 70 29 70 70 14 14 14 14 14 14 14 14 19 19 19 19 19 71 47 19 69  1  1  1
74 51 67 74 46 77 77 77 70 44 70 70 14 14 14 14 14 14 14 14 14 14 14 14 19 47 71 47 69 69  1  1  1
61 61 61 58 77 77 77 71 70 70 70 70 70 14 14 14 14 14 14 14 14 14 14 14 14 42 71 47 69 69  1  1  1
61 61 61 25 77 77 47 70 70 70 70 70 70 14 14 14 14 14 14 14 14 14 14 14 14  2  2 14 70 19 47 19 49  1  1  1
61 61 61 61 46 71 70 70 70 70 70 70 14 14 14 14 14 14 14 14 14 14 14 14 36 10  2 14 14 19 20 47 47  1  1  1
61 61 61 61 71 70 70 70 70 70 70 70 14 14 14 14 14 14 14 14 14 14 14 14 59 70 75 14 19 73 73 49  1  1  1
61 61 61 47 70 70 70 70 70 70 70 70 14 14 14 14 14 14 14 14 14 14 14 14 14 68 73 35  1  1  1
61 61 61 61 47 70 70 70 70 70 70 75 14 75 14 14 14 14 14 14 14 14 14 14 14 14 70 59  1  1  1
61 61 39 39 62 70 70 70 70 75 75 75 75 75 14 14 14 14 14 14 14 14 14 14 14 50 14 59  1  1  1
39 39 39 28 45 70 70 70 70 75 75 75 75 75 75 14 14 14 14 14 14 14 14 14 70 43 70 59  1  1  1
67 53 67 67 45 70 70 70 75 75 75 75 75 75 75 14 14 14 14 14 14 14 14 14 70 14 55  1  1  1
28 53 67 53 12 70 70 70 75 75 75 75 75 75 75 14 14 14 14 14 75 14 14 14 14 14 55  1  1  1
53 53 53 53 70 70 70 70 75 75 75 75 75 75 75 75 75 75 75 14 75 75 14 14 75 14 14 55  1  1  1
53 53 53 67 53 70 70 70 70 75 75 75 75 75 75 75 75 75 75 75 75 75 14 75 14 14 14 16  1  1  1
53 53 53 53 53 53 70 70 70 70 70 70 75 75 75 75 75 75 75 75 75 75 75 14 75 14 14 14 16  1  1  1
67 53 53 53 53 53 70 70 70 70 70 14 14 75 75 75 14 14 75 14 14 14 75 14 14 75 75 75 14 64  1  1  1
22  1  1  1  1  1  1  1  1  1  1  1  1  1  1 66  1 30 64 16  1 30  1 64 30 64  1  1  1  1  1  1  1  1  1
 1  1  1  1  1  1  1  1  1  1  1  1  1  1  1  1 22  1 57 16 16 15 55  1 55 57 16  1  1  1  1  1  1  1  1  1  1
 1  1  1  1  1  1  1  1  1  1  1  1  1  1  1  1  1  1  1  1  1  1  1  1  1  1  1  1  1  1  1  1  1  1  1  1
```

The bottom-right portion of the design.

Color Key

1	Medium Lavender	DMC 210
2	Medium Blue	DMC 826
4	Sky Blue	DMC 519
6	Very Light Old Gold	DMC 677
7	Light Antique Mauve	DMC 3727
8	Dark Cornflower Blue	DMC 792
9	Dark Parrot Green	DMC 905
10	Medium Delft Blue	DMC 799
11	Medium Wedgewood	DMC 3760
12	Very Light Avocado Green	DMC 471
14	Light Old Gold	DMC 676
15	Dark Lavender	DMC 209
16	Dark Brown Gray	DMC 3787
17	Pale Golden Brown	DMC 3827
18	Chartreuse	DMC 703
19	Medium Coral	DMC 350
20	Dark Dusty Rose	DMC 961
21	Light Pistachio Green	DMC 368
22	Light Blue Violet	DMC 341
23	Dark Antique Mauve	DMC 3726
24	Light Drab Brown	DMC 612
25	Medium Beige Gray	DMC 644
26	Mauve	DMC 3687
27	Light Salmon	DMC 761
28	Medium Parrot Green	DMC 906
29	Tan	DMC 436
30	Light Grape	DMC 3836
31	Dark Antique Blue	DMC 930
32	Very Dark Forest Green	DMC 986
33	Dark Desert Sand	DMC 407

Color Key

34	Light Brown	DMC 434
35	Medium Shell Pink	DMC 3722
36	Very Light Beige Brown	DMC 842
37	Coral	DMC 351
38	Ultra Dark Dusty Rose	DMC 3350
39	Dark Blue	DMC 158
40	Light Shell Gray	DMC 453
41	Light Terra Cotta	DMC 3778
42	Medium Salmon	DMC 3712
43	Light Blue	DMC 813
44	Light Orange Spice	DMC 722
45	Medium Yellow Beige	DMC 3046
46	Very Dark Beige Brown	DMC 838
47	Medium Mauve	DMC 3688
48	Light Beige Gray	DMC 822
49	Light Rosewood	DMC 3859
50	Medium Baby Blue	DMC 334
51	Light Khaki Green	DMC 3013
52	Light Mustard	DMC 372
53	Medium Yellow Green	DMC 3347
54	Moss Green	DMC 581
55	Dark Shell Gray	DMC 451
56	Medium Khaki Green	DMC 3012
57	Medium Dark Blue Violet	DMC 155
58	Very Light Mocha Brown	DMC 3033
59	Dark Beige Gray	DMC 642
60	Very Dark Salmon	DMC 347
61	Kelly Green	DMC 702
62	Medium Desert Sand	DMC 3773

continued

continued

Color Key

63	Light Turquoise	DMC 598
64	Dark Beaver Gray	DMC 646
65	Dusty Rose	DMC 3733
66	Light Antique Violet	DMC 3042
67	Medium Forest Green	DMC 988
68	Dark Melon	DMC 3705
69	Dark Coral	DMC 349
70	Light Desert Sand	DMC 950
71	Medium Rose	DMC 899
72	Light Raspberry	DMC 3833
73	Rose	DMC 335
74	Light Yellow Beige	DMC 3047
75	Tawny	DMC 945
76	Very Light Mahogany	DMC 402
77	Black Brown	DMC 3371
78	Medium Golden Olive	DMC 831
79	Pine Green	DMC 3364
80	Light Tawny	DMC 951

3 When, after a seemingly interminable period, you're finished stitching the piece, **remove** the stitched piece from the scroll frame and **wash** and **press** it as outlined in chapter 3 in the section "The Final Cut: Finishing Your Piece," also blocking it if necessary.

Sew the Pillow

4 Using your shears, **cut** two 10½-in. strips of decorative fabric that are 2½-in. wide. (These strips will become the top and bottom of your pillow.)

5 Using your shears, **cut** two 12½-in. strips of decorative fabric that are 2½-in. wide. (These strips will border the sides of your needlepoint piece.)

6 Using your shears, **cut** a 10½- × 12½-in. piece of decorative fabric.

7 **Sew** the 10½- × 2½-in. strips of fabric you cut in step 4 onto the top and bottom edges of the design, as close to the needlepoint stitches as possible. (You may need to pin the strips on first.)

Note: If you're using a sewing machine, a regular straight stitch will suffice for the steps in this project unless otherwise indicated. If you're sewing by hand, use a back stitch.

8 **Sew** the 12½- × 2½-in. strips of decorative fabric that you cut in step 5 onto the sides of your piece, also joining them with the fabric bordering the top and bottom edges. (Again, you may need to pin the strips on first.)

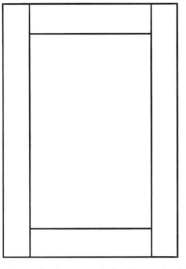

Frame the stitched piece with the decorative fabric.

9 **Pin** the front of the pillow to the pillow's back panel (the piece you cut in step 6) with their right sides together. Situate the pins at a right angle from the fabric's edges at ½-in. intervals.

10 **Stitch** the sides and top of the pillow together, leaving the bottom undone.

11 Using the opening you left in step 10, **turn** the pillow right-side out.

12 Again using the opening you left in step 10, **fill** the pillow with stuffing.

13 Use a needle and thread to **hand-stitch** the opening closed. (A slip stitch will do the trick.)

Variation

Double Crosser

This design could be easily converted to cross stitch. Just remember that each square in the diagram represents a square on your cross-stitch fabric rather than a thread intersection on canvas.

Cue the Violins

Do your co-workers act like Doug and Wendy Whiner? You know, the couple on *SNL* who whined all their lines, cornering anyone who would listen to complain about their diverticulitis. If so, this cubicle sign is the project for you. Use it to convey your anti-whining sentiments *without ever saying a word*.

Project Rating: Fling
Cost: $15
Necessary Skills: Cross stitch

Materials

- 1 12- × 12-in. piece Aida fabric, 18-count, white
- Embroidery hoop, 8 in.
- 1 skein cotton embroidery floss, black, DMC 310
- 1 skein cotton embroidery floss, light carnation, DMC 894
- Embroidery scissors
- Shears
- Cross-stitch needle, size 24
- 1 8 × 10-in. mat with a 41/2- × 6½-in. opening, white
- 1 8 × 10-in. frame, black

1 **Mount** the fabric into your hoop.

2 Using three strands of floss, **cross stitch** the charted design onto your fabric. (Note that the text should be black and the stars should be pink.) When you're finished, **tie off** and **snip** the excess thread.

3 **Remove** the stitched piece from the hoop and **wash** and **press** it as outlined in chapter 3 in the section "The Final Cut: Finishing Your Piece," also blocking it if necessary.

4 **Frame** your piece using the instructions in chapter 3 in the section "Ready, Frame, Admire: Mounting and Framing Your Piece."

Variation

Competence Is Sexy

If your beef with your co-workers relates less to whininess and more to incompetence, we suggest this signage alternative: COMPETENCE IS SEXY. For the morose among you, try CHEER UP OR DIE.

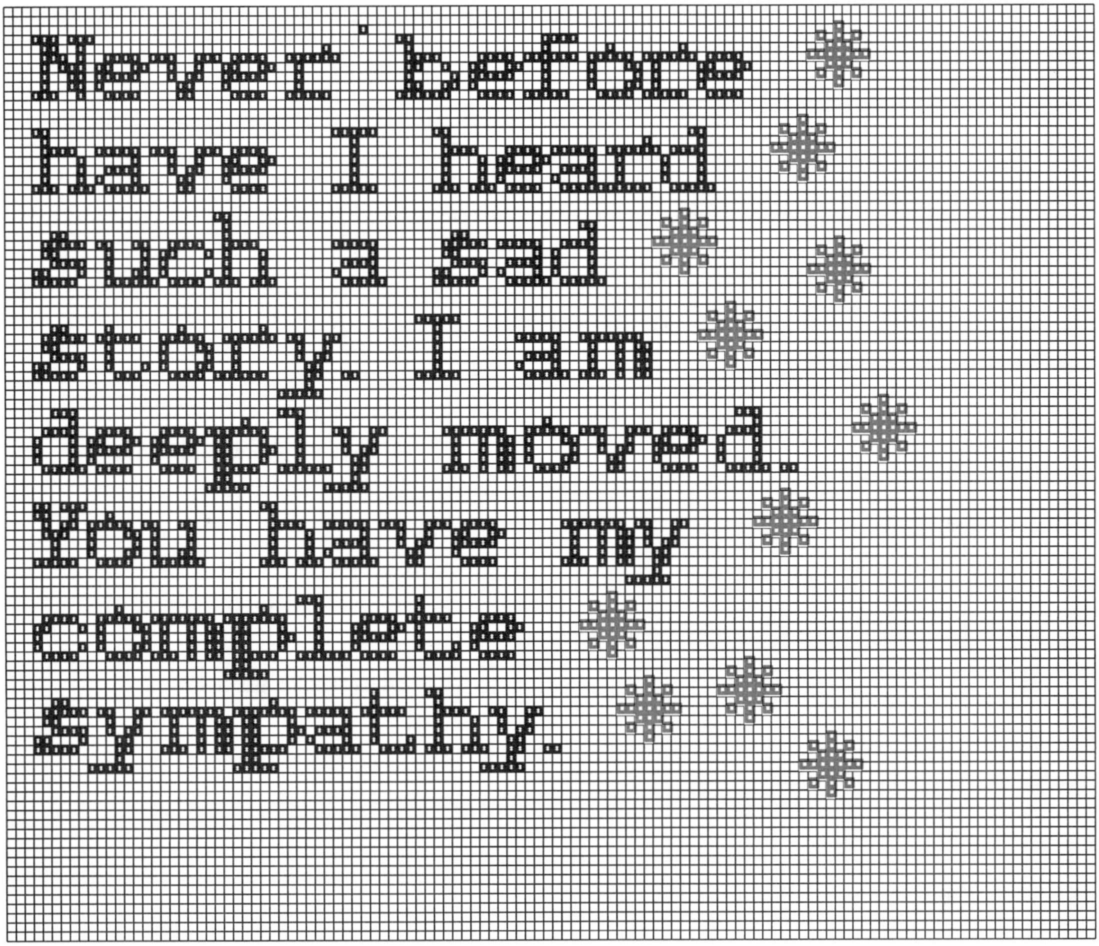

Never before
have I heard
such a sad
story. I am
deeply moved.
You have my
complete
sympathy.

Use this chart to stitch the design.

We Got Spirits Yes We Do!

If you did not matriculate from Mixology University or work a stint at Coyote Ugly, chances are your bartending skills are limited to a select few drinks. That's what makes this project so great: It's a repository for all your favorite cocktail recipes—and then some. Just jot down recipes on 3 × 5 index cards and store them in this drinks recipe box.

Project Rating: Fling

Cost: $7

Necessary Skills: Needlepoint

Materials

- 3 skeins cotton embroidery floss, light avocado green, DMC 470
- 3 skeins cotton embroidery floss, light blue, DMC 813
- 3 skeins cotton embroidery floss, white, DMC Blanc
- 3 skeins cotton embroidery floss, very light yellow green, DMC 772
- 3 skeins cotton embroidery floss, very light baby blue, DMC 775
- 3 skeins cotton embroidery floss, dark cornflower blue, DMC 792
- 3 skeins cotton embroidery floss, very light blue, DMC 827
- 3 skeins cotton embroidery floss, very light golden yellow, DMC 3078
- 3 skeins cotton embroidery floss, dark hunter green, DMC 3345
- 1 sheet heavy cardstock, light lime green
- 1 sheet transparency paper
- 1 sheet tracing paper

- Marker, fine-tip
- 2 sheets 10-count plastic mesh canvas
- X-Acto knife
- Shears
- Embroidery scissors
- 2 tapestry needles, size 22
- 1 pin
- Embroidery needle, size 5
- Pencil
- Permanent marker, fine-tip

Stitch the Cardstock

1 Using your shears, **cut** a 3½ × 2¼-in. piece of cardstock.

2 Using your shears, **cut** a 3½ × 2¼-in. piece of transparency paper.

3 Using the tracing paper and the fine-tip marker, **trace** the "Lush" design supplied here.

Lush

Use this design as your guide.

4 Lay the tracing paper over the card-stock you cut in step 1, centering it such that "Lush" appears where you want it. Then, using the pin, **follow** the lines of the letters, poking holes through the cardstock as you go. (When it's time to stitch, you'll draw the needle and thread through these holes; the more holes you add, the smoother the lines you stitch will appear.)

5 Using your embroidery scissors, **cut** a 15–18-in. length of white thread (DMC Blanc), **strip** the thread, **re-combine** two strands, and thread them onto your embroidery needle.

6 Start the thread using the method of your choice and, using a back stitch, **stitch** the letters on the cardstock, drawing the needle and thread through the holes you poked in step 4. When you're finished, **tie off** and **trim** any excess thread.

Note: If you find that the white thread doesn't really stand out on your cardstock, consider going over the white stitching with two strands of dark cornflower blue thread (DMC 792). The result is a nice three-dimensional effect that "pops."

Cut the Canvas

7 Using your shears, **cut** one rectangular piece of plastic canvas that's 56 × 29 holes. This will serve as the bottom of the recipe box.

8 Cut two rectangular pieces of canvas, both 56 × 36 holes. These will become the front and back panels of the box.

9 Cut two rectangular pieces of canvas, both 29 × 36 holes. These will become the box's side panels.

10 Cut one rectangular piece of plastic canvas that's 62 × 34 holes. This will serve as the top of the recipe box's lid.

11 Cut two rectangular pieces of canvas, both 62 × 10 holes. These will become the long sides of the lid.

12 Cut two rectangular pieces of canvas, both 34 × 10 holes. These will become the short sides of the lid.

13 Cut one rectangular piece of canvas that's 38 × 26 holes.

14 With your X-Acto knife, **cut** a rectangle out of the piece of 38 × 26-hole canvas you cut in step 13. **Use** the template that follows as your guide. This piece will frame your stitched paper on the top of the lid.

15 One last thing: **Lay** the frame you cut in steps 13 and 14 on the rectangular 62 × 34-hole piece of canvas you cut in step 10, aligning it as shown here. Then, using a thin permanent marker, trace the outline of the frame. There should be three holes to the left of the frame, three holes above, and five holes below.

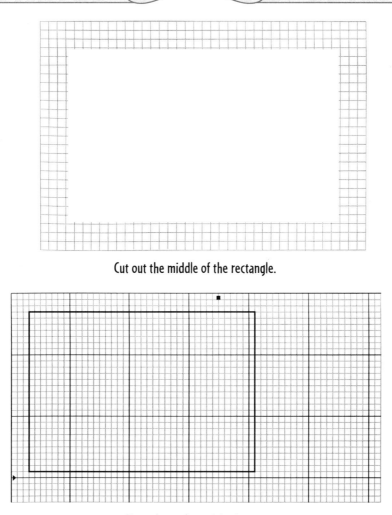

Cut out the middle of the rectangle.

Trace the outline of the frame.

Needlepoint the Box Pieces

16 Using your embroidery scissors, **cut** two 15–18-in. lengths of light avocado green thread (DMC 470), **strip** both lengths of thread so that you have 12 strands, **re-combine** 9 of the 12 strands, and thread them onto your needle.

Note: You'll use nine strands of thread throughout this project unless otherwise indicated.

17 **Start** the thread using the method of your choice and, beginning in the upper-left corner of either 29 × 36-hole side panel, **work** a diagonal row of condensed

cushion stitches. The thread in the stitches will move up and to the right, but the diagonal row will move down and to the right. (*Condensed cushion stitches* are exactly like condensed Scotch stitches, except that in this case each cushion stitch contains nine, rather than five, stitches.) When you're finished, **tie off** and **snip** your thread.

18 **Repeat** steps 16 and 17 with light blue thread (DMC 813), starting your thread in the upper-left corner, immediately to the right of the last condensed cushion stitch you added.

19 **Repeat** step 18 as many times as necessary to complete the right portion of the panel, starting with white thread (DMC Blanc) and cycling through the remaining thread colors.

20 **Rotate** the canvas 180 degrees so the blank portion is now in the upper-right corner rather than the lower-left. Then repeat step 18 using dark hunter green thread (DMC 3345). (You're reversing the order of the colors here to keep your pattern consistent.)

21 **Repeat** step 18 again, this time using very light golden yellow thread (DMC 3078).

22 **Repeat** step 18 as many times as necessary to complete the remaining portion of the panel, starting with very light blue thread (DMC 827) and cycling through the remaining thread colors in reverse order.

23 **Repeat** steps 16–22 to stitch the remaining 29 × 36-hole panel.

24 If you're all super perfect-y, **repeat** steps 16–22 on the bottom box panel (the one that's 56 × 29 holes). Or, if you're lazy like me, leave it *au naturel*, without a stitch on it. After all, no one will be able to see it.

25 **Repeat** steps 16–22 to stitch one of the 56 × 36-hole panels. This will become the back of your box.

26 To stitch the front of your box, first **repeat** steps 16 and 17, using light avocado green thread (DMC 470).

27 Rather than adding a diagonal row of light blue (DMC 813) condensed cushion stitches directly on top of the first row, follow the top line of the first row with light blue (DMC 813) *tent* stitches that, like the cushion stitches, point up and to the right. (If you're experiencing a bit of *déjà vu*, it's because this is very much like a Moorish stitch. It just substitutes the Scotch stitch with a cushion stitch.)

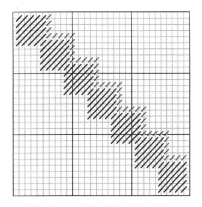

Work a modified Moorish stitch.

28 Repeat steps 26 and 27 with white thread (DMC Blanc) and very light yellow green thread (DMC 772).

29 Repeat steps 26 and 27 with very light baby blue thread (DMC 775) and dark cornflower blue thread (DMC 792).

30 Repeat steps 26 and 27 with very light blue thread (DMC 827) and very light golden yellow thread (DMC 3078).

31 Repeat steps 26 and 27 with dark hunter green thread (DMC 3345) and light avocado green thread (DMC 470).

32 Continue in this vein until you finish the right portion of the panel.

33 Rotate the canvas 180 degrees, so the blank portion is now in the upper-right corner rather than in the lower left. Then repeat step 29 using dark hunter green (DMC 3345). (You'll reverse the order of the colors here to keep your pattern consistent.)

34 Repeat steps 26 and 27 with very light golden yellow thread (DMC 3078) and very light blue thread (DMC 827).

35 Repeat steps 26 and 27 with dark cornflower blue thread (DMC 792) and very light baby blue thread (DMC 775).

36 Repeat steps 26 and 27 with very light yellow green thread (DMC 772) and white thread (DMC Blanc).

37 Repeat steps 26 and 27 with light blue thread (DMC 813) and light avocado green thread (DMC 470).

38 Continue in this vein until the panel is complete.

Needlepoint the Lid Pieces

39 Using your embroidery scissors, **cut** two 15–18-in. lengths of very light baby blue thread (DMC 775), **strip** both lengths of thread so that you have 12 strands, **re-combine** 9 of the 12 strands, and thread them onto your needle.

40 Situate either of your 62 × 10-hole panels horizontally in front of you. Then, starting in the bottom-left corner of the panel, count across to hole 32.

41 Start the thread using the method of your choice and draw your needle and thread through hole 32 from back to front.

42 Moving up and to the right, complete a tent stitch.

43 Draw your thread from back to front through the hole to the left of the one in step 41.

44 Moving up and to the right, pass your thread through the hole above the one in step 42.

45 Draw your thread from back to front through the hole to the left of the one in step 43.

46 Moving up and to the right, pass your thread through the hole above the one in step 44.

47 If you are feeling *déjà vu* all over again, it's because you just completed the first three stitches of a Scotch stitch.

Instead of completing the Scotch stitch, however, **repeat** the stitch you worked in steps 45 and 46, crossing three intersections in your canvas.

48 **Repeat** step 47 as many times as needed to reach the top of the column. When you run out of room to stitch across three intersections, "finish" the Scotch stitch by next stitching across two intersections, then by one. When you're finished, **tie off** and **snip** the excess thread.

Stitch the center column of one 62 × 10-hole panel.

49 **Repeat** steps 41–48 to complete a column of dark cornflower blue (DMC 792) stitches to the right of the very light baby blue column.

50 **Repeat** steps 41–48 to complete a column of very light blue (DMC 827) stitches to the right of the dark cornflower blue column.

51 **Repeat** steps 41–48, cycling through the remaining colors, until you've finished the right half of the lid's long side panel. (Note that the stitches in the rightmost row will cross two thread intersections rather than three.)

52 **Rotate** the canvas 180 degrees, so the blank portion is now on the right. Then **repeat** steps 41–48, starting with dark cornflower blue thread (DMC 792), then very light blue thread (DMC 827), and so on, so that they mirror the colors on the other half of the panel.

53 **Repeat** steps 41–52 to complete the second 62 × 10-hole piece and both 34 × 10-hole pieces. (Note that when repeating step 41, you'll want to start on hole 18 of each 34 × 10-hole panel.)

54 **Repeat** steps 41–52 to complete the top of the lid, leaving the holes within the outlined area unstitched. The stripes you sew on the top of the lid should line up with and be the same color as the stripes on each long side panel.

Needlepoint the Frame

55 Using your embroidery scissors, **cut** two 15–18-in. lengths of white thread (DMC Blanc), **strip** both lengths of thread so that you have 12 strands, **recombine** 9 of the 12 strands, and thread them onto your needle.

56 **Start** the thread using the method of your choice and, using a continental stitch, **stitch** around the outer ring of holes on the plastic canvas frame you cut in steps 13 and 14.

57 Still using white thread, **work** an overhand stitch around the inside edge of the frame.

Note: To prevent the plastic canvas from peeking through your overhand stitch, try first covering the entire length of the edging you're about to stitch with a length of thread the same color. Then, stitching in the opposite direction (i.e., along the path of the thread covering the edging), work your overhand stitch over the thread and the edging at the same time. In addition to

obscuring the plastic canvas, this extra thread also gives the edges a bit of padding. The same goes for the *lacing stitch* you'll use in a moment to bind the pieces of the box together.

58 Still using white thread, **work** an overhand stitch around the outside edge of the frame. When you're finished, the frame's inner ring of holes should be unstitched; **tie off** and **snip** any excess thread.

Affix the Frame

59 Your next move is to affix the frame to the top of the lid. First, **lay** the frame over the lid such that it defines the borders of the unstitched area.

60 **Start** a white thread using the method of your choice, drawing it through the lid from back to front as well as through the corresponding unstitched hole in your frame.

61 Moving up and to the right, **complete** a tent stitch, passing the needle and thread back down through the frame *and* the top of the lid.

62 Using a continental stitch, **stitch** the remaining empty holes along the top, right, and bottom edges of the frame, passing the needle and thread through both the lid and the frame each time. (Note that you left the left edge of unstitched holes as is; this is so you'll be able to slide your "LUSH" cardstock and the transparency paper into the frame. You'll do this a bit later.)

Finish the Panels

63 Still using white thread, **use** an overhand stitch to finish the top edge of the box's front panel. When you're finished, **tie off** and **snip** the excess. (Note that we're talking about the box's front panel here, not the lid. Either long edge of the panel can serve as the top.)

The inner holes of the frame should remain unstitched.

64 **Repeat** step 63 on the box's back panel.

65 **Repeat** step 63 on the top edge of both side panels. (Either short edge of the panel can serve as the top.)

66 Still using white thread, **use** an overhand stitch to **work** the bottom edges of the pieces comprising the sides of the lid. When you're finished, **tie off** and **snip** the excess.

Assemble the Box and Lid

67 Your next move is to stitch the pieces of your box together. To begin, **spread** the pieces of the box out on your workspace, face down. (Set the lid components aside for now.)

68 **Align** the back panel with the bottom panel, lining up the holes so they match.

69 Still using the white thread, **work** a lacing stitch from left to right to attach the back panel to the bottom panel.

70 On the side where your needle and thread are, **align** a side panel with the bottom panel, again lining up the holes so they match. Then continue with the lacing stitch to attach the side panel to the bottom panel.

71 **Repeat** step 70 to attach the front panel to the bottom panel.

72 **Repeat** step 70 to attach the remaining side panel to the bottom panel. When you're finished, **tie off** and **snip** the excess.

73 Your next step is to join the side panels with the front and back panels; let's begin with the back panel. **Start** a new white thread where the bottom panel meets the back panel and either side panel. Then work a lacing stitch to join the back and side. When you're finished, **tie off** and **snip** the excess.

74 **Repeat** step 73 to join the back panel with the remaining side panel. When you're finished, **tie off** and **snip** the excess.

75 **Start** *two* white threads, each on its own needle, on the two remaining corners of the bottom panel.

76 **Align** the front panel with the side panels and, using one of the two threads you just started, **work** a lacing stitch to join the front to one of the side panels. When you reach the top, **tie off** and **snip** any excess.

77 **Repeat** step 76 with the second thread to join the front panel to the remaining side panel.

78 **Repeat** steps 67–77 to assemble the lid.

Finishing Touches

79 **Place** the transparency paper on top of your stitched cardstock and **slide** both through the opening in your frame.

80 When the "LUSH" design is situated the way you like it, **start** a white thread and **use** a continental stitch to work the empty holes along the left side of the frame, passing the needle and thread

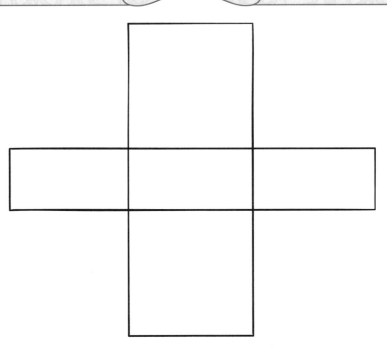

At this point, your box should be shaped like this.

through both the lid and the frame each time. When you're finished, **tie off** and **trim** the excess.

Note: Optionally, you can line the interior of your box with the remaining cardstock. I affixed mine using a very small amount of Krylon spray-on adhesive. (Beware: Using more than a light mist of the adhesive on the cardboard may result in discoloration of your thread on the outside of the box, which would *suck*.)

Variation

Recipe for Disaster

Okay, you aren't required to create a recipe box for drinks. You could instead stitch one up to house your favorite eats recipes. If you do, consider replacing "LUSH" with "GLUTTON."

Wash Your Damn Hands!

by Cindy Kitchel

Public restrooms inevitably contain the subtle reminder to the staff: "Employees must wash hands prior to returning to work." The towels in this project serve the same purpose but cut to the chase, reminding your party guests that if they're planning on diving into the tortilla chips you set out, a little personal hygiene can go a long way. The little cross stitch–ready guest towel used for this project, which is available at your local craft store or football field–sized superstore, make the perfect ladylike foil for *any* smart-ass message you want to convey.

Project Rating: **Fling**
Cost: **$5**
Necessary Skills: **Cross stitch**

Materials

- 1 cotton guest towel with cross-stitch inset (We used Charles Craft brand, 14 stitches to the inch inset.)
- 1 skein cotton embroidery floss, black, DMC 310
- 1 skein cotton embroidery floss, dark peacock blue, DMC 806
- 1 skein cotton embroidery floss, medium yellow green, DMC 3347
- Embroidery scissors
- Cross-stitch needle, size 24

1 **Find** the approximate center of the cross-stitch inset by folding the inset in half horizontally and then folding it in half vertically.

2 Beginning at the center of the chart on the following page, and using three strands of embroidery floss, **cross stitch** the charted design onto the insert. (Note that the x should be black, the ● should be blue, and the / should be yellow.) If you like, continue the flower motif on the bottom of the chart across the entire width of the towel.

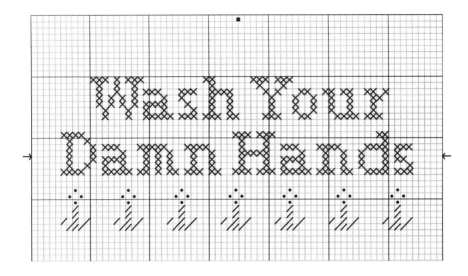

Use this chart to stitch the "Wash Your Damn Hands" design.

Variation

Hey! Buttface!

If you're like me, you don't wash bath towels after every single use. Instead, you fold them neatly over a towel rack—or toss them on the floor (guilty!). Has it ever occurred to you, though, that the next time you use said towel, you'll have no way of knowing which end was last used to wipe your face and which end was used to dry your nether regions? To resolve the gnawing anxiety this dilemma delivers, try stitching some helpful clues on opposite ends of the towel: BUTT and FACE.

1. Gather your supplies. You'll need a bath towel; a strip of 2-in. wide Aida that's long enough to fit across two towels plus 4 in. (the gauge you use is up to you); a skein of cotton embroidery floss, black, DMC 310; embroidery scissors; a tapestry needle, size 24; sewing thread that's about the same color as the Aida band; and a sharp sewing needle.

2. Fold the long edge of the Aida band in half and cut it on the fold. You now have two Aida bands, both about the width of the towel plus 2 in.

3. Find the center point of one of the Aida bands and cross stitch the FACE motif.

4. Cross-stitch the BUTT motif onto the second Aida band.

5. Fold the ends of the first band under 1 in. on each end. Then, using the sharp and sewing

thread, work a baste stitch to keep the turned-under edges in place.

6. Repeat step 5 with the second band. Both bands should now be the width of the towel.

7. Using your sharp and sewing thread, sew the FACE band into place on one end of the towel and the BUTT band on the other end.

Use this chart to stitch the BUTT/FACE design.

Case in Point

by Heidi Welsh with Kate Shoup Welsh

Obviously, not every drawing your kid does is a masterpiece. But every so often, one deserves to be preserved somewhere other than your refrigerator. Why not stitch it for posterity? Here, we stitched a drawing of my daughter's onto a pillowcase.

Project Rating: Flirtation

Cost: $10

Necessary Skills: Embroidery

Materials

- 1 pillowcase, white
- Transfer pencil
- Tracing paper
- Iron
- Embroidery hoop, 6 in.
- 1 skein cotton embroidery floss, black, DMC 310
- 1 skein cotton embroidery floss, very dark violet, DMC 550
- 1 skein cotton embroidery floss, very dark jade, DMC 561
- 1 skein cotton embroidery floss, tangerine, DMC 740
- 1 skein cotton embroidery floss, bright canary, DMC 973
- 1 skein cotton embroidery floss, light plum, DMC 3607
- 1 skein cotton embroidery floss, electric blue, DMC 3843
- Embroidery scissors
- Embroidery needle, size 5

1 **Wash** and **dry** the pillowcase. This prevents it from shrinking later, after you've embroidered it. Afterward, iron it.

2 Using the tracing paper and the transfer pencil, **trace** the design supplied here (or, if you're not sentimentally attached to a drawing by my kid, trace one of your own kid's). Note that we copied the heart in the center onto the tracing paper a few extra times as accents.

3 Using the iron, **transfer** the traced design to the edge of the pillowcase.

4 **Mount** the pillowcase in the hoop.

5 Using your embroidery scissors, **cut** a 15–18-in. length of light plum floss (DMC 3607), **strip** the floss, **re-combine** three of the strands, and **thread** the three strands onto your needle.

6 **Start** the thread using the method of your choice and, using a straight satin stitch, **stitch** the inner third of the girl's skirt. When you're finished, **tie off** and **snip** the excess.

7 Using your embroidery scissors, **cut** a 15–18-in. length of very dark violet floss

Trace this image for the pillowcase.

(DMC 550), **strip** the floss, **re-combine** three of the strands, and **thread** the three strands onto your needle.

8 **Start** the thread using the method of your choice and, using a straight satin stitch, stitch the outer two thirds of the girl's skirt.

9 Still with the very dark violet floss, using a straight satin stitch, stitch the girl's dog's bow. When you're finished, tie off and snip the excess.

10 Using your embroidery scissors, **cut** a 15–18-in. length of bright canary floss (DMC 973), **strip** the floss, **re-combine** three of the strands, and **thread** the three strands onto your needle.

11 **Start** the thread using the method of your choice and, using a straight satin stitch, **stitch** the girl's hair (leave the head-band area unstitched). When you're finished, **tie off** and **snip** the excess.

12 Using your embroidery scissors, **cut** a 15–18-in. length of tangerine floss (DMC 740), **strip** the floss, **re-combine** three of the strands, and **thread** the three strands onto your needle.

13 **Start** the thread using the method of your choice and, using a back stitch, **stitch** the lines comprising the boy's dog — including its eyes, nose, mouth, and whiskers.

14 Still with the tangerine floss, **use** a split stitch to stitch the boy's dog's leash.

15 Still with the tangerine floss, use a straight satin stitch to **stitch** the girl's headband.

16 Still with the tangerine floss, **use a** back stitch to stitch the lines comprising the girl's dog—including its eyes, nose, mouth, and whiskers. When you're finished, **tie off** and **snip** the excess.

17 Using your embroidery scissors, **cut a** 15–18-in. length of electric blue floss (DMC 3843), **strip** the floss, **re-combine** three of the strands, and **thread** the three strands onto your needle.

18 **Start** the thread using the method of your choice and, using a split stitch, **stitch** the girl's dog's leash.

19 Still with the electric blue floss, use a straight satin stitch to **stitch** the girl's cuff.

20 Still with the electric blue floss, use a straight satin **stitch** to stitch the heart above the boy and girl. When you're finished, **tie off** and **snip** the excess.

21 Using your embroidery scissors, **cut** a 15–18-in. length of very dark jade floss (DMC 561), **strip** the floss, **re-combine** three of the strands, and **thread** the three strands onto your needle.

22 **Start** the thread using the method of your choice and, using a back stitch, **stitch** the boy's eyes and mouth.

23 Still with the very dark jade floss, use a back stitch to **stitch** the girl's

eyes and mouth. When you're finished, **tie off** and **snip** the excess.

24 Using your embroidery scissors, **cut** a 15–18-in. length of black floss (DMC 310), **strip** the floss, **re-combine** three of the strands, and **thread** the three strands onto your needle.

25 **Start** the thread using the method of your choice and, using a straight satin stitch, stitch the boy's hair.

26 Still with the black floss, use a straight satin stitch to **stitch** the girl's sleeves and bodice. When you're finished, **tie off** and **snip** the excess thread.

27 **Start** a thread with two strands of black floss. Then, using a back stitch, **stitch** the outline of the boy's shoes, legs, torso, arms, hands, and head.

28 Still with the black floss, use a back stitch to **stitch** the outline of the girl's shoes, legs, dress, arms, hands, and head.

29 Using a straight satin stitch, **stitch** the accent hearts in the color(s) of your choice. We opted for light plum, tangerine, and electric blue.

Variation

Holy Sheet

Why stop at the pillowcases? Sheets make an excellent canvas for your (or my) kid's more ambitious works of art.

Coffee, Tea, or Me?

by Jenny Hart

It's my belief that those who profess to like tea have simply fallen prey to a conspiracy masterminded by a powerful tea lobby, which, for millennia, has convinced people that they're imbibing something delicious when in fact they're really just drinking hot water with a trace of revolting flavor. But that doesn't mean tea *towels*—especially this one—aren't a fabulous kitchen accessory. (By the way, if the colors used here clash with your *décor*, by all means choose ones you prefer!)

Project Rating: Fling
Cost: $7
Necessary Skills: Embroidery

Materials

- 100-percent cotton tea towel
- Embroidery needle, size 7
- Embroidery hoop, 6 in.
- 1 skein cotton embroidery floss, light violet, Presencia Finca Mouline 2606
- 1 skein cotton embroidery floss, plum, Presencia Finca Mouline 2246
- 1 skein cotton embroidery floss, dark plum, Presencia Finca Mouline 2406
- 1 skein cotton embroidery floss, dark violet, Presencia Finca Mouline 2635
- 1 skein cotton embroidery floss, dark yellow beige, Presencia Finca Mouline 7325
- 1 skein cotton embroidery floss, dark hazelnut brown, Presencia Finca Mouline 7408
- 1 skein cotton embroidery floss, dark topaz, Presencia Finca Mouline 8072
- 1 skein cotton embroidery floss, medium beaver gray, Presencia Finca Mouline 8567

- Embroidery scissors
- Iron
- Carbon transfer paper
- Ballpoint pen

1. Wash and dry the tea towel. This prevents it from shrinking later, after you've embroidered it. Afterward, iron it.

2. Photocopy the pattern provided here.

3. Using the carbon transfer paper and ballpoint pen, **transfer** the photocopied design onto your tea towel.

4. **Mount** the fabric into the hoop.

5. Using your embroidery scissors, **cut a** 15–18-in. length of dark yellow beige embroidery floss (Presencia Finca Mouline 7325), **strip** the floss, **re-combine** all six strands, and **thread** them onto your needle.

6. **Start** the thread using the method of your choice and, using a split stitch,

Use this image as your pattern.

stitch the dog's tail, hind quarters, and front legs—but not the outline of the sweater sleeve on the dog's left shoulder or the breast area. When you're finished, **tie off** and **snip** the excess.

7 Using your embroidery scissors, **cut** a 15–18-in. length of dark violet embroidery floss (Presencia Finca Mouline 2635), **strip** the floss, **re-combine** all six strands, and **thread** them onto your needle.

8 **Start** the thread using the method of your choice and, using a back stitch, **outline** the sweater. When you're finished, **tie off** and **snip** the excess.

9 Using your embroidery scissors, **cut** another 15–18-in. length of dark yellow beige embroidery floss (Presencia Finca Mouline 7325), **strip** the floss, **re-combine** all six strands, and **thread** them onto your needle.

10 **Start** the thread using the method of your choice and, again using a split stitch, **stitch** the dog's neck, the outer part of the right ear, the top of the head, the left ear, and the top of the snout. Then stitch to the dog's lower jaw and neck. When you're finished, **tie off** and **snip** the excess.

11 Using your embroidery scissors, **cut** a 15–18-in. length of dark topaz embroidery floss (Presencia Finca Mouline 8072), **strip** the floss, **re-combine** all six strands, and **thread** them onto your needle.

12 **Start** the thread using the method of your choice and, using a split stitch, **stitch** the inner portion of the dog's ear. When you're finished, **tie off** and **snip** the excess.

13 **Start** the dark topaz thread again and, still using a split stitch, **complete** the dog's *flews*—that is, the portions of the dog's muzzle that hang over her mouth. When you're finished, **tie off**, and **snip** any excess, and then go impress someone by correctly using the word "flews" in a sentence.

14 Using your embroidery scissors, **cut** a 15–18-in. length of dark hazelnut brown embroidery floss (Presencia Finca Mouline 7408), **strip** the floss, **re-combine** all six strands, and **thread** them onto your needle.

15 **Start** the thread using the method of your choice and, using a straight satin stitch, **stitch** the dog's nose. Then **work** some teeny stitches on the dog's left flew (that word again!) for its whiskers. When you're finished, **tie off** and **snip** the excess.

16 **Start** the dark hazelnut brown thread again and, using a back stitch, **stitch** the spiral comprising the outline of the dog's eye.

17 Still using the dark hazelnut brown thread, add the dog's pupil; use whatever stitch you like. When you're finished, **tie off** and **snip** the excess.

18 Using your embroidery scissors, **cut** a 15–18-in. length of medium beaver gray embroidery floss (Presencia Finca Mouline 8567), **strip** the floss, **re-combine** all six strands, and **thread** them onto your needle.

19 **Start** the thread using the method of your choice and, using whatever stitch you like, fill in the dog's iris. When you're finished, **tie off** and **snip** the excess.

20 Using your embroidery scissors, **cut** a 15–18-in. length of light violet embroidery floss (Presencia Finca Mouline 2606), **strip** the floss, **re-combine** all six strands, and **thread** them onto your needle.

21 **Start** the thread using the method of your choice and **apply** French knots on the dog's sweater. When you're finished, **tie off** and **snip** the excess.

22 Using your embroidery scissors, **cut** a 15–18-in. length of plum embroidery floss (Presencia Finca Mouline 2246), **strip** the floss, **re-combine** all six strands, and **thread** them onto your needle.

23 **Start** the thread using the method of your choice and, using a stem stitch, **stitch** the left heart in the lower cluster. When you're finished, **tie off** and **snip** the excess.

24 Using your embroidery scissors, **cut** a 15–18-in. length of dark plum embroidery floss (Presencia Finca Mouline 2406), **strip** the floss, **re-combine** all six strands, and **thread** them onto your needle.

25 **Start** the thread using the method of your choice and, using a back stitch, **stitch** the right heart in the lower cluster. When you're finished, **tie off** and **snip** the excess.

26 **Start** a new dark plum thread using the method of your choice and, using a back stitch, **stitch** the left heart in the upper cluster. When you're finished, **tie off** and **snip** the excess.

27 **Start** a new plum thread using the method of your choice and, using a stem stitch, **stitch** the right heart in the upper cluster. When you're finished, **tie off** and **snip** the excess.

Variation

Dog Run

This pup makes a great motif for a table runner; try switching up the color of the sweater and the positioning of the dog at different angles for a bit of variety.

The 25,000-Calorie Pyramid

You know that food pyramid the government puts out? According to the pyramid, you're supposed to eat a variety of foods—breads, cereals, rice, pasta, veggies, fruit, milk, meat . . . you know the drill. But what if, instead of reflecting what you *should* eat, the pyramid showed you what you *do* eat? If you're anything like we are, we're guessing your food pyramid would look like the one on this napkin.

Project Rating: Flirtation

Cost: $7 for the first napkin (because of the up-front cost of the thread); $3 for each napkin thereafter

Necessary Skills: Embroidery

Materials

- Cloth napkin
- Transfer pencil
- Tracing paper
- Iron
- Embroidery hoop, 8-in.
- Embroidery scissors
- 1 skein cotton embroidery floss, white, DMC Blanc
- 2 skeins cotton embroidery floss, black, DMC 310
- 1 skein cotton embroidery floss, red, DMC 321
- 1 skein cotton embroidery floss, peach, DMC 353
- 1 skein cotton embroidery floss, very light old gold, DMC 677
- 1 skein cotton embroidery floss, green, DMC 699
- 1 skein cotton embroidery floss, dark orange spice, DMC 720
- 1 skein cotton embroidery floss, very light topaz, DMC 727
- 1 skein cotton embroidery floss, medium tangerine, DMC 741
- 1 skein cotton embroidery floss, medium pink, DMC 776
- 1 skein cotton embroidery floss, dark topaz, DMC 782
- 1 skein cotton embroidery floss, medium topaz, DMC 783
- 1 skein cotton embroidery floss, baby pink, DMC 818
- 1 skein cotton embroidery floss, very dark hazelnut brown, DMC 869
- 1 skein cotton embroidery floss, light gray green, DMC 927
- 1 skein cotton embroidery floss, ultra dark coffee brown, DMC 938
- 1 skein cotton embroidery floss, medium sea-green, DMC 959
- 1 skein cotton embroidery floss, medium forest green, DMC 988
- 1 skein cotton embroidery floss, medium mocha brown, DMC 3032
- 1 skein cotton embroidery floss, very light beaver gray, DMC 3072
- 1 skein rayon floss, red, DMC 30321
- 2 embroidery needles, size 7

Prepare the Napkin

1 **Wash** and **dry** the napkin(s). This prevents it from shrinking later, after you've embroidered it. Afterward, iron it.

2 Using the tracing paper and the transfer pencil, **trace** the design supplied here.

3 Using the iron, **transfer** the traced design to the napkin.

4 **Mount** the bib in the hoop.

Stitch the Bottom Row of the Pyramid

5 Using your embroidery scissors, **cut** a 15–18-in. length of peach embroidery floss (DMC 353) and a 15–18-in. length of baby pink embroidery floss (DMC 818), **strip** both threads, **combine** two strands of peach floss with one strand of baby pink floss, and **thread** the three strands onto your needle.

6 **Start** the thread using the method of your choice and, using a straight satin stitch, **fill in** the liquid in the martini glass on the left. When you're finished, **tie off** and **snip** the excess thread.

7 Using your embroidery scissors, **cut** a 15–18-in. length of medium mocha brown embroidery floss (DMC 3032), **strip** the thread, **re-combine** three of the strands, and **thread** the three strands onto your needle.

Trace this image for the napkin.

8 **Start** the thread using the method of your choice and, using one long straight stitch, **stitch** the toothpick in the martini on the left. When you're finished, **tie off** and **snip** the excess thread.

9 Using your embroidery scissors, **cut** a 15–18-in. length of medium forest green embroidery floss (DMC 988), **strip** the thread, **re-combine** three of the strands, and **thread** the three strands onto your needle.

10 **Start** the thread using the method of your choice and **apply** a French knot on the toothpick in the martini on the left to represent the olive. When you're finished, **tie off** and **snip** the excess thread.

11 **Repeat** steps 5–10 on the remaining martini glass.

12 Using your embroidery scissors, **cut** a 15–18-in. length of white embroidery floss (DMC Blanc) and a 15–18-in. length of light beaver gray embroidery floss (DMC 3072), **strip** both threads, **combine** two strands of white floss with one strand of light beaver gray floss, and **thread** the three strands onto your needle.

13 **Start** the thread using the method of your choice and, using a vertical straight satin stitch, **stitch** the first coffee cup on the left in its entirety, covering the "logo."

14 Still with the same thread, using a very short vertical straight satin stitch, **work** the part of the lid that connects to the cup. Then **work** the side of the lid in the same manner.

15 Still with the same thread, **work** a *horizontal* straight satin stitch across the top of the lid. When you're finished, **tie off** and **snip** any excess thread.

16 Using your embroidery scissors, **cut** a 15–18-in. length of green embroidery floss (DMC 699), **strip** the thread, **re-combine** three of the strands, and **thread** the three strands onto your needle.

17 **Start** the thread using the method of your choice and, using a straight satin stitch, **stitch** the logo on the left-most coffee cup in spoke fashion. (This can be a simple green doughnut shape, meant only to *suggest* the logo for a company that shall go nameless here.) When you're finished, **tie off** and **snip** the excess thread.

18 **Repeat** steps 12–17 on the remaining two coffee cups.

horizontal satin stitch

short vertical satin stitch

short vertical satin stitch

long vertical satin stitch, stitched over the logo

spoked satin stitch

Stitch the coffee cups using these stitches.

19 Using your embroidery scissors, **cut** a 15–18-in. length of very light beaver gray embroidery floss (DMC 3072) and a 15–18-in. length of light gray green

embroidery floss (DMC 927), **strip** both threads, **combine** two strands of very light beaver gray floss with one strand of light gray green floss, and **thread** the three strands onto your needle.

20 **Start** the thread using the method of your choice and, using a vertical straight satin stitch, **stitch** the left-most soda can (leave the top unstitched for now). When you're finished, **tie off** and **snip** the excess thread.

21 **Combine** three of the remaining strands of very light beaver gray floss and **thread** them onto your needle.

22 **Start** the thread using the method of your choice and **work** a horizontal straight satin stitch across the top of the can. When you're finished, **tie off** and **snip** the excess thread.

23 **Combine** three of the remaining strands of light gray green floss and **thread** them onto your needle.

24 **Start** the thread using the method of your choice and **stitch** a French knot to represent the soda can's flip top. When you're finished, **tie off** and **snip** any excess thread.

25 Using your embroidery scissors, **cut** a 15–18-in. length of red *cotton* embroidery floss (DMC 321), **strip** the thread, **re-combine** two strands of it, and **thread** the two strands on a needle.

26 Using your embroidery scissors, **cut** a 15–18-in. length of red *rayon* embroidery floss (DMC 30321), **strip** the thread, **re-combine** four strands of it, and **thread** the four strands on a second needle.

27 **Start** both threads using the method of your choice and, using the first thread as the tying thread and the second thread as the laying thread, **stitch** a vertical swoop-y couched line on the left-most can. When you're finished, **tie off** both threads and **snip** the excess.

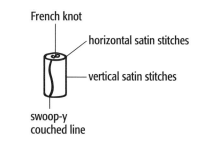

French knot

horizontal satin stitches

vertical satin stitches

swoop-y couched line

Work the cans using these stitches.

28 Repeat steps 19–27 on the remaining can.

Stitch the Second-from-Bottom Row

29 Using your embroidery scissors, **cut** a 15–18-in. length of red embroidery floss (DMC 321), **strip** the thread, **re-combine** three of the strands, and **thread** the three strands onto your needle.

30 **Start** the thread using the method of your choice and, using a vertical straight satin stitch, **stitch** the French fries container. When you're finished, **tie off** and **snip** the excess thread.

31 Using your embroidery scissors, **cut** a 15–18-in. length of dark topaz embroidery floss (DMC 782), **strip** the thread, **re-combine** three of the strands, and **thread** the three strands onto your needle.

32 **Start** the thread using the method of your choice and, using individual straight satin stitches, **stitch** some fries; each stitch should represent a single fry. When you've stitched about half the required number of fries to fill the container, **tie off** and **snip** the excess thread.

33 Using your embroidery scissors, **cut** a 15–18-in. length of medium topaz embroidery floss (DMC 783), **strip** the thread, **re-combine** three of the strands, and **thread** the three strands onto your needle.

34 **Start** the thread using the method of your choice and, again using individual straight satin stitches, **stitch** more fries to complement the ones you already have. When the container is full, **tie off** and **snip** the excess thread.

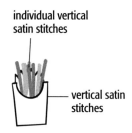

individual vertical satin stitches

vertical satin stitches

Stitch the French fries this way.

35 **Thread** the two remaining strands of medium topaz floss and one remaining strand of dark topaz floss onto your needle.

36 **Start** the thread using the method of your choice and, using a short, straight satin stitch, **stitch** the pizza crust—both the portion where one would grasp the pizza with her hand as well as the part underneath the sauce. When you're finished, **tie off** and **snip** the excess thread.

37 Using your embroidery scissors, **cut** a 15–18-in. length of dark orange spice embroidery floss (DMC 720) and a 15–18-in. length of medium tangerine embroidery floss (DMC 741), **strip** both threads, **combine** two strands of dark orange spice floss with one strand of medium tangerine floss, and **thread** the three strands onto your needle.

38 **Start** the thread using the method of your choice and, using a straight satin stitch, **stitch** the tomato sauce on the pizza. When you're finished, **tie off** and **snip** the excess thread.

39 Using your embroidery scissors, **cut** a 15–18-in. length of very dark hazelnut brown embroidery floss (DMC 869), **strip** the thread, **re-combine** three of the strands, and **thread** the three strands onto your needle.

40 **Start** the thread using the method of your choice and **stitch** several French knots over the sauce to represent sausage toppings.

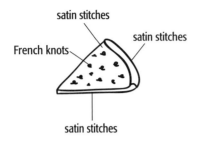

satin stitches

satin stitches

French knots

satin stitches

Stitch the pizza this way.

Stitch the Second-from-Top Row

41 Using your embroidery scissors, **cut** a 15–18-in. length of red rayon embroidery floss (DMC 30321), **strip** the thread, **re-combine** three strands of it, and **thread** the three strands onto your needle.

42 **Start** the thread using the method of your choice and, using a short, straight satin stitch, **stitch** the unopened part of the candy-bar wrapper along the top of the candy bar.

43 Using the same thread, use short, straight satin stitches to **work** the sides of the wrapper. When you're finished, **tie off** and **snip** the excess thread.

44 Using your embroidery scissors, **cut** a 15–18-in. length of light gray green embroidery floss (DMC 927), **strip** the thread, **re-combine** three strands of it, and **thread** the three strands onto your needle.

45 **Start** the thread using the method of your choice and, using a straight satin stitch, **stitch** the ripped foil portion of the candy-bar wrapper. When you're finished, **tie off** and **snip** the excess thread.

46 Using your embroidery scissors, **cut** a 15–18-in. length of very dark hazelnut brown embroidery floss (DMC 869), **strip** the thread, **re-combine** three strands of it, and **thread** the three strands onto your needle.

47 **Start** the thread using the method of your choice and, using a satin stitch, **stitch** the exposed portion of the candy bar, along the top.

48 Using the same thread, use short straight satin stitches to **work** the side of the candy bar. When you're finished, **tie off** and **snip** the excess thread.

49 Using your embroidery scissors, **cut** a 15–18-in. length of ultra dark coffee brown embroidery floss (DMC 938), **strip** the thread, **re-combine** two strands of it, and **thread** the two strands onto your needle.

50 **Start** the thread using the method of your choice and **stitch** a grid across the chocolate portion of the bar to indicate pieces. When you're finished, **tie off** and **snip** the excess thread.

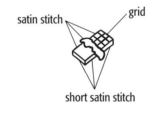

satin stitch

grid

short satin stitch

Stitch the chocolate this way.

51 Using your embroidery scissors, **cut** a 15–18-in. length of very light old gold embroidery floss (DMC 677) and a 15–18-in. length of very light topaz embroidery floss (DMC 727), **strip** both threads, **combine** two strands of very light old gold floss with one strand of very light topaz floss, and **thread** the three strands onto your needle.

52 **Start** the thread using the method of your choice and, using vertical straight satin stitches, **stitch** the cake portion. When you're finished, **tie off** and **trim** the excess thread.

53 Using your embroidery scissors, **cut** a 15–18-in. length of white embroidery floss (DMC Blanc), **strip** the thread, **re-combine** three strands of it, and **thread** the three strands onto your needle.

54 **Start** the thread using the method of your choice and, using a straight satin stitch, **stitch** the top layer of icing.

55 Still with the white thread, work a single long satin stitch horizontally across the cake portion to indicate a middle layer of icing. When you're finished, **tie off** and **trim** the excess thread.

56 Using your embroidery scissors, **cut** a 15–18-in. length of baby pink embroidery floss (DMC 818) and a 15–18-in. length of medium pink embroidery floss (DMC 776), **strip** both threads, **combine** two strands of baby pink floss with one strand of medium pink floss, and **thread** the three strands onto your needle.

57 **Start** the thread using the method of your choice and, using French knots, **stitch** the edging around the top of the cake. When you're finished, **tie off** and **trim** the excess thread.

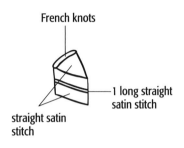

Stitch the cake this way.

Stitch the Top Row

58 Using your embroidery scissors, **cut** a 15–18-in. length of white embroidery floss (DMC Blanc) and a 15–18-in. length of very light beaver gray embroidery floss (DMC 3072), **strip** both threads, **combine** two strands of white floss with one strand of very light beaver gray floss, and **thread** the three strands onto your needle.

59 **Start** the thread using the method of your choice and, using a straight satin stitch, **stitch** half of one pill capsule.

60 **Repeat** step 59 for the remaining two capsules. When you're finished, **tie off** and **trim** the excess thread.

61 Using your embroidery scissors, **cut** a 15–18-in. length of medium seagreen embroidery floss (DMC 959), **strip** the thread, **re-combine** three strands of it, and **thread** the three strands onto your needle.

62 **Start** the thread using the method of your choice and, using a straight satin stitch, **stitch** the remaining half of each pill capsule. When you're finished, **tie off** and **trim** the excess thread.

Finish the Food

63 Using your embroidery scissors, **cut** a 15–18-in. length of black embroidery floss (DMC 310), **strip** the thread, and **thread** one strand onto your needle.

64 **Start** the thread using the method of your choice and, using a back stitch, **stitch** the outlines of all the food items in the pyramid. When you're finished, **tie off** and **trim** the excess thread.

Outline the Pyramid

65 Using your embroidery scissors, **cut** a 15–18-in. length of black

embroidery floss (DMC 310), **strip** the thread, **re-combine** three strands of it, and **thread** the three strands onto your needle.

66 **Start** the thread using the method of your choice and, using a double-running stitch, **stitch** the outline of the pyramid and the lines separating each food group.

Things You Hang on the Kitchen Wall

Here are the clues: Cabinets! Clock! Spice rack! The design you just stitched! The answer? Things you hang on the kitchen wall. This design makes a great piece of kitchen art—the perfect reminder that a moment on the lips is a lifetime on the hips.

Chapter Eight

◆◆◆

Present Tents: Nifty Needlecraft Gifts

Who's the Boss?

Anyone who's ever babysat knows babies aren't so much bundles of joy as tiny tyrants, diapered despots, Castro minus the beard. This bib just tells it like it is.

Sweet Emoticon

If emoticons can be used to replace facial expressions in e-mail and text messages, why not on greeting cards, too? This embroidered emoticon greeting card is the perfect way to say "I'm joking."

It's All Geek to Me

Whip up this embroidered journal cover for your favorite introverted, socially awkward writer.

Anklebiter

Embroider this wee dog T for your favorite ankle biter.

You Reek

Don't take it all personally. Everyone is capable of some serious stink. This punch-needle sachet works to counteract everyday odors with the reek of your choosing.

Who's the Boss?

by Amanda Smithers-Bentley

When moralist Martin Farquhar Tupper wrote "A babe in the house is a wellspring of pleasure, a messenger of peace and love, a resting place for innocence on earth, a link between angels and men," he obviously had never met *my* kid. I mean, she's cute and all, and I love her like crazy. But calling her a "messenger of peace" is like calling Paris Hilton a "homebody." If babies are anything, they're tiny tyrants. They're diapered despots. They're Castro, but wee and with less hair. Hence this refreshingly honest "dictator" bib.

Project Rating: Flirtation

Cost: $5

Necessary Skills: Embroidery

Materials

- 1 bib (We bought ours in packs of three at IKEA, but you can find good ones at Target as well. Pick one that isn't super thick or stiff because that will make it harder to embroider.)
- A 7 × 5-in. piece of cut-away interfacing (We used the kind that you iron on.)
- Transfer pencil
- Tracing paper
- Iron
- Embroidery hoop, 4 in.
- 1 skein cotton embroidery floss, red, DMC 321
- Embroidery scissors
- Embroidery needle, size 5
- Thin towel

1 **Wash** and **dry** the bib. This prevents it from shrinking later, after you've embroidered it. Afterward, iron it.

2 **Cut** the piece of fusible interfacing to fit the bib. (The interface may need to curve a bit on the edges to fit properly.)

3 Following the instructions that came with the fusible interfacing, **iron** the interfacing onto the back side of the bib. (Your iron should be hot, on the Cotton setting.)

4 Using the tracing paper and the transfer pencil, **trace** the "dictator" design supplied here.

Note: It appears in reverse here so that when you iron it on it comes out right.

5 Using the iron, **transfer** the traced design to the bib.

6 **Situate** the bib in the hoop.

rotatib (mirror-reversed "dictator")

Trace this image for the "dictator" bib.

7 Using your embroidery scissors, **cut** a 15–18-in. length of red embroidery floss, **strip** the floss, **re-combine** three of the strands, and **thread** the three strands onto your needle.

8 **Start** the thread using the method of your choice and, using a stem stitch, **embroider** the design. When you're finished, **tie off** and **snip** the excess thread.

Variation

Despot Measures

by Amanda Smithers-Bentley

In case "dictator" just doesn't convey the degree to which one's spawn rules with absolute power, ratchet up your language with a "despot" onesie. Simply get your hands on a onesie of the appropriate size, transfer the letters for the design (again, in reverse), and stitch away. (We used black thread.) When you're finished, trade in the kid's stroller for a litter and hire some able-bodied types to carry him on a walk.

TOPSED (mirror-reversed "DESPOT")

Trace this image for the "despot" onesie.

Sweet Emoticon

by Angela Plumb

Quintessential symbol of the Internet age, *emoticons* are used to replace facial expressions in e-mail and text messages. I say, why shouldn't they appear on greeting cards, too? This embroidered emoticon greeting card is the perfect way to say "I'm joking."

Project Rating: Fling

Cost: $5

Necessary Skills: Embroidery

Materials

- 1 8 × 8-in. square white flannel
- Transfer pencil
- Tracing paper
- Iron
- Embroidery hoop, 4 in.
- 1 skein cotton embroidery floss, black, DMC 310
- Embroidery scissors
- X-Acto knife
- 1 piece cardstock (3.5 × 4-in.) (Ours was yellow.)
- Ruler
- 1 blank white greeting card (4.5 × 5-in., folded)
- 1 white envelope
- Glue (Try "The Ultimate!" glue by Crafter's Pick.)
- Spray-on adhesive

1 Using the tracing paper and the transfer pencil, trace the emoticon design supplied here.

2 Using the iron, **transfer** the traced design onto the center portion of the white square of flannel.

The emoticon design.

3 **Mount** the flannel square in your hoop.

4 Using your embroidery scissors, **cut** a 15–18-in. length of black embroidery floss, **strip** the floss, **re-combine** three of the strands, and **thread** the three strands onto your needle.

5 **Start** the thread using the method of your choice and, using a satin stitch, **fill in** the eyes and the mouth. When you're finished, **tie off** and **snip** any excess thread.

6 **Remove** the flannel square from the hoop.

7 Using your X-Acto knife, **cut** a rectangle in the cardstock where you want the emoticon to appear.

8 With your ruler, **measure** a rectangle around the emoticon on the flannel that's ¼-in. larger than the rectangle you cut into the cardstock in step 7. Then use your embroidery scissors to **cut away** the flannel outside the rectangle.

9 **Glue** the emoticon onto the back side of the yellow cardstock, so it's visible through the rectangular window.

10 Using the spray adhesive, **adhere** the yellow cardstock onto the white card.

Variation

Play the Frame Game

These emoticon cards are great for framing, making a cheerful accent for any computer desk.

It's All Geek to Me

by Angela Plumb

Having recently found an old journal and read its contents, it's clear that I was a total geek. (Example: "Fritz turned me off a little when he couldn't remember my name.") Too bad I didn't have this excellent "geek" journal cover back then.

Project Rating: Fling

Cost: $7

Necessary Skills: Embroidery

Materials

- 1 composition book measuring 7½ × 9¾ -in., ¼-in. thick
- 16 × 6-in. piece khaki-colored canvas material (not needlepoint canvas; more like artist's canvas)
- Tracing paper
- Transfer pencil
- Iron
- Embroidery needle, size 7
- Embroidery hoop, 4 in.
- 1 yd. felt (Ours was orange.)
- 1 skein very dark coffee brown embroidery floss, DMC 898
- Embroidery scissors
- Shears
- Fabric glue
- Sewing machine (If you don't have one, use a sewing needle to stitch the journal cover by hand.)
- Sewing needle
- Sewing thread that matches the felt

1. Using the tracing paper and the transfer pencil, **trace** the "geek" design supplied here.

Note: It appears in reverse here so that when you iron it on it comes out right.

2. Using the iron, **transfer** the traced design to the canvas fabric.

3. **Mount** the canvas on the embroidery hoop.

4. Using your embroidery scissors, **cut** a 15–18-in. length of the very dark coffee brown embroidery floss, **strip** the floss, **re-combine** three of the strands, and **thread** the three strands onto your needle.

5. **Start** the thread using the method of your choice and, using a satin stitch, **fill in** the letters of the "geek" design. When you're finished, **tie off** and **snip** any excess thread.

6. **Remove** the fabric from the hoop.

7. Using your shears, **trim** the canvas around the word to measure 4½ × 2¼ in.

geek

(mirrored/reversed)

Trace this design.

8 Using your shears, **cut** a piece of felt that's larger than the canvas by about ¼ in. all the way around.

9 **Cut** a second piece of felt that's 21¼-in. wide and 10¼-in. high. This will comprise the journal cover. (If you're thinking the width seems a bit off, it's because it accounts for two 3-in. flaps that will fold around to the inside of the journal in order to hold the cover in place.)

10 Accounting for the 3-in. flap on the right side of the felt, use your shears to **cut out** a rectangular window in the felt through which the "geek" design will be displayed. The window should be slightly smaller than your canvas. We placed ours 2¼ in. from the top of the felt and about 4⅞ in. from the right edge of the felt.

11 **Lay** the felt face down and position the "geek" design, also face down, in the rectangular window. When you're satisfied with its placement, **dab** a wee bit of fabric glue on the felt to hold the canvas in place.

12 **Lay** the small piece of felt—the one you cut in step 5—over the back side of the canvas.

13 **Sew** the "geek" design into place. (Use a straight stitch if you're using a sewing machine, or a back stitch if stitching by hand.)

14 With the felt still face down, **fold** one side of the felt over to create a flap that's about 3-in. wide.

15 **Sew** the flap into place along the top and bottom edges of the felt. (Again, use a straight stitch if you're using a sewing machine or a back stitch if stitching by hand.)

16 **Repeat** steps 14 and 15 to create the other side flap.

17 **Slide** the felt cover onto the composition book. *Le geek, c'est chic*!

Patch Maker, Patch Maker, Make Me a Patch

The stitched geek design makes for a great patch, too. Alternatively, try stitching a different word; we opted for "nerd." Then, stitch the canvas onto a piece of felt that's slightly larger all the way around. Alternatively, follow the steps in the project "The Diet of Worms," in chapter 6, to create your patch.

Anklebiter

Why is it that the smallest dogs—the ones who could easily be mistaken for a member of the taxonomic order *rodentia*—are the most vicious? Thanks to this informative doggie T, forewarned is forearmed—*and* four legged.

Project Rating: Flirtation
Cost: $5
Necessary Skills: Embroidery

Materials

- 1 white doggie T (Ours is size small, purchased on eBay.)
- Transfer pencil
- Tracing paper
- Iron
- Embroidery hoop, 6 in.
- 1 skein cotton embroidery floss, black, DMC 310
- 1 skein cotton embroidery floss, very light carnation (DMC 894) or light blue (DMC 813)
- Embroidery scissors
- Embroidery needle, size 5

1 **Wash** and **dry** the doggie T. This prevents it from shrinking later, after you've embroidered it. Afterward, iron it.

2 Using the tracing paper and the transfer pencil, **trace** the "anklebiter" design supplied here or draw your own.

Note: It appears in reverse here so that when you iron it on it comes out right.

3 **Lay** the tracing paper face down on the back side of the doggie T, situating it so the letters appear where you want them. Then **apply** your hot iron to the back side of the paper to transfer the design.

4 **Hoop** the doggie T.

5 Using your embroidery scissors, **cut** a 15–18-in. length of very light carnation (DMC 894) or light blue (DMC 813) embroidery floss, **strip** the floss, **recombine** three of the strands, and **thread** the strands onto your needle.

Trace this image for the "anklebiter" doggie T.

6 Start your thread using the method of your choice and, using a satin stitch, **embroider** the body of each letter in your design. Stitch over any dots that fall within the body of a letter (for example, the two dots that appear in the letter *a*); you'll layer over the satin stitch to complete those in a moment.

7 Still using the very light carnation or light blue thread, use small straight stitches to **stitch** the lines embellishing the *e*s, the dot on the *i*, the dots over the letter *k*, as well as the two accent dots. When you're finished, **tie off** and **snip** the excess thread. When you're finished, **tie off** and **snip** the excess.

8 Using your embroidery scissors, **cut** a 15–18-in. length of black embroidery floss, **strip** the floss, **re-combine** three of the strands, and **thread** the three strands onto your needle.

9 **Work** a cross stitch for the two dots that appear on each of the following letters: *a, n, i, t,* and *r.* Alternately try using French Knots. When you're finished, **tie off** and **snip** the excess thread.

10 **Remove** the doggie T from the hoop.

11 If necessary, **iron** the doggie T again (apply the iron to the back side of the T) to smooth it out.

Variation

It's the Leashed You Could Do

If you shrink it down a bit, this "anklebiter" design could easily be stitched onto a wee leash or collar.

You Reek

It's not for nothing that the perfume industry is as old as the Pyramids in Egypt. The sad fact is, just about everything—and everyone—is capable of some serious stink. This punch-needle sachet works to counteract everyday odors with the reek of your choosing.

Project Rating: Flirtation

Cost: $5

Necessary Skills: Punch-needle embroidery, sewing

Materials

- Transfer pencil
- Tracing paper
- Iron
- Embroidery hoop, 4 in. (Note that special hoops and stands for punch-needle embroidery are available. As they do make the punch needler's life a bit easier, you might consider using one for this project.)
- Embroidery scissors
- Shears
- 5 × 5-in. piece punch-needle embroidery fabric (Ours is antique white.)
- ½-yd. decorative fabric (Fielder's choice here—this is for the back of the sachet. Ours is brown with yellow, coral, pink-ish, and peach-ish dots. Whatever you choose, go for something that will breathe a bit so the scent of your potpourri will waft through. Also, note that if your fabric differs widely from ours, you'll likely want to change the thread colors you use accordingly.)
- Punch needle
- Punch-needle threader

- 1 skein cotton embroidery floss, medium lavender, DMC 210
- 1 skein cotton embroidery floss, very light topaz, DMC 727
- 1 skein cotton embroidery floss, medium mocha brown, DMC 3032
- 1 skein cotton embroidery floss, apricot, DMC 3341
- 1 skein cotton embroidery floss, light mauve, DMC 3689
- 1 skein cotton embroidery floss, light apricot, DMC 3824
- Sewing machine (If you don't have one, you can stitch by hand using a sewing needle.)
- Sewing needle
- Sewing thread to match your fabric (Ours is brown.)
- Pins
- Potpourri (Ours is lavender.)

Prepare Your Materials

1. Using the tracing paper and the transfer pencil, **trace** the design supplied here.

Note: In this design, the text appears from left to right—which means when you transfer it onto your fabric, it'll appear backwards. Don't panic! Because you stitch punch-needle designs from the *back* side of the fabric, the design will read correctly on the fabric's front side.

Trace this image for the sachet.

Lay the tracing paper face down on the *back* side of your punch-needle embroidery fabric and **apply** your hot iron to the back side of the paper to transfer the design.

Mount the punch-needle embroidery fabric in your hoop, with the back side (i.e., the side onto which you transferred the design) facing up.

Stitch the Design

Using your embroidery scissors, **cut** a 36-in. length of very light topaz floss (DMC 727), **strip** the floss, **re-combine** three of the strands, and **thread** the three strands onto your punch needle.

Use your punch needle to **outline** the letter "R" in the "REEK" design; then **fill in** the letter. When you're finished, **remove** the thread from the punch needle and **snip** the excess, leaving a tail of about ¼ in.

Using your embroidery scissors, **cut** a 36-in. length of apricot floss (DMC 3341), **strip** the floss, **re-combine** three of the strands, and **thread** the three strands onto your punch needle.

Use your punch needle to **outline** the first letter "E" in the "REEK" design (that is, the top-most E); then **fill in** the letter. When you're finished, **remove** the

thread from the punch needle and **snip** the excess, leaving a tail of about ¼ in.

8 Using your embroidery scissors, **cut** a 36-in. length of light apricot floss (DMC 3824), **strip** the floss, **re-combine** three of the strands, and **thread** the three strands onto your punch needle.

9 Use your punch needle to **outline** the second letter "E" in the "REEK" design (that is, the bottom-most E); then **fill in** the letter. When you're finished, **remove** the thread from the punch needle and **snip** the excess, leaving a tail of about ¼ in.

10 Using your embroidery scissors, **cut** a 36-in. length of light mauve floss (DMC 3689), **strip** the floss, **re-combine** three of the strands, and **thread** the three strands onto your punch needle.

11 Use your punch needle to **outline** the letter "K" in the "REEK" design; then **fill in** the letter. When you're finished, **remove** the thread from the punch needle and **snip** the excess, leaving a tail of about ¼ in.

12 Using your embroidery scissors, **cut** a 36-in. length of medium lavender floss (DMC 210), **strip** the floss, **re-combine** three of the strands, and **thread** the three strands onto your punch needle.

13 Use your punch needle to stitch the border around the "REEK" design. When you're finished, **remove** the thread from the punch needle and **snip** the excess, leaving a tail of about ¼ in.

14 Using your embroidery scissors, **cut** a 36-in. length of medium mocha brown floss (DMC 3032), **strip** the floss, **re-combine** three of the strands, and **thread** the three strands onto your punch needle.

15 Use your punch needle to stitch the remaining empty spaces in the design between the letters and inside the border. When you're finished, **remove** the thread from the punch needle and **snip** the excess, leaving a tail of about ¼ in.

16 **Remove** the fabric from the hoop and **flip** the fabric around so it's right-side up.

Sew the Sachet

17 Using your shears, cut two 6-in. strips of decorative fabric that are about 1½-in. wide.

18 Using your shears, **cut** two 8-in. strips of decorative fabric that are about 1½-in. wide.

19 Using your shears, **cut** a 6 × 8-in. piece of decorative fabric.

20 Sew the strips of fabric you cut in step 17 onto the top and bottom edges of the design, as close to the punch-needle stitches as possible.

Note: If you're using a sewing machine, a regular straight stitch will suffice for the steps in this project. If you're sewing by hand, use a back stitch.

21 **Sew** the strips of fabric you cut in step 18 onto the sides of your piece, also joining them with the fabric bordering the top and bottom edges.

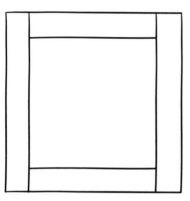

Frame the stitched piece with the decorative novelty fabric.

22 **Pin** the front of the sachet to the sachet's back panel (the piece you cut in step 19) with their right sides together. Situate the pins at a right angle from the fabric's edges, at ½-in. intervals.

23 Stitch the sides, top, and half of the bottom portions of the panels together, leaving enough room to turn the sachet right-side out and to cram the potpourri through.

24 Using the opening you left in step 23, **turn** the sachet right-side out.

25 Again using the opening you left in step 23, fill the sachet with potpourri. (Don't feel like you have to stuff it to the gills; a little bit of that stuff goes a long way.)

26 Use a needle and thread to hand-stitch the opening closed. (A slip stitch will do the trick.)

27 Inhale.

28 Exhale.

29 Repeat steps 27 and 28 as needed.

Variation

On Pins and Needles

You could easily use the steps in the "Sew the Sachet" section of this project to whip up a pincushion, using the design of your choice as the front. Just substitute fiber fill or wool for the potpourri. (Unlike with the sachet, you'll probably want to cram as much of the filling in as you can so that your pincushion doesn't look all deflated.)

Designer Bios

 **Jen Beeman** Born and raised in Chicago (where she still lives), Jen Beeman developed an abiding fascination with sewing at age 12, when her mom taught her the craft. Jen's interest with sewing naturally led her to explore other needlecrafts, including knitting and embroidery. Although Jen has a BFA in photography, she recently returned to school to study fashion design. When not completing class-related projects or indulging in her needlework habit, Jen can usually be found in Wisconsin, practicing her aim with her Red Ryder BB gun.

 **Roxane Cerda** Roxane Cerda dabbles in dozens of crafts. Because she can't stay focused on one thing for long, she has become a Jacqui of All Trades, master of none. Nonetheless, when she does whip up something spiffy, she loves to share, and she hopes you enjoy her projects. Roxane began to craft ages ago, and has only looked back to ensure she's not trailing bits of string and dropping beads all over the place.

 **Lindsay Evans** When not working at her day (and occasional night) job as a veterinarian in Australia, Lindsay Evans enjoys crafting. As well as embroidery, she particularly likes crochet, papercrafts, and beading, but is willing to try just about anything once. She prefers making random, unique, and occasionally slightly disturbing pieces.

Jenny Hart Jenny Hart is best known as the founder of Sublime Stitching, an independent design company that rocked the needleworking industry in 2001 with the first alternative patterns and resources for a new generation of stitchers. Sublime Stitching has been featured in such magazine publications as *Bust, Jane, Real Simple,* and *The Wall Street Journal*. Jenny is an internationally published artist/illustrator, an award-winning author of two titles for Chronicle Books, and a designer for Plaid/Bucilla. She lives and works in Austin, Texas, where she is also the founding member of the infamous Austin Craft Mafia.

Amy Holbrook Searching for a stress-relief activity, Amy Holbrook hit upon needlepoint, which, she discovered, kept her hands busy, calmed her nerves, and put her into a meditative state. After stitching numerous floral motifs, dog portraits, and pillows with cute sayings, Amy sought needlepoint designs that would better complement her urban lifestyle and home décor. She visited many needlepoint shops and searched online but couldn't find what she was looking for, so she decided to design her own. Amy launched AMH Design, a Brooklyn-based needlepoint design studio in 2004 to offer updated projects for a new generation of needlepointers. Easy, stylish, portable, and all-inclusive, AMH Design's contemporary needlepoint kits are perfect for beginner and veteran stitchers alike. Amy's needlepoints have been featured in several fashion and home décor magazines including *InStyle, Domino,* and *Jane*. For more information about AMH Design and to order Amy's kits, please visit her Web site at www.amhdesignonline.com.

Jenn Maruska A proud resident of Seattle, Jenn Maruska, with her husband and two cats, likes movies and books, and loves to cook—she makes a mean guacamole. Jenn is currently writing two children's books and designing handbags, as well as working on miscellaneous hand-crafted projects. You can see more of Jenn's work at www.maruskadesign.com.

Adam Moe Adam Moe lives in Chicago with his wife, Emily, and their intrepid border terrier, Spoof. He has always been a performer, writer, and musician, but recently found that embroidery filled some of those creative and political needs—without the necessity of leaving the house. Adam has worked as a high-school English teacher, a newspaper columnist, a log peeler, an actor, a fiddler, a singer, and once made an appearance on television with retired professional wrestler Mad Dog Vachon. When he isn't doing embroidery, Adam writes, directs, and acts for his theater company, Flying Leap Radio, which presents vintage and new radio theater for live audiences. He also plays the ukulele, and is not ashamed of it. You can contact Adam about anything you'd like, and find his embroidery for sale at www.moesewco.com.

 **Angela Plumb** Based in Ottawa, Canada, Angela Plumb is striving to make the world a softer place, one pillow at a time. The former science teacher and computer engineer started Pillowhead Designs in early 2006 as a side project (her main project being a stay-at-home mom). With an appreciation for clean, modern style, Angela expanded her line of hand-embroidered goods to include pillows, greeting cards, sachets, journals, and other accessories. In the fall of 2006, she launched www.mypillowhead.com to showcase her work. Aside from sewing and embroidery, Angela enjoys spending time with her little family, honing her culinary skills, and writing the odd science-fiction story here and there.

 **Amanda Smithers-Bentley** For Amanda Smithers-Bentley—who, at age 7, learned to stitch from her extremely talented mother—embroidery is more than just making something prettier; it's about creating a fully functional piece of art that more accurately reflects the role of women today. Smithers-Bentley's belief that embroidery is often unfairly relegated to the world of crafts and not taken seriously as an art form inspires her to embroider pieces that are surprising, interesting, and practical, and that challenge the way people think about the traditional arts, about women, and about feminism. For a more detailed look at Amanda's creations, visit www.pinprickdesigns.com.

 **KB VanHorn** Professional thing-maker KB VanHorn was born and raised in West Virginia but now resides on the other side of the country, in Hollywood, California. VanHorn started *kokoleo* in the summer of 2002 after her fabric collection became too vast to be contained in one room. Since then, baby clothes, purses, and stuffed toys have left the confines of her sewing studio and landed in the hands of those who appreciate one-of-a-kind designs. Her work can be found in several boutiques as well as alternative craft shows such as Bazaar Bizarre and Felt Club in Los Angeles. VanHorn is inspired by vintage fabrics, flea market finds, folk art, fashion, patchwork, and an appreciation for all things handmade. Visit her Web site at www.kokoleo.com.

Index

transferring designs to fabric
 by ironing, 49–50
 overview, 20–21, 49
 by painting, 50–51
 by tracing, 50
95 Theses (Luther), 11, 173

O

On Pins and Needles variation, 240
open herringbone stitch, 75–76
open pendant couching stitch, 89
opus anglicanum embroidery, 8, 9
organizing. *See* storing and organizing
overdyed (variegated) floss, 34, 35, 73
Overlord embroidery piece, 16

P

painting designs on fabric, 50–51
paper "fabric", 27
paper, graph, 21
patch projects, 128, 173–178, 234
patterns and charts. *See also* needlework
 buying, 19–20
 designing, 20–21
 interpreting, 54–55
 storing, 44
 using, 55
PC Stitch software, 21
pearl cotton thread, 31
Pelon, Pierre (book), 12

Penelope canvas, 26
perforated paper "fabric", 27
Persian wool yarn, 29, 33
petit point technique, 13
pillowcase (Case in Point), 212–214
pillow (You Bore Me), 189–197
pincushion and emery, 41
pincushion project, 240
pins, 41
plain-weave fabric, 22, 24
plastic canvas, 27
Play the Frame Game variation, 231
plies, thread, 26, 28
pouncing, 12
power looms, 14
printing press invention, 11, 12
project cards, 43, 46
Protestant Reformation, 11–12
punch needles, 37, 107
punch needlework, 107–109,
punch needle project (You Reek), 237–240

Q

Q Snaps, 40
quarter cross stitch, 73, 74
quill (long-arm feather) stitch, 86, 87–88

R

recipe box (We Got Spirits, Yes We Do!), 200–208
Rescue Me variation, 186
roller (scroll) frames, 39–40, 53
Rosey Grier's Needlepoint for Men (Grier), 1

rulers, 42
running stitches. *See also* cross stitch; line stitches
 double-running, 77, 78–79
 interlaced running, 78
 laced running, 78
 running, 77
 whipped running, 78

S

sachet project (You Reek), 237–240
samplers, 12–13
satin stitches. *See also* embroidery stitches
 long-and-short, 81, 83–84
 slanted, 81, 82
 straight, 81–82
scissors, 41
Scotch stitches. *See also* needle-point stitches
 checker, 98, 99
 condensed Scotch, 98, 101–102
 Hungarian diamond, 98, 104–105
 Moorish, 98, 102–103
 mosaic, 98, 104
 overview, 91, 98
 Scotch, 98–99
 Scottish squares, 98, 100–101
scroll frames, 39–40, 53
selvage, 22
sewing machines, 14, 42
sharps (needles), 37
shoes project, 162–163
shopping for goodies
 accessory tools, 40–42
 choosing colors, 34–35

Notes

About the Author

Kate Shoup Welsh Devoted crafter Kate Shoup Welsh has written or co-written several books, including *The Agassi Story* and *Not Your Mama's Beading*. She also co-wrote and starred in a feature-length film, and once worked as the sports editor of her local independent weekly. When not writing, Kate loves to ski (she was once nationally ranked), read, bead, and stitch. She also enjoys riding Lynda (her motorcycle), and she plays a mean game of 9-ball. Kate lives in Indianapolis with her husband, their daughter, their dog, and their cat.

Rescue Me
(variation of Laptop Dance; see page 186)

You Bore Me (see page 189)

Bomb Squad
(variation of The Diet of Worms; see page 177)

Laptop Dance (see page 179)

Germ Warfare (see page 169)

The Diet of Worms (see page 173)

British Invasion (see page 164)

Front of British Invasion

Double or Nothing (variation of Felt Up; see page 161)

Chuck Berries (see page 162)

Hip Code (to access this bonus pattern,
go to www.wiley.com/go/notyourmamas)

Felt Up (see page 157)

You're So Money (see page 137)

I'll Stop the World and Belt with You (see page 152)

Hoodie Two Chews (see page 125)

I Got My Eye on You (see page 129)

Tattoo You (see page 121)

Bull's-eye
(variation of Tattoo You; see page 123)

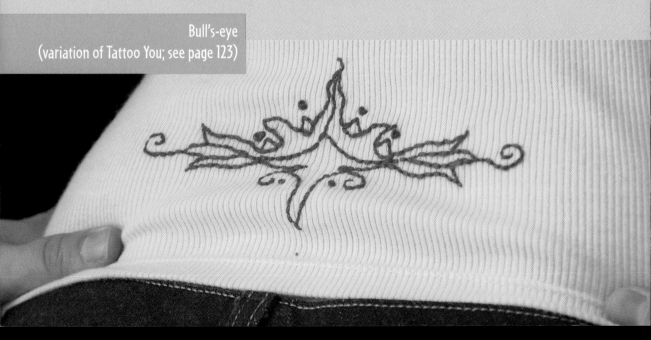

Tie Me Up (see page 116)

Sticking It to the Man
(variation of Tie Me Up; see page 120)

Patch Maker, Patch Maker, Make Me a Patch
(variation of It's All Geek to Me; see page 234)

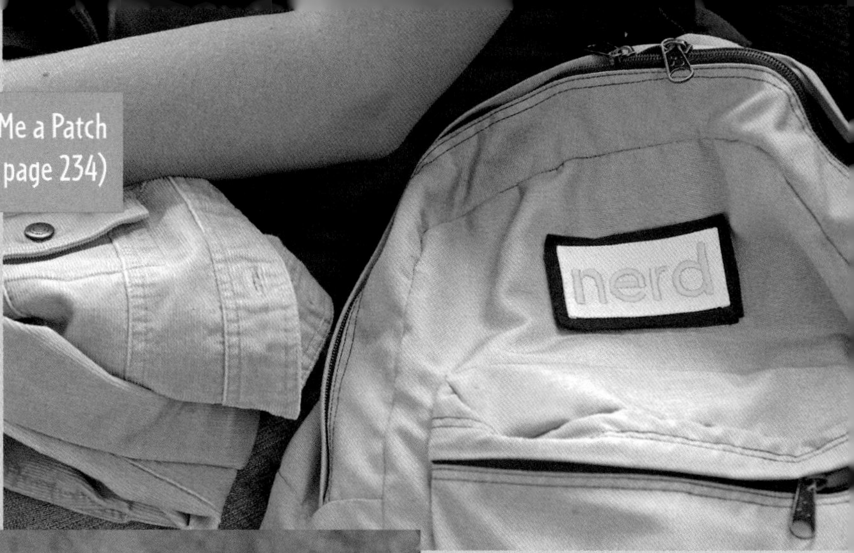

Anklebiter (see page 235)

You Reek (see page 237)

It's All Geek to Me (see page 232)

geek

Sweet Emoticon (see page 230)

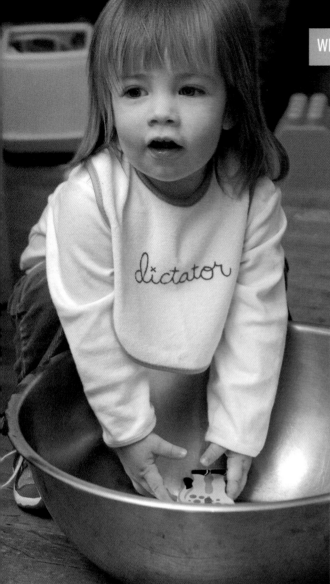

Who's the Boss? (see page 228)

Despot Measures
(variation of Who's the Boss?; see page 229)

Coffee, Tea, or Me? (see page 215)

The 25,000-Calorie Pyramid
(see page 219)

The Pyramid

Wash Your Damn Hands!
(see page 209)

Case in Point (see page 212)

Close-up of Case in Point

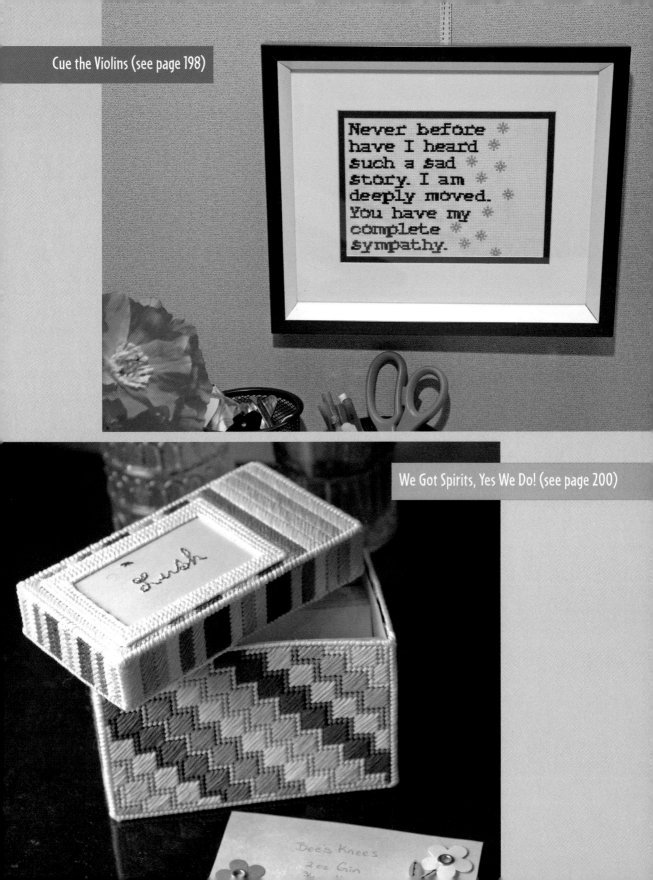

Cue the Violins (see page 198)

Never before
have I heard
such a sad
story. I am
deeply moved.
You have my
complete
sympathy.

We Got Spirits, Yes We Do! (see page 200)

Lush

Bee's Knees
2oz Gin

There's lots more in store with *Not Your Mama's*™ Craft Books!

Hip and savvy *Not Your Mama's* books are designed for confident crafters like you who don't need to start at the beginning and don't want to go back to basics and slave over every pattern and page. These books get right to the point so you can jump right into real projects. With easy-to-follow instructions plus hints, tips, and steps for customizing projects, you'll quickly have something to show for your efforts—fun, trendy items to add sass and class to your wardrobe or home.

not your mama's **knitting**
The cool and creative way to pick up sticks
by Heather Dixon

0-471-97382-3

not your mama's **crochet**
The cool and creative way to join the chain gang
by Amy Swenson

0-471-97381-5

not your mama's **beading**
The cool and creative way to string 'em along
by Kate Shoup Welsh

0-471-97380-7

It's knitting with a trés chic attitude. Projects include Pirate Socks, Boot-i-licious (boot jewelry), Girly (a sexy cardigan), Macho Picchu (a man's sweater), Techno Bag (a laptop case), Pampered Pooch Pullover, Hearts & Stars (cushions), and more.

Creative crochet is in today! Patterns include an Uber-Femme Capelet, Pseudo Kimono, Daisy Chain Neck Warmer, When the Jeans Don't Fit (recycled denim rug), Straight-Laced Tank and Shrug, Wowie Zowie Eco-Tote, Crocheted Bling, two super-cute plush toys, and more.

Do the bling thing. Projects include Financial Freedom (recycled credit card necklace), Tough Cuff, Catch Your Own Bouquet ring, Tipple Rings (wine stem markers), Girls Gone Bridaled (a tiara), Security Anklet, push pins with pizzazz, and more.

All *Not Your Mama's*™ Craft Books
$14.99 US/$17.99 CAN/£9.99 UK • Paper • 240-264 pp.
7 3/8 x 9 1/4 • Lots of illustrations and color photos

Available wherever books are sold.

WILEY
Now you know™
wiley.com